FISH & SEAFOOD COOKBOOK

KNACK

FISH & SEAFOOD COOKBOOK

Delicious Recipes for All Seasons

Doug DuCap and Linda Beaulieu

Photographs by Christopher Shane

KNACK
MAKE IT EASY

Guilford, Connecticut
An imprint of Globe Pequot Press

Editorial Director: Cynthia Hughes
Editor: Katie Benoit
Project Editor: Tracee Williams
Cover Design: Paul Beatrice, Bret Kerr
Text Design: Paul Beatrice
Layout: Melissa Evarts
Cover Photos by: Christopher Shane
Interior Photos by: Christopher Shane with the exception of those on page 4 (left): © wiedzma | Shutterstock; page 32 (left): © Robert Pernell | Shutterstock; page 69 (right): © Onestepbeyond | Dreamstime.com; and page 143 (left): © erkanupan | Shutterstock.

Library of Congress Cataloging-in-Publication Data

DuCap, Doug.
  Knack fish & seafood cookbook : delicious recipes for all seasons / Doug DuCap and Linda Beaulieu ; photographs by Christopher Shane.
     p. cm.
  Includes index.
  ISBN 978-1-59921-916-5
  1. Cookery (Fish) 2. Cookery (Seafood) I. Beaulieu, Linda. II. Shane, Christopher. III. Title.
  TX747.D82 2010
  641.6'92—dc22
                                                    2010015370

The following manufacturers/names appearing in *Knack Fish & Seafood Cookbook* are trademarks:
Boboli®; Clamato®; Cointreau®; DeLonghi® Fritos®; Goldfish®; Grands!®; Gran Marnier®; Kitchen Bouquet®; Mae Ploy™; Old Bay®; Pernod®; Ritz®; Rotel®; Sanyo®; Southern Comfort®; Special K®; Stove Top®; Tabasco®; Thermador®; Viking®; West Bend®; Wolf®

Printed in China

10 9 8 7 6 5 4 3 2 1

For Tabetha, my ever-fixed mark
Who looks on tempests and is never shaken.

~Doug DuCap

Acknowledgments

Many thanks to my editor, Katie Benoit, for her guidance and her unwavering kindness.

Special thanks go out to the mighty Pat Conroy for his generous praise and encouragement; to my dear friends Joe and Terri (and the many wonderful folks at Terri's Sports Bar) for their love and support; to Scott, George, and the rest of the D.F. Club (don't ask); and to the awesome Fred Dockery: friend, fisherman, and patient teacher.

My thanks to the fine and welcoming people of Charleston, South Carolina, and to the memory of the late Dr James Gulledge, whose abiding love for the Lowcountry led me to this beautiful place.

And especially: thanks to my "oldest and bestest," Thos W, always, for everything.

~Doug DuCap

Publisher's Acknowledgments

The publisher would like to thank the two talented authors who collaborated to create this delicious book and the photographer who brought the recipes to stunning color on the pages.

CONTENTS

INTRODUCTION

Let's face it. Seafood can be intimidating.

Unlike a meat market, with its relatively few and familiar choices of beef, pork, and chicken, a well-stocked fish market might have a bewildering and overwhelming display of several dozen different species of fish, mollusks, crustaceans, and cephalopods—often in their original state and all with different requirements.

Some might require scaling, gutting, and boning. Others might require seemingly arcane tools and special techniques to prepare. Some are far too expensive to risk mangling or overcooking them.

And the complexity doesn't end at the dinner table, either. Compared to seafood, meat and poultry are kid stuff. You don't need instructions to eat a steak. Even if you can't operate a knife and fork you can just pick it up and bite right into it with no harm done (except maybe to your reputation as a dinner guest). Try that with a steamed lobster or a whole, unboned sea bass and you might find yourself in big trouble (and possibly an ambulance)!

But seafood can also be delicious, exciting, and nourishing. It can be cooked quickly in a wide variety of ways and contains healthful nutrients like Omega-3 fatty acids. Doctors entreat us to incorporate more seafood into our diets, but given that seafood can seem so intimidating, who could be blamed for not wanting to swim upstream?

That is why most folks stick to their old standby preparations (the 'Salmon-in-the-Foreman' syndrome) or rely on prepackaged, precooked microwaveables. But even if you never get up the courage to gut fish or crack crabs on your own, there's still a deliciously vast array of possibilities open to you—and it's closer than you think.

Sources in the seafood industry estimate that close to 90 percent of all retail seafood purchases, both fresh and frozen, are made in the supermarket. The *Knack Fish & Seafood*

Cookbook focuses mainly on the varieties of fish and seafood most commonly found in supermarkets and provides original step-by-step recipes, helpful photographs, and practical techniques for making outstanding, restaurant-quality meals from them. (You'll also find several recipes for some very appealing up and coming choices, like skate wing and basa, that are available in larger fish markets.)

The seafood departments of modern supermarkets often stock a comparatively small but well-chosen mix of perennial favorites like salmon and flounder along with slightly more exotic options like mahimahi and grouper. Many sizes of uncooked shrimp, high quality crabmeat, and lobster tails are also available. Some supermarkets will steam your shellfish (seasoned or unseasoned) for free while you shop—a great timesaver for weekday meals.

In the frozen section, pre-cut fish fillets, raw and cooked shrimp, baby clams, mussels, and more can be found in vacuum-sealed, FAS (Frozen at Sea), and IQF (Individually Quick Frozen) forms. Thanks to modern handling methods, the quality of frozen seafood has improved dramatically, and can sometimes be better than the "fresh" choices available at the seafood counter (some of which arrive frozen and are thawed "for your convenience"—at a higher price).

As you cook your way through the recipes in this book, you'll find yourself becoming comfortable with fish and shellfish and may want to learn about and experience the more exotic varieties available. One of the best ways to do this is to develop a relationship with your local vendor, whether it's the manager of the supermarket's seafood department or your regular guy at the fish market. They can be a valuable source for information and practical advice on handling, storing, and cooking just about everything that swims. In addition, they often have access to a wide network of resources and can order anything you need, from the ordinary to the obscure.

Don't be afraid to ask questions about the characteristics of any fish or shellfish you're unfamiliar with, as well as any questions about source and quality. A good seafood vendor takes pride in his stock and will welcome your interest. (Be wary of any who seem impatient or circumspect; they might have something to hide!) They can show you firsthand what to look for and what to avoid.

If you happen to live near a coastal area where small-scale commercial fishermen dock, you might try inquiring about purchasing the day's catch. Depending on the state, many are licensed to make sales directly to the customer. It may or may not be less expensive than buying retail, but you can't beat "right-off-the-boat" seafood for freshness and flavor.

Once you start enjoying these recipes, you'll find that cooking fresh seafood is exciting, rewarding, and not so intimidating after all—and you'll never again settle for the ho-hum, the commonplace, and the "everyday."

Because when you think about it, every day is a gift, and every meal can be a celebration.

A Note on Choices: As of this writing, the stocks of the fish species chosen for these recipes are considered to be sustainable or in the process of becoming fully sustainable. When in doubt, check with one of the online resources like the Monterey Bay Aquarium's Seafood Watch Program (www .montereybayaquarium.org/cr/seafoodwatch .aspx) for the most up-to-date information on populations and health advisories.

BUYING FISH

The 3 senses you will rely on for judging freshness are sight, smell, and feel

The freshness of the fish you purchase is more important than any recipe you use to prepare that fish.

First, look at the fish carefully. If whole, the fish's eyes should be clear and full, not cloudy or sunken. Gills should be deep red. Fish that has been cut up should appear firm and moist with no bruising or dark spots. The color should be the true color of the fish—sole will be white, salmon bright orange, mackerel grayish-brown. Most fresh fish is fragrant and does not smell "fishy." Look for the pleasant smell of the sea.

The flesh of fresh fish should be firm to the touch and elastic, not mushy. When pressed, your finger should not leave an indentation. Whole fish should be firm, not floppy.

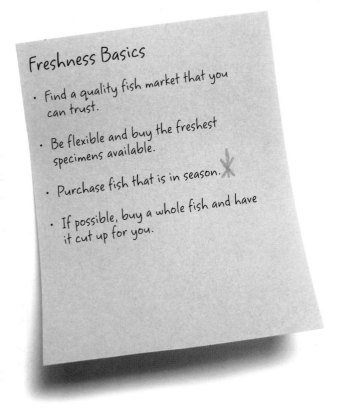

Freshness Basics

- Find a quality fish market that you can trust.
- Be flexible and buy the freshest specimens available.
- Purchase fish that is in season.
- If possible, buy a whole fish and have it cut up for you.

Fillets and Steaks

- Fresh fish is moist and cleanly cut, with no browning around the edges.
- It should be fragrant, not fishy smelling.
- It should be firm and elastic to the touch.
- Fish should be kept on a bed of ice.

It's important to find a fish market that you can trust. The people behind the counter should be able to answer all your questions on the fish they are selling. Fresh fish has a shelf life of about 5 days, if handled properly. Fish should always be refrigerated, preferably kept on a bed of crushed ice, which helps maintain moisture.

When it comes to buying fish, a good tip is to be flexible. Buy the freshest specimens available even if it's not the type of fish you had in mind for a particular recipe. Many different kinds of fish can be used in any given recipe.

Ideally, buy a whole fish and have the fishmonger cut it up for you while you wait. This way you'll have steaks or fillets as well as the bones, which you can use to make your own fish stock.

Shop around for the best quality and price. Try to buy fish that's in season. Also be adventuresome—try a variety of species.

Buying Whole Fish

- The best way to buy fresh fish is to buy it whole.

- The eyes should be bright and bulging.

- The fish should have a pleasant smell, not a fishy odor.

- The scales should be intact and have a glossy sheen.

Tuna and Swordfish

- Steaks should be moist and shiny.

- The flesh should be firm and resilient.

- Edges should be clean and smooth, with no browning.

- Steaks should not be sitting in a pool of liquid, a sign of poor freezing techniques.

BUYING SHELLFISH

The variety of available crustaceans and mollusks is vast, from tiny shrimp to giant crabs

Some cooks shy away from shellfish because of a lack of knowledge. So it's important that you have an understanding of shellfish basics. If shellfish has a family tree, it consists of 2 branches—crustaceans and mollusks. Crustaceans such as crab, crayfish, lobster, and shrimp have an external shell and joints for movement.

Further down the family tree, the mollusks have 2 branches of their own. Univalves such as abalone and conch have 1 shell, and bivalves such as clams, mussels, oysters, and scallops have 2 shells. Cephalopods, animals that carry their shells within their bodies, are also members of the shellfish family.

✱ Shrimp

- Raw shrimp is not sold live; often it arrives at a fish market in a frozen state.

- Shrimp is sold in its shell as well as peeled and deveined, and cooked, peeled, and deveined.

- Shrimp is often sold by the count—that is, how many shrimp to the pound.

- Raw shrimp should be grayish white and translucent, with tight shells and no black spots (a sign of bacteria).

Crabs and Lobsters

- Lobsters and crabs can be purchased live or cooked. Live specimens will be dark blue, green, or black.

- Live or cooked, lobsters and crabs should feel heavy for their size.

- Limbs should be intact and shells should be hard with no signs of discoloration.

- Live lobsters and crabs should be active and lively, not sluggish.

2

Most shellfish is purchased alive or cooked. The exceptions to this rule are shrimp, squid, and soft-shell crab.

As with buying fresh fish, rely on your sense of sight, smell, and touch when you purchase shellfish. Here are some general guidelines for buying shellfish:

Live crustaceans should be lively with their claws intact. However, lobsters and crabs that are missing a claw cost less, if you are looking to save money. Crustaceans should feel heavy for their size. Watch out for foaming around the mouth, a sign the creature is dying.

Univalves are sold either in the shell or freshly shucked. Most bivalves are sold alive in their shells. Look for hard shells that are whole and unbroken. The shells should smell of the sea, a pleasant smell, not "fishy." Buy shells that are tightly closed. If the shells do not close after you tap on them, do not purchase them. They are dead.

Cephalopods such as octopus and squid should look fresh, not grayish or dry looking, and they should have a fresh, almost sweet smell.

Scallops and Oysters

- Fresh scallops are available shucked on the half shell, or without the shell. Each scallop should be slightly rounded with smooth edges.

- Scallops are ivory or cream colored, not grayish, and they should not have any dark markings.

- Oysters are sold live in their shells, freshly shucked, and stored in salt water.

- Look for tightly closed shells and oyster meat that is shiny, moist, and plump.

Clams and Mussels

- Clams and mussels should be purchased live in their shells.

- The shells should be unbroken and tightly closed, a sign they are still alive.

- These bivalves should have a fresh sea smell.

- If the shells do not close after tapping on them, it's a sign that they are dead and should not be used.

HANDLING & STORING FISH

From the market to your table, it's crucial that you keep fish fresh

Every effort should be made to keep fish fresh once you've made your purchase at a reliable fish market. To ensure safe food handling, put your fresh fish purchase in a cooler or insulated bag for the trip home. And when you get home, refrigerate the fish immediately.

If you have a whole fish that you caught yourself, the fish should be gutted and cleaned before it is refrigerated. Keep freshly caught fish on ice for a maximum of 2 days.

When it comes to fish purchased at a market, it's best to use the fish in a recipe within 24 to 48 hours. When you get home with your fresh fish purchase, unwrap it and rinse the fish under cold running water. Pat it dry and wrap it in waxed paper to store in the coolest part of the refrigerator until it's time to cook.

If you have no immediate plans to prepare and cook your fresh fish, it should be frozen. If this is done quickly

Cleaning

- Freshly caught fish should be gutted and cleaned as soon as possible.

- Rinse the cavity thoroughly to remove any blood to help prevent spoilage.

- Rinse fish under cold running water to remove an ammonia smell, which sometimes occurs when fish is stored in plastic bags.

- A quick rinse will remove any scales that might still be clinging to a freshly caught fish.

Keeping It Cool

- Ideally, fresh fish should be kept on ice, preferably ice chips or shavings.

- The fresh fish should be wrapped in plastic wrap as airtight as possible.

- Keep an eye on the ice. Never let the fish sit in a pool of melted ice water.

- Store freshly purchased fish in the coldest part of your refrigerator, closer to the bottom.

and correctly, the fish will be moist and flavorful when you eventually thaw it out for cooking.

Plan to freeze the fish in the quantities you will need at any one time. Wrap the fish in plastic wrap as airtight as possible to prevent freezer burn. Mark the package with the type of fish and the date. In general, lean white-fleshed fish can be frozen for up to 6 months, and oily fish for 3 months. Thawing the frozen fish unwrapped in the refrigerator will take about 12 hours. Make sure to use a plate or paper towels to catch any liquids.

Many cooks recommend cooking the fish while it is still partially frozen as this minimizes any loss in moisture, which occurs during the thawing process.

Sealing in Favor

- Fresh fish can be wrapped in plastic wrap, waxed paper, or aluminum foil.

- It's important that the fish is wrapped as airtight as possible to seal in freshness.

- If you plan to freeze the wrapped fish, every package should be labeled with the type of fish and the date.

- Divide the fish to be frozen into just the right amounts you will need in your recipes.

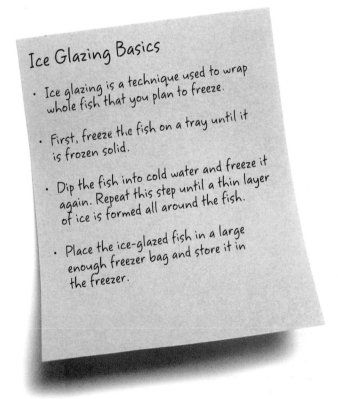

Ice Glazing Basics

- Ice glazing is a technique used to wrap whole fish that you plan to freeze.

- First, freeze the fish on a tray until it is frozen solid.

- Dip the fish into cold water and freeze it again. Repeat this step until a thin layer of ice is formed all around the fish.

- Place the ice-glazed fish in a large enough freezer bag and store it in the freezer.

5

HANDLING & STORING SHELLFISH
With shellfish food safety is of the utmost importance

A good cook does more than turn out delicious dishes. A good cook is always aware of the importance of food safety, which can be easily achieved by following proper handling and storage techniques.

When you get home with live lobsters, keep them in a cool spot until you're ready to cook. A large sink is ideal for this. Keep the lobsters covered with wet newspaper. Some experts recommend placing live lobsters into the freezer for

up to an hour. This is considered to be a more humane death than plunging the live lobster into a pot of boiling water.

Frozen or cooked lobsters and crab should be stored in the coldest section of your refrigerator, which is typically toward the bottom. Wrapped in foil or plastic wrap, they can be kept for up to 2 days.

Shrimp can also be refrigerated for up to 2 days, preferably with their shells on to retain moisture. Raw shrimp can easily

Shrimp

- Place shrimp in a plastic bag filled with water. Seal the bag tightly and place it in the freezer.

- Shrimp frozen in an ice block will not experience freezer burn.

- Shrimp can also be placed on a tray and frozen in

about an hour. Then the frozen shrimp can be transferred to an airtight plastic bag for storage in the freezer.

- The individually frozen shrimp can be easily removed from the bag in any desired amount.

Crab and Lobster

- Crabs and lobsters should be stored in the coldest part of your refrigerator.

- It's easy to twist off the legs of a cooked crab or the claws off of a cooked lobster.

- The legs and claws can be frozen for future use.

- Or, the legs and claws can be cracked open so the tender meat can be extracted.

be shelled under cold running water. There are 2 ways to freeze shrimp: in an ice block or individually on a tray in the freezer. Frozen shrimp will keep up to 2 months in the freezer. They can easily be thawed slowly in the refrigerator.

Shellfish should be stored in a large bowl covered with a damp towel. Oysters and scallops on the half shell should be refrigerated in a single layer on a tray covered with damp paper cloth. The oysters should be stored cup side down so the meat inside is submerged in the oyster liquor. Scallop meat is best kept in an airtight container in the refrigerator.

Clams and mussels can be kept in a large paper bag in the refrigerator, which allows the shellfish to breathe.

If any shellfish dies while being stored in the refrigerator, do not hesitate to throw it out.

Scallops and Oysters

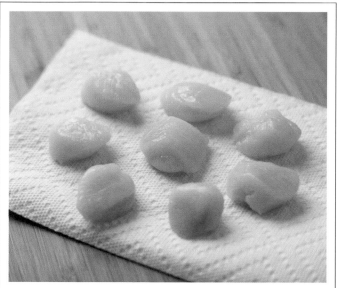

- Scallops are generally more perishable than other bivalves because they can't close their shells tightly.

- Keep fresh scallops in an airtight container in the refrigerator for up to 2 days.

- Oysters should be scrubbed with a brush before shucking.

- Oysters should never be submerged in water for long because they will suffocate.

Clams and Mussels

- Keep clams and mussels in a bowl covered with a damp towel in the refrigerator.

- Clams and mussels can be stored in the refrigerator for up to 24 hours.

- Bivalves can also be stored in a large paper bag in the refrigerator, which enables them to breathe.

- Bivalves need a thorough rinsing under cold water and can even be scrubbed with a brush to remove sand and mud.

PREPARING FISH

A few basic steps are recommended before you start to cook your fish

You're doing everything right—finding a reputable fish market, selecting the freshest fish available, storing it properly once you're home for food safety reasons. Now it's almost time to start cooking, but first there are a few steps you need to take to ensure success in the kitchen.

After you unwrap the fish, check for any ammonia smell, which can occur when fish is wrapped in plastic. Simply rinse the fish under cold running water to eliminate the odor.

Next, examine the fish, checking carefully for bones of any kind. Don't just rely on your eyes. Your sense of touch is needed here as well. Run your index finger across the surface of the fish to detect any small bones. A pair of tweezers is a handy utensil for removing such bones.

You also want to check for ragged or discolored edges, which should be trimmed so that the fish fillet or steak looks perfect. Use a small knife for this job, one that is very sharp.

Check for Bones

- Use your eyes and your fingers to check for small bones in fresh fish.

- Run a finger across the surface of the entire fillet and especially along any visible seams in the flesh.

- Use a pair of tweezers to remove the bones.

- Clean and rinse the fish thoroughly.

Trim Rough Edges

- Place the fish fillet on a clean cutting board.

- Use a small knife to trim the rough edges from a fish fillet.

- Make sure your knife is very sharp, which will make this task easier to accomplish.

- The scraps of raw fish can be frozen and used at a later time to make fish stock.

You can also use a sharp knife to remove the skin from fish. Place the fillet on a clean work surface, skin side down. Begin at the tail end, holding the tail firmly with your fingers. Run your knife between the flesh of the fish and its skin, staying as close to the skin as possible. The flesh will separate from the skin as you press down firmly and move the knife away from the tail.

With some fish, such as salmon steaks, it's a good idea to use butcher's twine to tie the thick slice of fish into a tidy bundle for easy cooking. This will result in a cooked fish steak that is more moist because the edges did not dry out during the cooking process.

Shaping Fish Steaks

- Some fish steaks need to be formed into neat bundles for proper cooking.

- Butcher's twine is ideal for this technique.

- The steak can be compacted and secured with twine.

- This allows the fish steak to cook evenly and results in a neat presentation.

Removing Skin from Fillets

- A very sharp knife is essential when you want to remove the skin.

- Always begin at the tail end, holding the tail firmly with your fingers.

- Dipping your fingers in salt first will help you hold onto the fish.

- Run your knife between the flesh of the fish and its skin. Stay as close to the skin as possible.

PREPARING SHELLFISH

Different steps are needed for the variety of shellfish you will be cooking

Some shellfish need to be cleaned before cooking, but not lobsters. Some cooks have no problem thrusting live lobsters into a pot of boiling water, while others feel it is more humane to place the lobsters in the freezer for up to a hour prior to cooking.

Crabs, on the other hand, should be rinsed carefully under cold running water. Sometimes a kitchen brush is needed to clean crabs that are especially dirty.

Shrimp need a quick rinse under cold running water before being used in a recipe. Their shells can be removed either before or after cooking. Shrimp also needs to be deveined.

Mollusks in the shell, such as oysters and clams, need

Shrimp

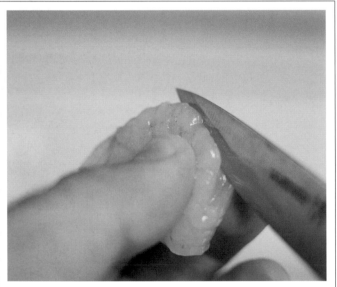

- Shrimp should be deveined. That means removing the thin dark vein that runs along the back of each shrimp.

- Rinse the shrimp and remove the shells, but leave the tail intact for serving, if desired.

- Run a small, very sharp knife along the outer back of each shrimp.

- To butterfly the shrimp, cut in just far enough to open up the shrimp without cutting all the way through.

Crabs and Lobsters

- Place a lobster tail on a clean cutting board.

- Using a very sharp chef's knife, cut the lobster tail lengthwise from end to end.

- Because the shell is hard, it will take some effort to cut

- the tail, but it can be done with a strong knife.

- Once the knife is all the way through, you can split the lobster in half. Make sure you remove the intestinal tract running throughout the tail.

serious cleaning. Use a kitchen brush to get rid of sand and mud imbedded in the shells. Clams should be rinsed in several changes of fresh cold water. They can also be soaked in a large pot of cold water for up to an hour, during which time the clams purge themselves of any sand inside the clams. Some cooks recommend sprinkling the pot of water with cornmeal, which encourages the clams to purge even more.

Mussels need a good rinsing as well. They also need to be debearded. That is, the wiry beard on many mussels needs to be pulled out by hand, or removed with a small sharp knife.

Squid, or calamari, can be bought already cleaned and ready to cook. Simply rinse the squid under cold running water. If bought whole, remove and discard the head and tentacles. Be sure that the transparent quill or cartilage has been removed from the squid and discarded. Remove the skin and fins, then rinse well. The squid can be left whole or cut into rings, depending on your recipe.

Scallops and Oysters

- A kitchen brush is an essential tool when it comes to cleaning oysters and other shellfish.

- Scrub the shellfish with the brush under cold running water.

- When opening oysters, keep the rounder shell on the bottom.

- This technique allows you to save as much of the oyster liquor as possible.

Clams and Mussels

- Clams and mussels can be cleaned with a kitchen brush under cold running water.

- Discard any clams or mussels that are unusually heavy, a sign that they may be filled with mud or sand.

- Mussels require individual attention. After rinsing each one, remove the beard.

- Holding the mussel in 1 hand, grasp the beard firmly, and yank it off.

COOKWARE FUNDAMENTALS
With the right equipment, you can poach, bake, broil, grill, fry, and steam seafood

It's really not hard to cook fish and seafood, especially if you have the right tools and equipment. With various pots, pans, and gadgets in your kitchen, you can tackle any recipe.

Poaching, or cooking fish in a simmering liquid, can be done on the stovetop or in the oven. A fish poacher is ideal for this technique.

The dry heat method of cooking known as baking is done in the oven, using everything from glass casseroles to clay baking dishes.

For broiling, you will need a broiler pan or baking sheet as well as an extra long spatula.

Grilling, of course, requires a grill of some sort. Some cooks

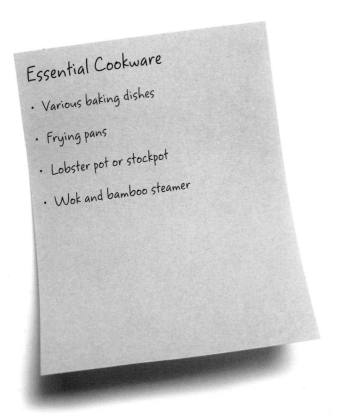

Essential Cookware

- Various baking dishes
- Frying pans
- Lobster pot or stockpot
- Wok and bamboo steamer

Essential Bakeware

- A variety of baking dishes comes in handy when fish and seafood need to be cooked.

- Bakeware can be ovenproof glass, ceramic, metal, or cast-iron.

- Whether you're cooking for 1 or for a crowd, bakeware in different sizes is always a good idea.

- Baking sheets also come in handy, especially when you're cooking a lot of fish.

are lucky enough to have an indoor grill in their kitchens. Grilling baskets are handy, and grilling tools such as long-handled tongs are essential.

For frying, various skillets, pans, and a wok are needed. A deep-fryer is useful, as well.

Moist-heat cooking, or steaming, can be done in various ways using a large pot, wok, or bamboo steamer.

Boiling seafood such as lobsters and crab should be done in a lobster pot or large stockpot. Other basic necessities include sharp knives and tweezers for removing fish bones.

ZOOM

Special tools are required for opening and serving shellfish. These tools include an oyster knife, clam knife, clam opener, shrimp sheller, shrimp deveiner, small seafood forks, nutcrackers, nut picks, lobster crackers, and lobster picks. Butter warmers make a nice presentation. These are small ceramic bowls positioned over a candle, which keeps your melted butter warm for dipping.

MATERIALS & TECHNIQUES

Multipurpose Pots and Pans

- Many tools can be used to cook other foods as well as fish and seafood.

- A wok and a bamboo steamer are essential for cooking Asian food as well as fish.

- A lobster pot can also be used for cooking pasta.

- A large heavy pot with a lid can be used for stewing fish as well as other foods.

Iron for High Temperatures

- Good cooks often have a well-used cast-iron pan in their cookware collection.

- Remember that cast-iron skillets heat up and cool down slowly.

- Cast-iron pans are excellent for cooking outdoors over an open fire or on a grill.

- Fish should be fried in hot oil or butter (a combination of both is recommended).

ESSENTIAL UTENSILS
Cooking fish and seafood is so much easier with the right tools

Some kitchen tools are very specific in their use, while other utensils can be used for a variety of tasks. When it comes to cooking fish and seafood, you'll find yourself reaching for spatulas and ladles that you use every day. And once in a while, you'll use a gadget that has a dedicated purpose that makes a certain job easier to accomplish.

The multipurpose kitchen tools include a wide assortment of large spoons, high-quality knives that are sharpened

regularly, spatulas for turning cooked food over, and ladles for dishing out soups and chowders.

There are other tools that you don't use often, but when you do, you're glad to have that particular utensil in your collection. For example, you use tweezers to remove bones from fresh fish and specialized knives for opening clams and oysters.

If you cook fish often, you'll want a fish knife in your knife

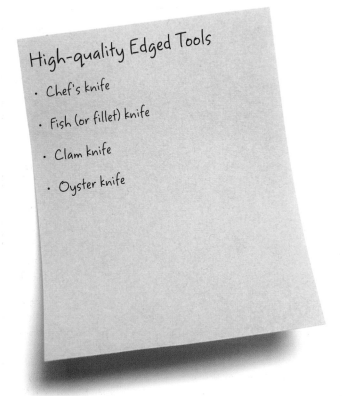

High-quality Edged Tools

- Chef's knife

- Fish (or fillet) knife

- Clam knife

- Oyster knife

Turners and Spatulas

- Various turners and spatulas come in handy when cooking fish.

- Be sure to use plastic turners and spatulas when cooking fish in nonstick pans.

- Always use metal turners and spatulas when cooking fish on a hot grill.

- The new silicone spatulas can withstand extremely high heat.

drawer. This is a long flexible knife that can be used for removing the skin from a fish.

You also will want a special spatula called a fish slice, which is extra wide and allows you to turn over an entire piece of fish without it breaking into pieces.

Spoons and Ladles

- All kinds of spoons come in handy when cooking fish and seafood.

- Metal, wooden, and plastic spoons, some with long handles, are recommended.

- Metal and plastic ladles can be used to scoop up everything from steamed clams to lobster bisque.

- A slotted ladle can be used to lift out food without any of the cooking liquid.

Specialty Items

- The extra-wide metal fish spatula, called the fish slice, is a handy tool.

- Because of its width, the fish slice can easily turn fish over to cook on the other side.

- When the fish is done, the fish slice can lift up the entire piece of fish without it falling apart.

- The fish slice is especially handy when you are cooking small whole fish.

OTHER VERY USEFUL TOOLS
Kitchen gadgets of all sorts will help you become an even better cook

There's a saying: "The older you get, the better you cook." Maybe that's because cooks amass a terrific collection of gadgets that really do help in the kitchen.

Once you begin to use these tools, whether it's a thermometer or multi-event kitchen timer, you'll wonder how you ever cooked without them.

Gourmet shops and their catalogs are filled with all sorts of gizmos. These are great places to shop for gifts for friends and relatives who love to cook.

You might want to create a wish list for yourself. Possible items include new cutting boards, a garlic press, measuring cups and spoons, colanders and strainers, oversized flexible

Helpful Appliances
- Thermometer
- Kitchen timer
- Chef's thermometer fork
- Seafood scissors/deveiner

Oil Thermometer

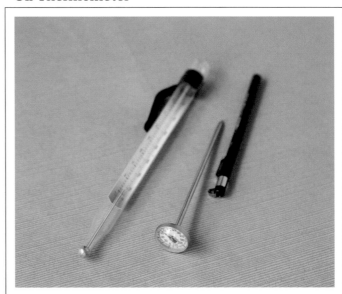

- An oil thermometer is a precision instrument that helps ensure successful frying results.

- Oil thermometers clip to the rim of the pot. Digital thermometers flash and beep.

- They are calibrated to measure the wide range of heat required when cooking with oil.

- They measure temperatures from 100 to 400°F.

spatulas, splatter screens, locking tongs, and kitchen shears.

Herb choppers and mincers are useful when cooking fish and seafood, as well as microplane graters, and spider and mesh skimmers. Seafood scissors can help you uncover the meat of crabs and lobsters with ease. The curved carbon-steel blades make shelling a snap. Or you can purchase a shrimp deveiner, which will help you quickly and easily remove the vein-like intestine from shrimp. Its curved blade matches the contour of the shrimp's shell.

ZOOM

Timers and thermometers are available in all price ranges from a basic inexpensive digital thermometer to a more advanced stainless steel triple timer. Professional chefs have used instant-read thermometers for years, and now they are widely available. You might also try a chef's thermometer fork. Stick the fork into the cooked item, and you get an instant temperature reading on the handle.

Multi-event Timer

- Multi-event timers are very handy when more than 1 dish is being prepared.

- Separate cooking tasks of varying lengths can be monitored at the same time.

- One dial can time a dish that takes a long time to cook, while another dial can be used to time another dish that doesn't take that long.

- Each timer has its own audible alert to let the cook know when time is up.

Grilling Baskets and Toppers

- Grilling baskets are hinged metal cages that come in a variety of shapes and sizes.

- A whole fish can be placed in a grilling basket that is in the shape of a fish.

- A grilling grate or fine mesh grill (round or square) can be used for grilling pieces of seafood such as scallops.

- The basket or grate can be turned or lifted off the grill without food sticking to the grill.

17

PANTRY STAPLES

A well-stocked pantry will help you answer the question: What's for dinner tonight?

A pantry is a small closed space connected to a kitchen, often with a door, in which food can be stored. It can be a cupboard with shelves or a walk-in closet. A smart cook will keep the pantry well stocked with condiments, herbs, and spices.

Condiments range from barbecue sauce to Worcestershire sauce. In between you'll find jars and bottles of capers, chili paste, chutney, hoisin sauce, honey, horseradish, hot pepper sauce, ketchup, maple syrup, marmalades, molasses, dried or canned mushrooms, mustards, a variety of oils, olives (black and green), pickles, soy sauce, teriyaki sauce, sun-dried tomatoes, and different kinds of vinegar. Most condiments have a very long shelf life but should be refrigerated once opened.

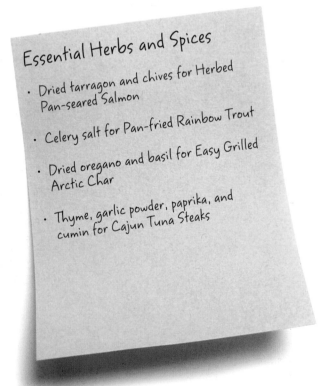

Essential Herbs and Spices

- Dried tarragon and chives for Herbed Pan-seared Salmon

- Celery salt for Pan-fried Rainbow Trout

- Dried oregano and basil for Easy Grilled Arctic Char

- Thyme, garlic powder, paprika, and cumin for Cajun Tuna Steaks

Oils, Vinegars, and Wines

- Olive oil, canola oil, sesame oil, and peanut oil can all be used to prepare fish and seafood.

- Some oils are infused with herbs and savory flavors.

- The 3 basic vinegars are balsamic, cider, and wine (red and white).

- Red and white wines are also used in various fish and seafood recipes.

Basic herbs and spices often used in cooking fish and seafood include dried basil, bay leaves, chili powder, coriander, cumin, curry powder, dill weed, fennel seeds, 5-spice powder, garlic powder, ground ginger, dried marjoram, dried mint, dried ground mustard, onion powder, oregano, paprika, pepper, peppercorns, rosemary, sage, salt, sesame seeds, dried tarragon, dried thyme, and turmeric. Herbs and spices will lose their potency after 6 months so buy only what you need and in small amounts. It is best to store them in a cool dark place.

• • • • • • • • • GREEN ● LIGHT • • • • • • • • •

Different kinds of oils and vinegars are called for in many different recipes. Keep your pantry stocked with olive oil, canola oil, sesame oil, and peanut oil. Oils can go rancid so buy only what you plan to use in the next 6 months. Store oil in a cool dark space. There are 5 types of vinegar to keep on hand—balsamic, cider, red wine, white wine, and rice vinegar. Unlike oils, vinegar has an extremely long shelf life.

Versatile Necessities

- The addition of capers, olives, or sun-dried tomatoes adds that special touch to a recipe.

- Capers are a flavor enhancer in many French, Italian, and Greek dishes.

- Olives, both green and black, can be used whole, sliced, or chopped.

- Sun-dried tomatoes are ripe tomatoes that have been dried in the sun to remove their water content.

Sauces and Savory Potions

- A wide range of ethnic sauces are now available to home cooks.

- Sauce staples include hot sauce, Worcestershire sauce, and tomato sauce.

- There are many Asian sauces, including soy, hoisin, and teriyaki.

- Some of the more exotic sauces include Jamaican jerk sauce, spicy mango Creole sauce, coconut curry sauce, and chipotle barbecue sauce.

MARINATING, GLAZING & CRUSTING
Add these cooking techniques to your repertoire and you'll dazzle your dinner guests

Cooking is like any other skill. First, you have to learn the basics, and then you can broaden your skills with a wide range of techniques. Three techniques you will use again and again are marinating, glazing, and crusting.

Marinating involves soaking a raw food product in a marinade that is made up of oil, seasoning, and an acid such as wine, vinegar, or lemon juice.

Glazing is accomplished when a thick liquid is applied over the surface of food being cooked, usually resulting in an appealing sheen. Some glazes are reduced, highly concentrated stocks.

Crusting can be achieved in a number of ways. Flour or

Marinades That Infuse

- A simple marinade for fish can be made by combining oil, lemon juice or white wine, and flavorings.

- Flavorings could be members of the onion family—scallions, shallots, and leeks.

- Flavorings also could be root vegetables such as carrots and celery.

- Herbs and spices such as bay leaves and thyme infuse a great deal of flavor into fish.

Marinades That Cook

- Pieces of raw fish can be "cooked" in a marinade made with lime juice or some other citrus fruit.

- This type of marinade that cooks the fish is called ceviche and originated in South America.

- You can use any firm white fish, scallops, or shrimp to make ceviche.

- Flavorings include red onion, mild and hot chile peppers, fresh cilantro, and garlic.

cornmeal are usually the basis of the crumb coating, which results in a golden and crispy finished product. Various seasonings can change the dish completely. When crusting fish, it is coated in flour, then in a beaten egg, and finally in cornmeal or bread crumbs before being fried. The coating can be plain or exotic with the addition of shredded coconut, curry powder, coriander, cumin, or chili powder. The coating of the fish can be done in a bowl. Or to avoid a mess, the fish and coating mixture can be combined in a plastic bag that is then shaken to coat the fish thoroughly.

Flavor-rich Glazes

- A glaze can be achieved by coating fish with a thick paste during cooking.

- This thick paste can be a simple coating of mustard, or a more exotic combination of ingredients.

- Fish can also be coated with a sweet glaze made with honey, sugar, or mirin (sweet sake).

- A popular glaze for swordfish is made by combining honey and mustard.

Crusting for Tasty Textures

- Seasoned flour and beaten eggs are needed to prepare fish with a delicate crust.

- A golden, crispy fish fillet is made easily with a simple cornmeal coating.

- Dry bread crumbs can also be used to coat fish that is going to be fried.

- Exciting flavors can be added to the coating mixture, everything from shredded coconut on shrimp to spices on fish.

BREADING & BATTERING

Elevate flounder, cod, and calamari to new taste levels with crispy and flavorful coatings

All kinds of fish and seafood can be breaded or battered for added flavor and texture.

Breaded coatings are made with many different ingredients including fine bread crumbs, cornmeal, crushed crackers, flour, crushed potato chips, dried herbs, panko (Japanese) bread crumbs, and even breakfast cereals. One popular restaurant dish is fried shrimp with a coconut coating.

The trick is to cook the fish without the breading falling off. One solution to this problem is to allow the fish to sit at room temperature for 20 minutes to dry as much as possible. It also helps to always use very fine crumbs when you make the breading and make sure the oil in your frying pan is very hot.

Basic Coatings 101

- Plain flour
- Flour and water batter
- Club soda batter
- Bread crumbs
- Panko (Japanese) bread crumbs
- Egg white batter
- Baking powder batter

Breadings for Crunch

- Panko or Japanese bread crumbs create an outer crust that is relatively thick, very crunchy, and most appealing.

- A batter made with club soda will give you light and crispy results.

- A club soda batter has to be made at the last minute because the carbon dioxide in the soda dissipates rapidly.

- Batter made with baking powder is light and very crunchy, but results in a slightly tougher coating.

In hot oil, the coating forms a protective seal around the fish, which prevents the fish from absorbing too much oil.

A batter is quite different. It's a liquid mixture usually containing beaten eggs, flour, and either baking soda or baking powder, which makes the batter rise when cooked. Deep-fried fish and chips from England are often made with a beer batter. The Japanese pride themselves on their tempura dishes featuring seafood and fresh vegetables dipped in a batter made with cake flour.

Coconut Shrimp ✳✳ ✳

Batter-sealed Flavor

- The clean flavor of fresh fish comes shining through when a simple flour and water batter is used.

- Leavened batters also seal in the ocean-fresh flavor of fish and seafood.

- Equal amounts of flour and beer plus a beaten egg and salt are the ingredients for a classic beer batter.

- The secret to a good tempura batter is using ice water, which results in added crispness.

Other Tasty Ideas

- Buttered bread crumbs are easily made by combining 1 cup of fresh bread crumbs with 2 tablespoons of melted butter.

- Any kind of white fish or oily fish fillets can be coated with a mix of flour, sesame seeds, lemon pepper, and lemon rind.

- A rather unusual but delicious coating can be made with flour, ground cashews, and spices.

- For a spicy fried fish, coat with flour, ground coriander, ground cumin, and chili powder.

BROILING & BAKING

Two dry-heat methods can be used to prepare fish and seafood in the oven

What's the difference between broiling and baking?

With broiling, food is cooked by a very high heat source above the food. Typically, food is broiled by placing it on the top shelf in an oven and setting the dial to broil, with the oven door left slightly open. Recipes usually indicate how many inches the food should be placed below the broiler unit. It's best to broil fish fillets that are in a shallow pan, which can catch the juices released from the fish as it cooks. Brush the top surface of the fillets with oil or melted butter. A nicely broiled piece of fish will be slightly crusty with golden brown specks.

Baking, which is similar to roasting, takes place when food

Broiling Fillets and Steaks

- Because oven broiling involves intense heat, it's better to broil thin pieces of fish, which will then cook evenly.

- Most broiling is done about 4 inches from the heat source.

- A broiling pan with a grated insert will allow juices to fall into the pan below, not on the floor of your oven.

- In case of a broiler flare-up, always have a box of baking soda nearby that can be used to douse the flames.

Savory Skewers and Kebabs

- Fish and seafood that has been skewered can be cooked under the broiler or on the grill.

- Small pieces of fish, such as chunks of swordfish, large sea scallops, or shrimp, are threaded on long thin rods.

- Skewers can be made of either bamboo or metal.

- Bamboo or wooden skewers must be soaked in water before being used to prevent them from burning.

is cooked in a pan in the oven, with the heat coming from the bottom. All kinds of fish, and all kinds of cuts, can be baked with perfect results. It's essential that you start with an oiled baking pan, which will allow you to remove the cooked fish without it sticking and breaking into pieces. The oven-proof baking pan should have slightly raised sides. If you use a glass baking dish, remember to lower the oven temperature called for in the recipe by 25 degrees.

MAKE IT EASY

Whether you are broiling or baking fish in the oven, make sure you have the right tools when it is time to remove the fish from the pan in which it was cooked. An extra wide spatula is ideal or use 2 spatulas together to lift each piece of fish. If you are baking a whole fish, it's wise to serve it right from the baking dish. If you try to lift a whole fish, it will most certainly break into pieces.

Easy Baked Fish

- Large whole fish, fish steaks, and fillets—all kinds and all cuts—can be baked in the oven.

- Baking pans need to be oiled before use so food does not stick.

- Fish should be arranged in a single layer in the baking pan for even cooking.

- A whole baked fish should be served in its baking dish at the dinner table.

Foil Packets and Parchment

- Cooking in a package of either foil or parchment is an excellent method for cooking fish.

- Dry heat from the oven generates steam within the package, which then cooks the fish.

- This method, called *en papillote*, keeps the fish moist and succulent.

- Each guest is served an aromatic packet of cooked fish on a dinner plate.

COOKING METHODS

COOKING IN LIQUIDS

If done right, moist-heat cooking methods preserve the flavor and texture of seafood

Moist-heat cooking methods include steaming, poaching, boiling, braising, and stewing. Steaming is considered the most natural method of moist-heat cooking. All kinds of fish and shellfish can be steamed in about 1 inch of a liquid, often water or wine, which can be flavored with herbs and spices. Steaming is done in a pot that has a tight-fitting lid.

The liquid is brought to a boil, and the seafood is cooked by the surrounding steam in the pot.

Poaching is a gentler method of cooking, done in a simmering liquid on the stovetop or in the oven. It's important to watch the clock to prevent overcooking. Poaching is recommended for firm-fleshed fish such as salmon, tuna, and halibut.

Steaming in Flavor

- Steam only non-oily fish such as bass, cod, trout, red snapper, salmon, and tuna.

- Shellfish especially good for steaming are clams, mussels, and shrimp.

- Steaming can be done in a large pot with a tight-fitting lid, or Chinese bamboo baskets.

- A properly steamed fish has a more delicate texture than fish that's been poached.

Gentle Poaching with Aromatics

- Poaching seafood preserves its texture and flavor.

- A classic vegetable stock with its subtle flavor is the ideal poaching liquid.

- Onions and carrots in the poaching liquid add a bit of sweetness to the flavor.

- A dash of cayenne pepper brings the dish into perfect balance.

Boiling will break up the tender flesh of fish and should be used only to cook shellfish such as lobster and crab.

Braising and stewing are slow-cooking methods that tenderize the foods being cooked. Ingredients being braised are not quite submerged in a liquid, and they stew and steam at the same time. With stewing, the ingredients are totally submerged and simmer for a long time. Because it takes so long to braise or stew food, it's better to do these dishes the day before. When reheated, the flavors are more pronounced.

MAKE IT EASY

How can you tell when fish is done? Scallops turn opaque, while shrimp turns pink. Medium-done tuna and salmon are darkish pink at the center. White fish should look moist and opaque rather than translucent at its center. One way to identify cooked fish is to pierce it with a sharp knife. If it goes through with ease, the fish is done and should be removed from the heat immediately.

Boiling Shellfish

- Most fish is too delicate to be boiled.

- Only shellfish such as clams, crab, and lobster should be cooked in boiling water.

- Shellfish can be boiled in water, or water combined with beer, wine, and/or herbs.

- Bring the liquid to a vigorous boil, drop in the shellfish, and start timing when the liquid returns to a boil.

Braising and Stewing

- Braising and stewing are slow-cooking methods.

- Braised foods are partially submerged in a liquid, while stewed foods are completely submerged.

- Braised dishes and stews are best cooked the day before and reheated.

- Cod, blackfish (aka tautog), squid, porgy, and tilefish are excellent for braising and stewing.

SAUTÉING, SEARING & STIR-FRYING

Three more cooking techniques, all done on the stovetop, but with completely different results

Standing at the stove, you can sauté a delicate piece of fish, you can sear a fish steak, and you can create an Asian stir-fry. These are 3 more cooking techniques worth mastering.

When you sauté, you are cooking food quickly in a small amount of fat over very high heat. This is done in a sauté pan or skillet. The fat can be hot olive, peanut, or safflower oil,

clarified butter, or a combination of oil and butter.

Searing is the way to brown food quickly in a pan or under the broiler. This is done at the outset of the cooking process in order to seal the surface. In fact, searing is the first step in sautéing. When you sauté fish, you shake it in the hot pan so that it sears and cooks quickly.

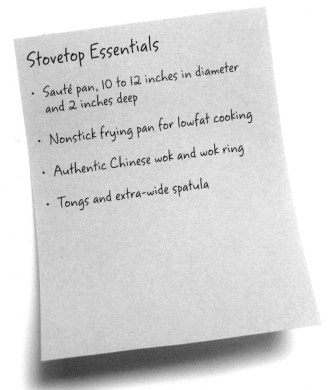

Stovetop Essentials

- Sauté pan, 10 to 12 inches in diameter and 2 inches deep

- Nonstick frying pan for lowfat cooking

- Authentic Chinese wok and wok ring

- Tongs and extra-wide spatula

Multipurpose Sautéing

- A sauté pan or frying pan can be used to sauté foods in little fat.

- A straight-sided sauté pan can be used for sautéing, braising, frying, and making quick sauces.

- This pan should have a lid so food can be covered and simmered over low heat.

- In a nonstick sauté pan, you can cook fish in even less oil or butter.

Stir-fry is the Asian cooking technique of frying small pieces of food quickly in very little fat in a wok over very high heat. A cook must constantly stir the ingredients for a proper stir-fry. It's a form of sautéing but uses higher heat. Fish is sliced into bite-size pieces and cooked in hot peanut or safflower oil, often with a dash of Asian sesame oil for added flavor.

ZOOM

An authentic wok is bowl-shaped and sits on a wok ring over the heat source. Some woks have flat bottoms for use on electric stoves. Most chefs agree that electric woks do not reach the high temperatures needed for stir-frying. A wok should never be washed with soap and water. You can season a wok by wiping it with vegetable oil and then placing it over medium heat for 2 minutes.

Searing Adds Flavor

- When you sear a piece of fish, it is subjected to very high heat, which seals in the juices.

- Fish fillets can be placed in a very hot pan and turned around until a crust forms on the surface of the fish.

- Searing caramelizes the juices and creates a flavorful crust.

- After the fish is seared, reduce the heat to finish the cooking process.

Speedy Stir-frying

- The art of stir-frying lies in the technique of quickly frying small pieces of food in a small amount of fat over very high heat.

- To stir-fry successfully, a cook must constantly toss and stir the ingredients.

- Peanut oil and safflower oil are used to stir-fry food, with a little Asian sesame oil added for extra flavor.

- Soy sauce or rice wine vinegar may be added to a stir-fry dish at the end of the cooking process to moisten the fish.

OUTDOOR GRILLING

Hot off the grill—sometimes the oldest cooking methods are the best

Nothing is older—or better—than cooking over an open fire. Almost any seafood can be grilled in the great outdoors. It's a healthy alternative to hot dogs and hamburgers.

Easy steps for successful outdoor grilling start with marinating fish, or rubbing it lightly with oil, to keep it from sticking on the grill.

While the fish is marinating, check to see if the grill is clean, again so the food won't stick. Grilling baskets and fine mesh grates help in this area.

Always use a hot fire to grill seafood. How can you tell when the grill is ready? Hold your hand above the grill 4 to 5 inches from the hot coals. If you can hold it there for only 3 to 4

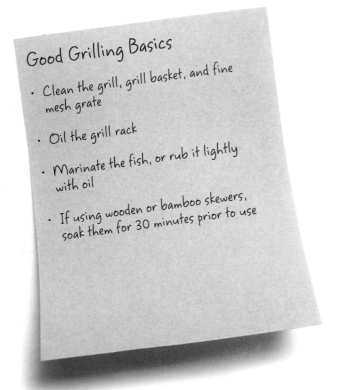

Good Grilling Basics

- Clean the grill, grill basket, and fine mesh grate
- Oil the grill rack
- Marinate the fish, or rub it lightly with oil
- If using wooden or bamboo skewers, soak them for 30 minutes prior to use

Gas or Charcoal

- Most households do some sort of grilling, on a simple hibachi or a state-of-the-art gas grill.

- Cooks who use charcoal or a wood-burning grill are passionate about the smoky flavor of their food.

- People who prefer gas grills cite their convenience.

- Aromatic wood chips can be added to charcoal grills and to some gas grills.

seconds, the temperature is perfect and you can start grilling.

If you're cooking fish fillets, put the flesh side down first. Cook for about ⅓ of the total cooking time given in your recipe (usually 10 minutes per inch of thickness). Turn the fish over once to finish cooking.

Kabobs are fun and stretch your seafood dollar. Fish and vegetables should be cut into uniform 1-inch cubes. Leave mushrooms and cherry tomatoes whole. Medium to large shrimp are great on skewers.

ZOOM

Fish cooks quickly on the grill so be careful to avoid overcooking, which will dry out the fish. Delicate fish can be cooked on a sheet of heavy-duty aluminum foil that's been perforated and oiled. The holes allow grill smoke to penetrate and flavor fish. Charcoal and wood-burning grills can be messy, but they provide that distinctive charcoal flavor. Try using hickory, mesquite, or alder wood chips.

Aromatic Infusions

- Three types of wood are used in grilling: basic, fruity, and specialty.

- The basic woods are white and red oak, pecan, hickory, maple, and mesquite.

- The fruity woods include apple and cherry.

- Specialty woods consist of the woody stems of herbs (especially rosemary), lilac, olive, grapevine, and seaweed.

Marinades Enrich Flavor

- Marinades are used to enhance the flavor of fish and seafood.

- A basic marinade can be made with oil, lemon juice or wine, and various flavorings.

- Flavorings can include onions, celery and carrots, as well as herbs like thyme and bay leaves, and spices.

- Marinades can be derived from the cuisines of China, Japan, India, and Thailand.

EASY GRILLING INDOORS

When outside just isn't an option, you can grill indoors with the right equipment

Grilling aficionados can now grill their favorite foods year-round and in all kinds of weather, thanks to new indoor grills that are safe to use.

There are 3 types of indoor grills:

The open grill is a freestanding electric unit that looks a lot like a small outdoor grill.

The countertop contact grill is basically an electric panini press that allows you to grill your food on both sides at the same time.

Some kitchen stoves come with stovetop grills and griddles. These accessories either sit on top of the stove, or they replace stovetop heating coils. This is the best way to do any

Stovetop Grills

- Some stove manufacturers (Viking, Thermador, Wolf, and others) offer built-in grill accessories.

- Some grills can double as a griddle by swapping the grill grate for a flat griddle pan.

- The advantages include convenience and safety.

- The disadvantages include the lack of wood smoke flavor.

Grill Pans

- Another way to grill food indoors is with a grill pan.

- Durable cast-iron grill pans retain and distribute heat evenly and effectively.

- The ridged cooking surface inside the pan creates grill marks on the food being cooked.

- Grill pans with deep ridges prevent the food from contacting the grease and fat in the bottom of the pan.

indoor grilling because the smoke can be easily removed by turning on the stove's overhead exhaust hood.

Indoor grills require a cook's complete attention. The smoke can be a problem, so it's a good idea to trim excess fat from food that's about to be cooked. The less fat you have, the less smoke there will be. If possible, keep your indoor grill near an open window or turn on your stove's exhaust hood. You also have to be aware of the fire risk. Always keep a fire extinguisher on hand. A list of the latest and best indoor grills can be found online. Simply search "indoor grills."

Speedy Contact Grills

- Contact grills have both top and bottom cooking surfaces.

- These grills are designed to cook both sides of the food at the same time.

- They offer a faster cooking time than open grills.

- Contact grills with removable grill plates are easier to clean.

Grills for Entertaining

- An indoor electric grill with a large cooking surface is ideal when cooking for a crowd.

- The Sanyo Smokeless Indoor Electric Grill gets favorable reviews for its large capacity and easy cleanup.

- The West Bend Electric Indoor Grill is large enough to cook for a family.

- The DeLonghi Perfecto is another highly rated open grill with a glass lid that minimizes splatters.

COOKING METHODS

DEEP-FRYING & PAN-FRYING

Frying is probably the single most popular method of fish cookery in the world

Throughout America, the fish fry is a popular culinary tradition. The fish may vary from region to region, but the process is basically the same everywhere. Fresh fish is breaded lightly and fried in oil. With a crispy golden exterior, the fish is sweet and moist. This combination of delicate fish flavor and crusty batter is hard to beat.

For most fish recipes, the oil should be deep enough in the frying pan to come about halfway up the side of the fish being cooked.

It's best to coat fish with breading or a batter before frying. This seals in the natural flavor and juiciness of the fish, without absorbing a lot of oil.

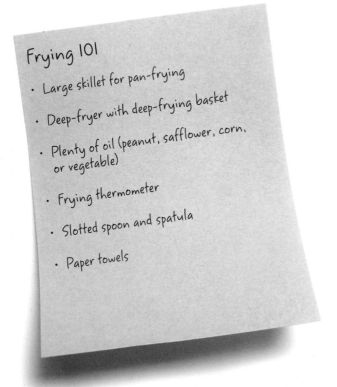

Frying 101

- Large skillet for pan-frying
- Deep-fryer with deep-frying basket
- Plenty of oil (peanut, safflower, corn, or vegetable)
- Frying thermometer
- Slotted spoon and spatula
- Paper towels

Stovetop Deep-frying

- A deep pot with 2 handles and a wire basket insert can be used for deep-frying on top of the stove.

- When the fish is cooked, the basket is used to lift out and drain the fish.

- Often the baskets have rests for propping the food above the oil to drain.

- Frying oil can be used again and again, but it should be refrigerated and reserved for fish only.

When frying fish, it's crucial that the oil be between 350 and 375°F at all times. Rather than guess, you can use a fat thermometer to check the temperature. If you are frying up a large batch of fish, allow the oil to come back to temperature between batches.

When you remove the fish from the frying pan, place it on plenty of paper towels to drain off any excess fat. Keep the cooked fish in a warm oven until all the fish has been fried. This will keep the coating crispy.

Electric Deep-fryers

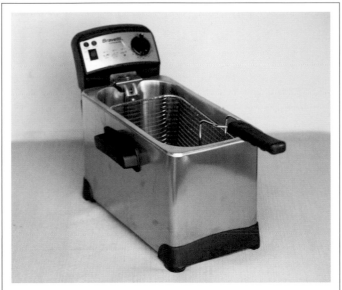

- An electric deep-fryer is a deep electric pot with a wire frying basket.

- It has a temperature control, which helps the cook maintain an even frying temperature.

- Electric deep-fryers come in a variety of sizes for the home cook as well as the professional chef.

- Electric deep-fryers fit easily on a countertop and have very quick temperature recovery time.

Easy Pan-frying

- Pan-frying can be done in a large skillet, preferably with straight deep sides.

- A specialized frying thermometer will help you maintain an even temperature in non-electric frying pans.

- Electric skillets offer a temperature control for even pan-frying.

- Cast-iron skillets can be used for pan-frying, but they heat up and cool down slowly.

COOKING METHODS

HERBED PAN-SEARED SALMON

Tangy mustard and savory herbs give this easy-to-make salmon a flavorful crust

Fast, easy, and so delicious! A simple coating of Dijon mustard, tarragon, and chive flavors the fish and seals in the natural juices during the cooking. Afterwards, the pan is deglazed with wine and butter and the resulting sauce bathes the salmon in even more flavor.

The key to a perfect crust in this dish is a hot pan and a little patience. Don't try to move the fillets around; let them form a crust and they will release naturally after a minute or 2.

Salmon can range from pale pink to fiery orange. More important than color is texture and aroma: Fresh salmon is resilient and has a clean smell; old salmon is mushy and smells "fishy." *Yield: 2 servings*

Ingredients:

2 (6-ounce) salmon steaks or skinless fillets

2 tablespoons Dijon mustard

2 tablespoons dried tarragon

2 tablespoons dried chives

1 tablespoon light olive oil

1/2 cup dry white wine

2 tablespoons butter

Herbed Pan-seared Salmon

- Dry salmon well. Spread half the mustard over 1 side of fish. Coat with half of the herbs. Turn salmon over and repeat.

- Heat a heavy sauté pan or skillet until hot. Drizzle oil into pan; immediately add salmon.

- Cook 1 to 3 minutes per side (depending on thickness) until a golden crust forms. Remove from pan to a heated plate.

- Pour wine into pan and cook until reduced by half. Whisk in butter; spoon sauce over the fish. Serve immediately.

Mushroom-dusted Spaghetti Squash: Cut a medium spaghetti squash in half lengthwise; remove seeds and fiber. Place in a microwave-safe dish, cut-side down, and cover with plastic wrap. Cook on high 10 to 15 minutes until tender. Remove strands with a fork; drain well. Grind 2 tablespoons dried wild mushrooms in a mortar or spice grinder until nearly powdered. Toss squash strands with salt, pepper, and mushroom powder. Serve as a side dish.

Salmon with Spiced Apple Mustard: Dry 2 salmon fillets or steaks well. Drizzle a tablespoon of oil in hot heavy skillet; add salmon. Cook 1 to 2 minutes per side. Remove; keep warm. To the pan, add 1 tablespoon whole grain mustard, 1/2 cup apple juice, and 1/4 teaspoon ground allspice. Stir until heated; whisk in 1 tablespoon butter. Spoon sauce over fillets.

Coat Fish with Herbs

- The salmon steaks or fillets are coated on each side with a generous amount of Dijon mustard.

- After each side is coated, the tarragon and chives are sprinkled into the mustard.

- Fish can also be coated with a thick glaze and then dusted with herbs and spices, which forms a nice crust as it cooks.

- Some basic glazes are reduced, highly concentrated stocks.

Whisk Butter into Pan

- After the salmon is sautéed in light olive oil, it's removed from the pan.

- White wine is added to the pan to deglaze it, and it is cooked until reduced by half.

- Butter is then added to the pan to make a creamy wine and butter sauce to serve with the salmon.

- This is similar to a classic beurre blanc, but simpler.

SALMON

SALMON & VEGETABLE PASTA

Salmon, peas, and toasted walnuts in a creamy sauce make for elegant comfort food

Pasta and peas are a natural combination and a favorite Italian comfort food. Here, we add a touch of dill, some toasted walnuts, and the lush flavor and delicate color of lightly poached salmon fillet. Bring them all together with an easy, creamy sauce and you've got a meal that is perfect for a cool evening in any season.

In addition to salmon fillets, you can also use leftover grilled salmon fillets or steaks broken into chunks.

Frozen peas have wonderful flavor and are a fine substitute for fresh (don't use canned peas —they're too mushy).

Use fresh dill for its bright flavor and save a few small fronds to garnish the dish for an elegant finish. *Yield: 4 servings*

Ingredients:

1 pound penne rigate pasta

1 pound skinless salmon fillet

1 (15-ounce) can chicken broth

1 cup chopped yellow onion

2 tablespoons canola or vegetable oil

2 tablespoons flour

1 cup milk

1/2 cup fresh or thawed frozen green peas

1/4 cup chopped fresh dill

1/4–1/2 teaspoon white pepper

1/4 cup chopped walnuts, lightly toasted

Dill fronds for garnish

Salmon and Vegetable Pasta

- Cook pasta in salted water according to package directions; drain and set aside. Poach salmon in simmering broth 3 to 5 minutes. Remove and keep warm. Reserve broth.

- Sauté onion in oil until softened; add flour and cook 2 minutes more. Slowly add broth and milk, stirring constantly, until thickened.

- Stir in the peas, dill, and pepper; cook 3 minutes more and toss with pasta.

- Divide pasta between 4 bowls; top with chunks of salmon and sprinkle with walnuts and dill fronds.

Toasting Nuts

Mincing Fresh Herbs

- Nuts can be toasted in a frying pan or roasted in an oven.

- Nuts must be watched carefully because they can quickly burn.

- To toast nuts, spread them in a single layer in a large frying pan over medium-high heat for a few minutes.

- To roast nuts, spread them in a single layer on a baking sheet and place the sheet in a 375°F oven for 5 minutes, shaking the pan after a couple of minutes.

- To mince fresh herbs, you must chop them very fine.

- First, chop the herbs roughly, forming them into a neat pile.

- With 1 hand on the tip of the knife blade and the other hand on the handle, rock the blade back and forth.

- With your knife blade, continue moving from 1 end of the pile to the other; repeat crosswise.

SALMON

ASIAN SALMON LETTUCE WRAPS

An exciting "roll your own" meal idea for parties or family dinner fun

More than ever before, people like to customize. From cell phones to body art, personal expressions of creativity are everywhere. So why not on the dinner plate, too?

This excitingly different approach to dinner takes its cue from a style of eating that's quite popular in Asian cultures. Each diner fills a lettuce leaf with his choice of ingredients, rolls it up, and enjoys his tasty creation. Then they all do it again, varying ingredients and quantities to suit their taste.

Buy the freshest salmon you can find, preferably filleted from a whole fresh fish, and feel free to add other goodies to the choices offered—more is always better when it comes to variety. *Yield: 4 servings*

Ingredients:

1 1/2 pounds skinless sashimi-grade salmon fillet, cut into strips (approx 1/4-inch thick by 2 to 3 inches long)

2 tablespoons Sriracha or similar hot chili sauce

1 teaspoon toasted sesame oil

1/2 teaspoon sugar

3 scallions, green and white parts minced separately

1 1/2 cups jasmine rice or other long grain rice

2 1/2 cups water

1 tablespoon grated or minced fresh ginger

2 tablespoons toasted sesame seeds

1 teaspoon salt

1 large head green leaf lettuce, rinsed and separated into leaves (stems cut out)

1 medium cucumber, peeled, seeded, and cut into 1/4-inch strips

1 cup matchstick-cut carrots

Asian Salmon Lettuce Wraps

- Mix salmon strips with Sriracha, sesame oil, sugar, and green parts of scallions. Refrigerate.

- Bring rice and water to a boil; add white parts of scallions, ginger, sesame seeds, and salt. Cover and cook 15 minutes on lowest heat.

- Separate lettuce leaves. Rinse, dry well, and cut in half lengthwise.

- Serve rice in individual bowls. Divide lettuce leaves among guests. Place salmon and vegetables on individual plates or on a communal platter. Serve with Sweet Peanut Sauce.

Sweet Peanut Dipping Sauce: Combine 3/4 cup of Asian-style sweet chili sauce (such as Mae Ploy brand) with 1 teaspoon (or more) *nuoc mam* or similar fish sauce, 1 tablespoon fresh squeezed lime juice, and 2 tablespoons finely chopped roasted peanuts. Mix well and serve in small bowls for dipping.

Slammin' Salmon Hand Rolls: Prepare salmon, rice, cucumber, and carrots as for main recipe. Lightly toast 10 sheets of sushi nori over a low flame (about 5 seconds per side). Cut each sheet in half lengthwise. Place a small handful of rice at 1 end; place some of the salmon and vegetables on rice diagonally. Fold corner over onto rice and roll into a cone. Seal end with water.

Slice Salmon into Strips

Seeding Cucumbers

- Cut the salmon fillets into strips that are approximately 2 to 3 inches long and ¼ inch thick.

- Make sure you are using sashimi-grade salmon.

- In a bowl, combine the hot chili sauce, hot sesame oil, sugar, and minced scallions (green part only).

- Pour the mixture over the salmon strips, and refrigerate the salmon until needed.

- For this recipe, use a regular cucumber, not the English variety, medium in size.

- Peel the cucumber, trimming the ends, and cut it in half lengthwise.

- Using a soup spoon, scoop out the seeds, making sure you scrape out all the pulp.

- Cut the cucumber into ¼-inch strips.

SALMON

TOMATO & FENNEL BRAISED SALMON

Fennel, a Mediterranean favorite since ancient times, pairs beautifully with thick, moist salmon steaks

This dish uses fennel in 3 ways: the white bulb is braised in butter and wine, aromatic fennel seeds season broth, and feathery fronds contribute their bright, spring-fresh flavor.

Sometimes labeled "anise" in the produce section, fennel has a mild licorice taste that mellows with cooking. Eaten raw, slices of the white bulb are crisp and refreshing in salads or as crudités. Try paper-thin slices with a little olive oil, a few drops of fresh lemon juice, freshly grated black pepper, and shaved Parmesan as a summer salad with grilled foods.

The green stalks can be stringy, but are a flavorful addition to the stockpot. The feathery fronds make an excellent garnish. *Yield: 2 servings*

Ingredients:

2 cups sliced (approx. 1/4 inch) fennel bulb (white part)

2 tablespoons butter

3/4 cup white wine

1/4 cup chopped sun-dried tomatoes

2 teaspoons fennel seeds

1/2 teaspoon dried basil

1/8 teaspoon white pepper

1 cup chicken stock

2 salmon steaks (approx. 1 1/2-inch thick)

Fennel fronds for garnish

2 teaspoons grated or shaved Parmesan (optional)

Tomato and Fennel Braised Salmon

- Braise the fennel in butter and wine until just soft. Remove the fennel from pan; keep warm.

- Add sun-dried tomatoes, fennel seeds, basil, pepper, and stock to pan.

- Bring to a simmer; add salmon, cover, and simmer 5 minutes. Remove any foam from broth, spoon broth over salmon, and cook 1 to 2 minutes more.

- Divide broth between 2 shallow bowls. Place salmon in center; mound braised fennel on top, sprinkle with fennel fronds and grated or shaved Parmesan.

Baked Salmon with Slow-roasted Fennel: Toss 4 cups sliced fennel bulb (white part) with 2 tablespoons olive oil, 1 minced garlic clove, and ¼ teaspoon salt in a roasting pan; bake 30 to 40 minutes at 325°F, stirring regularly until lightly colored. Sprinkle 2 salmon fillets (approx. 8 ounces each) with salt and pepper and lay on fennel. Cover with foil and bake 15 minutes or until salmon is opaque.

Salmon, Fennel, and Radicchio Salad: Poach 2 salmon fillets in 1 cup chicken broth and ½ cup white wine until barely opaque (3 to 5 minutes). Let cool. Slice 1 small fennel bulb very thinly and toss with ¼ cup bottled vinaigrette. Separate 1 head of radicchio into leaves on 2 plates. Place salmon fillets on radicchio; top with fennel slices and dressing.

Slice the Fennel

Plating the Fish

- Wash the fennel under cold running water, and remove any tough or discolored outer parts.

- Using a chef's knife, cut off the stalks and feathery fronds.

- Slice the fennel bulb into ½-inch pieces for braising in this recipe.

- Set the fennel fronds aside to garnish the finished dish, and use the fennel stalks to make a vegetable stock.

- Two shallow bowls with wide rims are ideal for serving this salmon dish.

- Divide the broth between the 2 bowls, and place the cooked salmon in the center of each bowl.

- Mound the braised fennel nicely on top of the salmon.

- Sprinkle each bowl with shaved Parmesan cheese and garnish with fennel fronds.

SALMON

MEXICAN SALMON & CORN SALAD

Sweet and smoky grilled corn meets boldly flavored salmon in this easy and impressive dish

Carts selling *elote*, freshly grilled ears of corn seasoned with mayonnaise, Cotija cheese, lime juice, and chili powder, are a familiar sight in Mexico and California. Cotija has a delightfully tangy, salty flavor similar to feta but milder. It's an increasingly popular and versatile cheese.

This method cooks the corn quickly and keeps it moist while imparting a nice smoky flavor. The zesty salmon grills up juicy and delicious, and the snow peas add a bright flavor and a satisfying crunch.

It can be prepared entirely outdoors and makes a lovely summertime dinner. *Yield: 4 servings*

Ingredients:

4 large ears sweet corn, husks and silk removed

Mayonnaise for brushing

4 (4- to 6-ounce) skinless salmon fillets

1 tablespoon olive oil

1 tablespoon dried thyme

2 tablespoons chili powder

$1/2$ teaspoon salt

$1/4$ cup mayonnaise

2 tablespoons grated Cotija cheese

2 tablespoons finely chopped cilantro leaves

$1 1/2$ teaspoons fresh lime juice

$1/2$ teaspoon cayenne

$1/2$ teaspoon freshly ground black pepper

8 ounces snow pea pods, cut into thin strips

Mexican Salmon and Corn Salad

- Brush corn with mayonnaise and grill, turning frequently, for about 10 minutes until browned in spots.

- Brush salmon with olive oil. Sprinkle top and bottom of each piece with thyme, chili powder, and salt. Grill salmon for 2 to 3 minutes per side until lightly firm.

- Cut the corn kernels off the cob using a sharp knife. Mix corn kernels with remaining ingredients.

- To serve, divide snow peas between the plates and spoon elote mixture in the center. Top with grilled salmon.

••••••••• GREEN ● LIGHT •••••••••

Here's a "corny" idea you'll love: Don't throw away those corncobs; save them in the freezer and add them to the pot next time you're making stock. Corncobs have a surprising amount of sweet corn flavor that will enrich your homemade chicken, vegetable, or beef stock.

•••• RECIPE VARIATION ••••

Caribbean Confetti Salad: Grill corn as for the main recipe. Brush the salmon with prepared jerk seasoning; grill 2 to 3 minutes per side. Cut the corn kernels from the cob and mix with $1/4$ cup each diced red and green bell pepper, $1/2$ cup chopped mango, 2 tablespoons flaked coconut, 1 tablespoon lime juice, and $1/4$ teaspoon each cayenne and salt.

Grill the Corn

Removing the Kernels

- Test fresh corn by pinching a kernel between your fingers; the juice should taste fresh and sweet.

- When removing husks from corn, leave stem on as a handle. Cut the tip off the cob to steady it on the cutting board.

- Grill salmon according to thickness and the heat of the grill. Press with your finger to gauge doneness.

- Rainy day blues? Make this under the broiler! Turn corn frequently; broil salmon 2 minutes per side.

- If corn gets too dark in spots, just scrape off the charred bits before cutting.

- Hold corn by the stem and stand it up on a cutting board. With a sharp knife, make downward cuts along the cob to remove the kernels.

- Find Cotija in the supermarket with the international cheeses or near the refrigerated tortillas.

- If you can't find Cotija, substitute grated dried ricotta (ricotta salata) or Parmesan.

SALMON

45

SALMON & ONION BISCUIT PIES

These little flaky pies are a sweet and smoky treat for lunch, brunch, or get-togethers

Everyone loves these tasty pies with their combination of homemade onion marmalade and salty, peppery smoked salmon. This marmalade comes together quickly and doesn't require a lot of cooking—just enough to soften the ingredients and meld the flavors. The base of the pie is a golden layer of flaky biscuit dough; use a roll of refrigerated "flaky-layer"

biscuits and separate each biscuit into 2 or 3 thinner ones.

Each of these "mini-biscuits" is perfect for making a flaky little tart crust in the bottom of a muffin cup. Press the dough slightly up the sides, top with the ingredients, and bake.

Use the thick-cut style of "hot smoked" salmon coated with coarse black pepper for this recipe. *Yield: 18 to 20 appetizers*

Ingredients:

1 tablespoon butter

1 tablespoon canola or vegetable oil

2 cups chopped sweet onions

1/2 cup chopped dried apricots

1/2 teaspoon sugar

1/4 teaspoon salt

2 tablespoons water

1 roll (10-12 ounces) refrigerated "flaky layer"-type biscuits

8 ounces black pepper-coated smoked salmon

Fresh lemon juice (optional)

Salmon and Onion Biscuit Pies

- Cook onions in butter and oil until softened; add apricots and cook until onions are caramelized. Add sugar, salt, and water; cook 5 minutes more. Let cool.

- Preheat oven to 375°F. Lightly coat 18 to 20 muffin cups with cooking spray. Separate each biscuit at the

middle layers into 2 thinner biscuits.

- Press biscuits into muffin cups. Divide onion mixture between them and top with a chunk of smoked salmon.

- Bake 10 to 15 minutes until biscuits are golden. Sprinkle with lemon juice.

Ever wonder why some smoked salmon looks different from other smoked salmon? The difference is in the method of smoking. All smoked salmon is salted and cured, but some types are "cold smoked" (smoked at low temperatures for long periods) and others are "hot smoked" at higher temperatures that dry, darken, and cook the flesh. Cold smoked salmon retains its natural color better.

• • • • RECIPE VARIATION • • • •

Sun-dried Tomato and Shallot Marmalade: Slowly cook ¹/₂ cup each of finely chopped shallots and sweet onions in 2 tablespoons butter until lightly caramelized. Add ¹/₂ cup chopped sun-dried tomatoes, 1 teaspoon sugar, a pinch of salt, and 2 tablespoons water. Cook, stirring gently, over very low heat for 10 minutes, adding a bit more water if necessary.

Dividing the Biscuits

Filling the Muffin Cups

- Pop open a tube of the flaky-layer biscuit dough from the refrigerator section of your supermarket.

- Separate the biscuit dough as directed on the package, and then separate each biscuit into 2 thinner biscuits.

- This is easy to do because the biscuit dough is made up of many layers.

- Press the biscuit dough into muffin cups.

- Press the biscuit dough into muffin cups, stretching the dough slightly up the sides of each cup.

- Place an equal amount of onion marmalade mixture in each cup.

- Top the onion marmalade mixture with a chunk of smoked salmon.

- Bake in a 375°F oven 10 to 15 minutes, or until biscuits are golden.

WINE-POACHED SALMON

Gently poached salmon is finished with cream and sliced grapes for a classic touch

Poaching is a great way to infuse fish with flavor, but many people shy away from poached salmon. Why? Because the poached salmon of the past was often dry and chalky.

Properly poached salmon, though, is both tender and moist. The key is to cook it very gently and for just long enough to barely cook it through. Overcooking and high heat make for dry fish with little flavor. Poaching in wine not only flavors the fish but gently firms the flesh; leaving the skin on during cooking helps hold the fillets together and helps retain the natural juices. The skin is removed before serving.

The quick pan sauce of cream and sliced grapes recalls the classic French *veronique* preparation. *Yield: 4 servings*

Ingredients:

3 cups champagne or dry white wine

1 cup low-sodium chicken broth

3–4 small sprigs fresh dill, plus a sprig reserved for garnish

8–10 peppercorns

Juice of 1 lemon

4 (6- to 8-ounce) salmon fillets (preferably skin-on)

8 seedless white grapes, cut in half lengthwise

1/2 cup light cream or half and half

1/8 teaspoon white pepper

Salt to taste

Lemon slices for garnish (optional)

Wine-poached Salmon

- Bring the wine, broth, dill, peppercorns, and lemon juice to a simmer in a non-aluminum pan. Cover and simmer 5 minutes.

- Add the salmon, skin-side down; cook at just below simmering for 6 minutes. Remove pan from heat.

- Remove ¾ cup of poaching liquid, strain, and briefly heat in a saucepan with the grapes. Stir in the cream and pepper. Adjust salt.

- Remove salmon from poaching liquid; discard skin. Place on warmed plates; spoon sauce over the fish.

Poached Whole Salmon: Poaching a whole small salmon is easier with a fish poacher, but it can also be done in a narrow roasting pan on the stovetop. Place a few lemon slices and some herbs inside the cavity, tie around the body in a few places with kitchen twine to close; place on an inverted roasting rack and poach for 10 minutes per inch.

Uncoated aluminum pots and pans are not suitable for cooking with acidic liquids such as vinegar, citrus juices, most marinades, and tomatoes. The acids react with the aluminum and can cause discoloration and off flavors in the foods, and can cause pitting and discoloration in the aluminum itself. Use either non-aluminum pots and pans or aluminum cookware with a coated interior for acidic foods.

Making the Poaching Liquid

- The poaching liquids commonly used include water, wine, fish stock, milk, and beer.

- Herbs and spices may be added to the poaching liquid to enhance the flavor.

- This recipe calls for wine, chicken broth, fresh dill, peppercorns, and lemon juice in the poaching liquid.

- They are combined in a non-aluminum pan in which the salmon will be poached.

Poaching the Salmon

- Bring the wine, chicken broth, fresh dill, peppercorns, and lemon juice to a simmer.

- Cover the pan and cook gently for 5 minutes.

- Add the salmon skin side down, and cook barely at a simmer for 6 minutes.

- Remove the pan from the heat. Remove the salmon from the poaching liquid. Discard the skin. Place the salmon on a warm plate.

MORE SALMON & TROUT

EASY GRILLED ARCTIC CHAR
Less well-known than its cousin, Arctic char is delicious and delicately flavored

More delicate in flavor than salmon, Arctic char has a fine texture that grills up beautifully. Though most char is farm-raised, it can vary in color from a creamy pinkish-white to fiery red depending on its habitat, diet, etc.

It's only available fresh for a short period of the year (most often as fillets or whole fish), but char fillets can be found in IQF (Individually Quick Frozen) form year round.

The marinade is easy to make, but if you're pressed for time you can use a bottled, red wine–based Italian dressing. But make certain that the dressing doesn't contain more than a small amount of sugar, as too much sugar will darken and burn on the grill. *Yield: 2 servings*

Ingredients:

2 (8-ounce) Arctic char fillets, skin on

³/₄ cup olive oil

¹/₄ cup red wine vinegar

¹/₂ teaspoon dried oregano

¹/₂ teaspoon dried basil

2 cloves garlic, minced

2 teaspoons minced shallot

¹/₄ teaspoon black pepper

¹/₂ teaspoon celery salt (or plain salt with a pinch of celery seed)

4 medium scallions, whole

2 medium yellow squash

6–8 asparagus spears

1 large or 2 medium portobello mushrooms, cut lengthwise into ¹/₄-inch thick slices

Minced parsley for garnish (optional)

Easy Grilled Arctic Char

- With a sharp knife, make shallow crosshatched cuts on both sides of the fillets and place in a bowl.

- Combine next 8 ingredients and blend thoroughly. Pour half of dressing over fish, turning to coat. Refrigerate 15 minutes.

- Dip or brush vegetables with reserved dressing and cook on a hot grill (or grill pan) until well marked. Keep warm.

- Grill the fillets, skin side down, 2 to 3 minutes. Turn fillets and grill for an additional 1 to 2 minutes until lightly firm.

Spice-crusted Planked Char: Soak 2 alder planks in water 2 hours. Preheat grill. Combine 1 tablespoon each crushed coriander seeds, crushed cumin seeds, crushed yellow mustard seeds, and crushed pink peppercorns. Rub char or salmon fillets with light olive oil; season with sea salt. Sprinkle with spice mix. Place fish on planks; grill, closed, 12 to 15 minutes. Check regularly; spray flare-ups on with water.

Creamy Cool Cucumber Sauce: Grate 1/2 of a peeled, seedless English cucumber and drain well or squeeze in a towel. Mix together 8 ounces sour cream, 1 teaspoon minced fresh mint leaves, and 1/4 teaspoon ground cardamom. Fold in the grated cucumber; add salt and pepper to taste. Refrigerate at least 30 minutes to allow flavors to blend. Serve with grilled salmon or other seafood.

Scoring the Fillets

- You can score the Arctic char by making shallow crosshatched cuts through the skin on both sides of each fillet.

- A very sharp knife is needed to make the shallow cuts, first in 1 direction and then in the other.

- Scoring helps to tenderize the fish, and it helps the fillet keep its shape.

- The marinade passes through the shallow cuts and seeps into the flesh of the fish.

Grilling the Vegetables

- All kinds of vegetables can be grilled and served either hot or at room temperature.

- Brush the vegetables with oil or marinade before placing them on the grill.

- Cut the vegetables in such a way so they do not fall through the grill into the hot coals.

- A fine mesh grill screen placed over the grill can be used to cook certain vegetables, such as asparagus.

MORE SALMON & TROUT

CRISPY CHEDDAR SALMON CAKES

Crunchy on the outside, tender on the inside, and full of tasty goodness

Do you remember those dry and dreaded "fish cakes" served in your school cafeteria? Well, these tasty treats will banish those bad memories forever!

Salmon and cheddar may not sound like a natural pairing, but once you try these you'll find that melted cheddar and savory salmon get along, well, swimmingly.

Freshly cooked salmon is used here, but this recipe is a great way to use leftover poached salmon or even canned salmon (just remove the skin and bones—yes, they're edible, but they're not very attractive). Serve with Southern Peach Salsa.

You can add more minced jalapeño pepper to your taste; the cakes are not hot, just flavorful. *Yield: 4 servings*

Ingredients:

2 cups chicken stock or 1 can (15 ounces) regular chicken broth

1 pound skinless salmon fillets

4 ounces medium or sharp cheddar, cut into ¼-inch cubes

1 cup fresh bread crumbs

¼ cup minced onion

1 tablespoon minced parsley

1 small jalapeño pepper (seeds removed), minced

1 tablespoon of Worcestershire sauce

¼ teaspoon black pepper

1 egg, beaten

¾ cup cornmeal or plain dry bread crumbs

Canola or peanut oil for frying

Crispy Cheddar Salmon Cakes

- Bring stock to a simmer in a covered pan. Cook salmon in stock until just barely cooked through. Remove salmon; let cool.

- Flake salmon and combine with next 8 ingredients. Form into 8 cakes, about ½ inch thick. Roll in crumbs; cover and chill 15 minutes.

- In a heavy skillet or frying pan, heat ¼ inch of oil over medium-high heat.

- Fry salmon cakes in hot oil until golden brown (about 2 minutes per side). Drain on paper towels.

ZOOM

Canned salmon has a mixed reputation because of the dry salmon cakes of old, but it is really quite moist and delicious. The large cans have some dark skin and soft bones included; these are completely edible, but unappealing, and the bones are chalky so it's best to remove them. Small cans (and the newer foil packets) are usually boneless and skinless.

Cubing the Cheddar

- To cut the cheddar cheese into cubes, first cut the block of cheese into slices that are ¼ inch thick. A chef's knife is recommended for this task.

- Next, cut the slices in half lengthwise.

- Then cut the halves into strips that are ¼ inch long.

- Finally, cut the strips into ¼-inch cubes.

Forming the Salmon Cakes

- In a bowl, flake the salmon and add the cheese cubes, bread crumbs, minced onion, parsley, jalapeño pepper, Worcestershire sauce, black pepper, and beaten egg. Mix well.

- Divide the mixture into 8 equal portions.

- Form each portion into a cake about ½-inch thick.

- Roll the cakes in the cornmeal or bread crumbs. Refrigerate the cakes for 15 minutes.

MORE SALMON & TROUT

SMOKED SALMON PIZZA

Surprise your guest or your family with this sophisticated variation on an old favorite

Dinner parties, whether for a few friends or a large crowd, can be great fun. Slaving over a hot stove to cook for them? Not so much. That's what makes this dish so great: It comes together quickly, cooks in no time, and there's almost no cleanup afterwards.

You can use individual pre-made crusts, refrigerated rolls of pizza dough cut to size, or fresh homemade dough (super easy to make in a food processor). You can also make a large rectangular pizza and cut it into appetizer-sized squares.

Feel free to vary the ingredients to suit your tastes: arugula or radicchio, for instance, can be lively and interesting substitutes for the spinach. *Yield: 4 servings*

Ingredients:

4 (8- to 10-inch) pre-baked pizza crusts (such as Boboli)

1 (8-ounce) container chive-flavored cream cheese

3-4 cups baby spinach leaves, rinsed and well dried; large stems removed

1 cup well drained "petite-cut" tomatoes

8-12 ounces thinly sliced smoked salmon or gravlax

$1/2$ cup sliced black olives, well drained

Small capers, well drained (optional)

Sour cream

Snipped fresh chives in 1- to 2-inch lengths (optional)

Smoked Salmon Pizza

- Preheat oven to 425°F. Spread pre-baked crusts with the chive cream cheese. Top evenly with spinach leaves.

- Bake for 4 to 6 minutes until spinach is wilted. Remove from oven and top pizza evenly with the tomatoes, smoked salmon, olives, and a sprinkling of capers (if using).

- Bake 2 to 3 minutes more until toppings are warmed. Remove from oven.

- Just before serving, dab a little sour cream over the pizza. Top with a few snipped chives, if desired.

Food Processor Pizza Dough: Using the steel blade, briefly pulse together 2 cups flour and 1 teaspoon salt. Dissolve 1 packet of active dry yeast in 1 cup warm water and add slowly while processing until the dough begins to form a ball. Knead on a floured surface, coat with olive oil; place in a bowl, covered, in a warm place to rise until doubled. Repeat kneading and rising steps.

Smoked Salmon and Apple Galette: Unroll refrigerated pie crust, spread with softened cream cheese, leaving a 1-inch border. Sprinkle with allspice, lemon zest, and black pepper. Starting from center, top with alternating, overlapping rings of Nova or gravlax and thinly sliced peeled apples. Sprinkle top with lemon juice, raw sugar, and additional pepper. Fold and crimp edges. Bake at 375°F until golden.

Bake the Crusts

- Fully cooked pizza crusts are now available in supermarkets.

- Home cooks can easily and quickly produce a gourmet pizza simply by topping one of these crusts and heating it in the oven.

- These pizza crusts can be baked on a pizza stone or right on the oven rack.

- Follow the instructions on the package. Generally, these pizza crusts bake for 8 to 10 minutes in a 425 to 450°F oven.

Adding the Toppings

- Pizzas prepared at home can be quite basic and topped simply with pizza cheese, tomato sauce, and seasonings.

- Or you can make gourmet pizzas at home with the addition of cream cheese, spinach, and smoked salmon.

- Other pizza possibilities include a fresh clam pizza flavored with pancetta.

- A spicy shrimp chorizo pizza combines the shrimp and sausage with blue cheese and green onions.

55

MORE SALMON & TROUT

PAN-FRIED RAINBOW TROUT

Crispy trout fillets are paired with a ginger-apple slaw for a "great outdoors" delight!

Pan-fried rainbow trout is an American classic. It has a flavor that speaks of glimmering streams, fragrant cook fires, and blackened skillets sizzling with promise.

Here, the fillets are dredged with a simple cornmeal and flour mixture for a golden crust. They are paired with a deliciously different take on coleslaw that features the tart

sweetness of Granny Smith apples and zing of fresh ginger.

Look for fillets that are firm and moist, not mushy or dried out. They should smell fresh, with only the slightest hint of a pleasant fish scent. Better still, have your seafood purveyor cut the fillets from whole fish that have moist eyes, a clean scent, and reddish (not brown) gills. *Yield: 4 servings*

Ingredients:

2 Granny Smith apples

1 tablespoon lemon juice

2 cups finely shredded Savoy cabbage

³/₄ cup matchstick carrots

1 teaspoon sugar

2 tablespoons grated or finely minced ginger root

¹/₂ cup flour

1 cup yellow cornmeal

1 teaspoon celery salt

¹/₂ teaspoon black pepper

Pinch of cayenne (optional)

8 small (3- to 4-ounce) skinless rainbow trout fillets

6 tablespoons butter, divided (3 tablespoons for each batch)

Salt and pepper to taste

Pan-fried Rainbow Trout

- Grate the apples and immediately stir to coat with lemon juice. Stir in the next 4 ingredients. Cover and refrigerate.

- Mix the flour, cornmeal, and spices. Dredge the fillets and place them on a tray to rest.

- Heat half the butter in a large skillet or frying pan over medium-high heat. Re-dredge the fillets and fry in 2 batches, 2 to 3 minutes per side or until golden.

- Drain fillets on paper towels. Stir apple slaw well before serving.

Trout Almandine: Sauté ¼ cup sliced almonds in 2 tablespoons butter until lightly browned; remove. Dust 4 medium trout fillets with salt, pepper, and flour. Melt another tablespoon of butter in pan and add fillets. Fry until golden 2 to 3 minutes per side; remove. Add ¼ cup white wine, 2 tablespoons lemon juice, and almonds to pan; stir until thickened. Pour over fillets. Sprinkle with minced parsley.

Rainbow Trout Caponata Crostini: Remove skin from 4 ounces of hot-smoked trout fillets and flake; sprinkle with 2 teaspoons red wine vinegar and ¼ teaspoon marjoram. Spread 24 crostini (or toasted baguette slices) with about ½ tablespoon caponata (available in jars in the supermarket) and warm briefly in the oven. Top with a dab of the marinated smoked trout and serve.

Grating the Apples

- Grating is the method used to break up a solid, such as an apple, into small particles.

- This is done by rubbing the apple against some sort of grater, a metal tool with sharp-edged holes.

- A box grater set over a large mixing bowl works well for grating apples.

- As soon as the apple is grated, add the lemon juice and stir well to prevent the bits of apple from turning brown.

Pan-frying the Trout

- Pan-frying is a wonderful method for cooking small whole fish or fillets.

- The fish should be dredged in flour, which will seal in moisture as it cooks.

- A medium-high heat is appropriate for pan-frying. The fish will cook quickly in 2 to 3 minutes per side.

- Fry the fish in a fat that doesn't burn at high temperatures.

MORE SALMON & TROUT

STUFFED WHOLE TROUT WITH BACON

This variation on a classic uses mushrooms, bacon, and dried cranberries in the stuffing

A whole stuffed trout is a true delight: The savory juices from the fish infuse the filling, while the aromatic vegetables and seasonings flavor the meaty flesh of the trout. This recipe uses classic American flavors like bacon and cranberries that bring the dish to a new level.

You can use dried cherries, dried apricots, or even dried apples in the stuffing. You can also substitute ¼ cup of wild rice for ¼ cup of the white rice.

You can remove the skin after cooking (or you can pass it under a hot broiler for a minute to crisp it up) and the flesh will be moist and flaky and will separate from the bones easily. *Yield: 2 servings*

Ingredients:

½ cup finely chopped mushrooms

½ cup chopped onions

¼ cup chopped celery

2 tablespoons butter

¼ cup dried cranberries

¼ cup crisp-cooked bacon, crumbled

¼ teaspoon black pepper

1¼ cups cooked rice

Salt to taste

2 dressed rainbow or other medium trout (about 1¾–2 pounds total)

Light olive oil or canola oil

Salt and pepper

Stuffed Whole Trout with Bacon

- Sauté the mushrooms, onions, and celery in butter until well softened. Add the cranberries, bacon, black pepper, and cooked rice; heat through. Adjust salt.

- Rinse and dry the trout; rub with oil. Sprinkle inside and out with salt and pepper. Fill the trout with stuffing and secure with toothpicks, if necessary.

- Place the fish on an oiled broiler pan and bake in a preheated 400°F oven about 15 to 18 minutes.

- Serve as is or with Lemon Sage Butter.

• • • • RECIPE VARIATIONS • • • •

Lemon Sage Butter: Make a chiffonade of 4 fresh sage leaves by stacking them on top of each other, rolling them up lengthwise, and slicing them very thinly. Toss to separate. Heat the juice of ½ of a medium lemon with 1 tablespoon of strained pan juices; whisk in 3 tablespoons butter. Stir in the sage chiffonade and pour over fish.

Indian-style Stuffed Trout: Combine 1¼ cups cooked basmati rice, ½ teaspoon each toasted coriander and mustard seeds, 2 tablespoons each chopped cashews and sultanas (golden raisins). Moisten with a little chicken stock and lemon juice; adjust seasonings. Prepare trout as for main recipe, fill with stuffing; secure with toothpicks, if necessary. Place the fish on an oiled broiler pan and bake as for recipe.

Thoroughly Rinse the Cavity

- The freshest trout is covered with a slippery layer of slime, but most trout is sold already gutted and ready to cook.

- Rinse the trout under cold running water, making sure the cavity is clean.

- Trout is one of the longest lasting fish you can buy, and it will keep for several days in the refrigerator.

- A fresh trout has a very delicate flavor, herbaceous and grass-like.

Stuffing the Trout

- After you rinse each trout thoroughly, especially the gutted cavity, dry the fish with a paper towel.

- Season the trout inside and out with salt and pepper.

- Fill the trout's gutted cavity with the stuffing that you have prepared.

- Secure the cavity with toothpicks to prevent the stuffing from falling out. Place the trout on an oiled broiler pan for baking in the oven.

CAJUN TUNA STEAKS

Versatile tuna gets a kick of Cajun flavor in this Big Easy entree

France, Africa, Spain, and Italy have all had a significant culinary influence on New Orleans cuisine. But, surprisingly enough, it was Canada that made New Orleans one of the most famous food cities in the world. Cajun cooking, made popular by the great Paul Prudhomme, came about when displaced Acadians from Canada migrated south to Louisiana. They brought with them their language and their cooking traditions, and adapted them to the local foodstuffs.

This recipe is no stranger to bold flavor, but it's not overly hot. You can add or subtract cayenne to taste. Choose firm red or pink (not brown) tuna steaks and make sure you have adequate ventilation during the searing, as there will be some smoke. *Yield: 4 servings*

Ingredients:

1 pound bag frozen corn kernels

2 tablespoons butter

2 cloves garlic, minced

$1/2$ cup chopped green bell peppers

$1/2$ cup chopped red bell peppers

$1/2$ cup chopped yellow onion

1 large ripe tomato, seeded and chopped

1 teaspoon sugar

$1/2$ teaspoon salt

$1/2$ teaspoon black pepper

$1/4$ teaspoon cayenne

$1/4$ cup half-and-half or milk

1 tablespoon hot pepper sauce

$1/2$ cup melted butter

1 teaspoon each dried thyme, garlic powder, paprika, cumin, salt, and black pepper

4 (6- to 8-ounce) tuna steaks

Cajun Tuna Steaks

- Pulse frozen corn briefly in food processor until coarsely chopped.

- Melt the butter in a covered pan; sauté corn with garlic and vegetables for 7 minutes. Add sugar, spices, and milk; cover and simmer 20 minutes.

- Stir hot sauce into butter; brush over tuna. Combine all the spices and dust tuna liberally.

- Heat a heavy-bottomed skillet until very hot. Sear tuna 1–3 minutes per side. Let rest 1 minute; slice and serve over maque choux.

Make the Maque Choux

Searing the Tuna Steaks

- In a food processor, pulse the frozen corn kernels until they are coarsely chopped.

- In a sauté pan (1 that has a cover), melt the butter.

- Add the chopped corn kernels, minced garlic, and chopped vegetables. Stir to combine, and sauté everything for 7 minutes.

- Add the sugar, salt, black pepper, cayenne pepper, and half-and-half or milk. Cover and simmer for 20 minutes.

- Searing is a cooking method in which meat or fish is subjected to very high heat in order to seal in the juices.

- Heat a heavy-bottomed skillet until very hot. Cast-iron pans are good for searing.

- Brush the tuna steaks with a mixture of melted butter and hot sauce. Dust the tuna liberally with the combined spices.

- Place the tuna in the hot pan. Sear on both sides, 1 to 3 minutes. Let rest 1 minute.

MEDITERRANEAN BRAISED TUNA

Give tuna an incredible depth of flavor by braising it with Italian-style marinated vegetables

This dish is so easy and so quick that you'll be amazed at how flavorful it is. In little more than the time it takes to boil pasta, you'll have a wonderfully fragrant, restaurant-style meal.

You can add more and/or different marinated vegetables to suit your taste. Marinated artichokes are a nice addition, as is marinated grilled zucchini. If you have leftover grilled vegetables such as asparagus, you can marinate them yourself in good olive oil with some crushed garlic and Italian seasoning.

Serve the tuna and sauce on a bed of the pasta in a shallow bowl. Drizzle a little fresh lemon juice over the top and make sure you have some crusty bread nearby. *Yield: 4 servings*

Ingredients:

1 jar (approximately 12 ounces) Italian marinated vegetables (any combination of mushrooms, eggplant, peppers, onions, etc.)

1 (14.5-ounce) can roasted garlic-flavored stewed (or chopped) tomatoes

1 pound pasta (small shells or other small shape)

4 (6- to 8-ounce) tuna steaks

Olive oil

1/2 cup frozen green peas, thawed

3 tablespoons chopped fresh parsley leaves

Lemon wedges

Mediterranean Braised Tuna

- Drain the marinated vegetables, reserving marinade. Simmer together marinated vegetables and canned tomatoes for 10 minutes.

- Cook pasta in salted water according to package directions. Drain well. Toss pasta with 2 to 3 tablespoons of marinade. Keep warm.

- While pasta is cooking, sear the tuna steaks in a little olive oil 1 minute per side. Pour the sauce over; cover and simmer 5 to 7 minutes. Stir in green peas; remove from heat.

- Toss pasta with parsley. Serve tuna with lemon wedges.

Tuna au Vin: Cook 6 ounces thick bacon cut in small pieces in a deep, covered skillet; remove bacon. Add 4 thick tuna steaks, 6 ounces each pearl onions, baby carrots, and white mushrooms; brown tuna lightly and remove. Add 1 cup each red wine and chicken stock, 1 teaspoon sugar, and 1 large bay leaf. Simmer, covered, 20 minutes. Return tuna and bacon to pot; simmer 10 minutes.

• • • • • • • YELLOW ● LIGHT • • • • • • • •

There are many species of tuna available, but some choices are better than others. While real bluefin tuna is the top choice for its deep color and rich flavor, it is seriously over-fished and very expensive. However, yellowfin and bigeye tuna (both also called ahi) from the Atlantic are delicious and more readily available—both in the ocean and in the supermarket—and are a responsible choice.

Simmer the Sauce

Add the Green Peas

- Using a sieve, strain the marinated Italian veg-etables, reserving the marinade.

- You will need the reserved marinade later in the recipe to flavor the cooked pasta.

- In a large pot, combine the marinated vegetables with the stewed tomatoes, including the juice from the can.

- Bring mixture just to a boil, reduce the heat, and sim-mer for 10 minutes.

- After you sear the tuna steaks in a large skillet (one that has a cover), pour the sauce over the tuna.

- Cover and simmer 5 to 7 minutes.

- Stir in frozen peas. Remove the pot from the heat.

- Adding the frozen peas at the very end of the cooking ensures that they will be tender and bright green when the dish is served.

TUNA "STEAK & POTATOES"–STYLE
Fish fanciers and serious steak lovers alike will love this bold, juicy "steakhouse" tuna

Perhaps you have a friend who would eat steak 3 times a day if he could. He dismisses fish as "not real food." Well, this juicy flavorful slab of grilled tuna might just change his mind.

Use a thick-cut tuna medallion that's at least 1½ inches thick and as close in shape and size to a cut of filet mignon as possible.

Let it marinate at least 45 minutes for a deep, dark color. Then grill it over a hot fire just a few minutes per side. You want to cook it to no more than medium so it retains a rich, red center.

Present this meal with a hefty steak knife for a truly authentic touch. *Yield: 4 servings*

Ingredients:

¼ cup ponzu sauce

1 tablespoon Kitchen Bouquet (or similar browning sauce)

¼ teaspoon black pepper

4 thick (6- to 8-ounce) tuna medallions

2 pounds unpeeled small red potatoes, washed

6 cloves garlic, minced

1 teaspoon salt

2–3 tablespoons butter

¼ cup half-and-half or light cream

¼ teaspoon white pepper (plus more to taste)

2–3 tablespoons freshly grated Parmesan cheese

1 tablespoon butter, softened

Coarse salt

Tuna "Steak and Potatoes"–Style

- Combine first 4 ingredients in a zip-top bag. Shake well; refrigerate.

- Cut potatoes into chunks. In saucepan, cover potatoes and garlic with water; add salt. Bring to boil; cover and simmer until tender (15 to 20 minutes).

- Drain well, add next 4 ingredients, and mash with a fork until chunky. Keep warm.

- Preheat broiler or grill. Remove tuna and pat dry; rub lightly with butter. Broil or grill on high 2 to 3 minutes per side. Sprinkle with coarse salt and serve immediately.

• • • • RECIPE VARIATIONS • • • •

Mushroom Shallot Garnish: Melt 2 tablespoons butter with 1 tablespoon cognac or brandy. Add 8 ounces sliced cremini mushrooms; season lightly with salt and pepper and cook slowly until mushrooms soften and absorb all liquid. Keep warm. Thinly slice 2 small shallots lengthwise and dredge in seasoned flour. Deep-fry until just golden. Mound mushrooms on tuna; top with fried shallots.

Low-carbing? Try these Garlic Faux-tatoes instead: Pulse 1 pound cauliflower tops and 3 cloves garlic in food processor until finely chopped. Simmer in lightly salted water until tender; drain well. Return cauliflower to pan over low heat and stir 2 to 3 minutes to dry. Stir in 2 tablespoons butter. Whip in $1/4$ cup (or more) light cream using an immersion blender. Season with salt and white pepper.

Making the Smashed Potatoes

- Cut the small red potatoes into chunks of equal size.

- In a saucepan, combine the potatoes and garlic with enough salted water to cover.

- Bring to a boil, cover and simmer until tender, about 15 to 20 minutes. Drain well.

- Add 2 to 3 tablespoons of butter, half-and-half, or light cream, white pepper, and grated Parmesan cheese. Mash with a fork until chunky.

Grilling the "Steaks"

- Prepare the grill, or preheat the broiler. Grilling will result in steaks with nice grill marks.

- Remove tuna steaks from the marinade. Drain the steaks, and pat them dry.

- Rub both sides of the tuna steaks lightly with softened butter.

- Grill or broil the steaks 2 to 3 minutes per side for medium doneness. Sprinkle with coarse salt. Serve immediately.

ASIAN SEARED TUNA SALAD

A little-known sushi style is the basis for this pleasing mix of color and flavor

Most people are familiar with maki sushi (the versatile "rolled" style) and nigiri sushi (fish or egg-topped "fingers" of rice), but an equally delicious style remains virtually unknown.

Chirashi sushi could best be described as "country-style" sushi. It consists of a bowl of seasoned rice topped with a variety of bite-sized ingredients: raw and pickled vegetables,

small slices of raw or cooked fish, small pieces of seafood, egg, etc. It's often sprinkled with sesame seeds and served with small squares of lightly toasted nori, (seaweed sheets).

Sear the tuna just enough to color the exterior and warm the interior. This releases the complex flavors and creamy richness of the fish. *Yield: 2 servings*

KNACK FISH & SEAFOOD COOKBOOK

Ingredients:

¹/₂ cup rice vinegar

3 tablespoons sugar

1 teaspoon salt

¹/₄ cup matchstick carrots

¹/₄ cup thinly sliced red radish

¹/₄ cup bean sprouts

1 cup short-grain rice

1¹/₂ cups water

1 teaspoon toasted sesame oil

1 tablespoon ginger root matchsticks

¹/₄ teaspoon salt

2 (4-ounce) tuna medallions

2 tablespoons ponzu sauce

2-inch section seedless cucumber, split lengthwise and cut into ¹/₄-inch "half moons"

¹/₄ cup baby lettuce leaves

Toasted sesame seeds

Asian Seared Tuna Salad

- Heat first 3 ingredients until dissolved. Chill.

- Place carrots, radishes, and sprouts in separate bowls; dress each with 1 tablespoon of vinegar mixture.

- Rinse rice and place in a heavy saucepan; add water, sesame oil, ginger, and salt.

Bring to boil, cover, reduce heat; cook 15 minutes. Toss rice with remaining vinegar. Keep warm.

- Brush tuna with ponzu; sear 1½ to 2 minutes per side; slice. Drain vegetables; arrange tuna with vegetables on rice. Sprinkle with sesame seeds.

Sushi Squares: Prepare the sushi rice, pickled carrots, bean sprouts, and tuna as for the recipe. Line the bottom of a small baking pan with toasted nori and spread half the rice over it. Add the pickled vegetables, sprinkle with sesame seeds; top with remaining rice. Press down well. Cut tuna slices into squares; arrange in rows over rice and cut into serving pieces.

There's nothing quite like fresh ginger root, with its exotic fragrance, bright taste, and subtle fire. But trying to peel ginger can be tricky because of its knobby, fractal shape. An easy way to get around the nooks and crannies: Use the edge of a spoon to scrape off the papery skin. Try it and you'll never peel ginger again!

Making the Sushi Rice

- Rinse the short-grain rice under cold running water, and place the rice in a heavy saucepan.

- Add the water, sesame oil, ginger root, and salt.

- Bring to a boil. Cover the saucepan, and reduce heat to a simmer. Cook the rice for 15 minutes.

- Toss the rice with the remaining vinegar mixture. Keep the rice warm until it is served.

Decorating the Rice Bowls

- Presentation is very important in Asian cuisine, and the brightly colored garnishes whet our appetite.

- In 3 separate bowls, have matchstick carrots, thinly sliced red radishes, and bean sprouts ready for use. Dress each bowl with some of the vinegar mixture.

- Garnish each salad plate with some of the carrots. Add a few radishes to each plate.

- Bean sprouts complete the artful arrangement on the salad.

BROILED HAWAIIAN TUNA SKEWERS

Fun and festive, these sweetly exotic tuna skewers make any meal a party

Back in the days when cavemen clubbed dinner over the head, cooking food on sticks was a cutting-edge culinary technique. Today, with a wide array of sophisticated kitchen equipment at our fingertips, we still cook food on sticks. Why? Because it's still a good technique—and it's good fun!

Tuna is a natural for skewering: Its flesh is firm and meaty

and holds up well under fire (or over it). This sweet and savory version infuses big cubes of tuna with shallots, pairs it with sweet mango chunks, glazes it with teriyaki, and tops it with tasty macadamias. Serve with Lime Sultana Basmati Rice.

These South Pacific delights are equally good made under the broiler or made outdoors on a hot grill. *Yield: 3 servings*

Ingredients:

2 pounds tuna steak

2 tablespoons canola oil

1 teaspoon minced shallots or minced onion

1/4 teaspoon salt

1/4 teaspoon pepper

6 flat metal skewers

2 slightly firm mangos, peeled and cut into 12 large chunks

12 cherry tomatoes

1/2 cup teriyaki sauce

1 tablespoon fresh lime juice

3/4 cup coarsely crushed macadamia nuts

Broiled Hawaiian Tuna Skewers

- Cut tuna into 24 pieces (approximately 3/4-inch cubes). Mix tuna, oil, shallot, salt, and pepper in a bowl or zip-top bag. Refrigerate for 15 to 20 minutes.

- Thread each skewer in this order: tuna, mango, tuna, tomato, tuna, mango, tuna, tomato. Mix the teriyaki

sauce with lime juice and baste the skewers.

- Preheat broiler to high. Place skewers on a broiling rack and broil, basting, 2 to 3 minutes per side until tuna is lightly firm.

- Dredge or sprinkle skewers with crushed macadamias.

• • • • RECIPE VARIATION • • • •

Lime Sultana Basmati: Remove 1 teaspoon of zest from a medium lime; reserve. In a saucepan, stir together $1\frac{1}{2}$ cups basmati rice, $\frac{1}{2}$ teaspoon salt, 2 minced scallions, and $\frac{1}{2}$ cup sultanas (aka golden raisins), then add the juice of half of the lime and $2\frac{1}{2}$ cups water; bring to a boil. Reduce heat to very low and cook covered 12 minutes. Toss with lime zest.

MAKE IT EASY

When choosing a mango, rely on your hands and your nose, rather than your eyes: Mangos come in a wide variety of colors, none of which are sure indicators of ripeness. Choose a mango that feels slightly soft when gently squeezed. Ripe mangos often have a sweet fruity scent at the stem end. Slightly underripe mangos will ripen at room temperature (faster inside a paper bag).

Threading the Skewers

- Cut the tuna steaks into ¾-inch cubes. You should end up with about 24 chunks of tuna. Marinate the tuna in the refrigerator for 15 to 20 minutes.

- Thread each skewer beginning with tuna and alternating the tuna with chunks of mango and tomato.

- In a small bowl, mix teriyaki sauce with the lime juice.

- Baste the skewers with the teriyaki-lime mixture before and during the cooking process.

Add Macadamias for Crunch

- To crush the macadamia nuts, use a food processor or blender.

- Or you can place the nuts in a plastic bag, and pound the nuts with a meat tenderizer or hammer.

- Place the crushed nuts on a baking sheet, long enough to hold the skewers.

- After you baste the skewers, dredge or roll each skewer through the nuts on the baking sheet. The basting liquid will help the nuts stick to the tuna.

BUFFALO TUNA WITH BLUE CHEESE

Tuna may not have wings, but it does have buffalo flavor in this dish

Buffalo wings may just be the most popular regional food specialty in America. The spicy, tangy, buttery flavor—a spur of the moment creation from Buffalo, New York's now legendary Anchor Bar—is fiendishly good and thoroughly addictive.

Here, a thick tuna steak is deeply flavored with buffalo-style sauce on the outside; inside is a pocket stuffed with a creamy version of the traditional buffalo wing accompaniments.

You can use your favorite bottled wing sauce, or you can make your own. Use toothpicks or thin skewers to hold the pockets closed during cooking. Remove them just before serving so some of the cream cheese filling oozes out appealingly.

Serve with skin-on french fries, coleslaw, and plenty of cold beer. *Yield: 4 servings*

Ingredients:

¹/₂ cup buffalo-style wing sauce

¹/₂ teaspoon black pepper

1 teaspoon dried oregano

4 (6- to 8-ounce) tuna steaks (about 1 to 1¹/₂ inches thick)

¹/₄ cup finely diced celery

4 ounces blue cheese crumbles

4 ounces cream cheese, slightly softened

Buffalo Tuna with Blue Cheese

- Mix sauce, pepper, and oregano. Place tuna in a zip-top bag; pour in sauce. Press out air, seal tightly, and refrigerate. Let marinate 20 to 30 minutes.

- While the tuna is marinating, mix remaining ingredients. Cover and refrigerate.

- Cut a deep pocket in each piece of tuna. Fill with some of the blue cheese mix and secure with toothpicks.

- Brush tuna with additional marinade and broil or grill over high heat about 3 to 5 minutes per side.

• • • • RECIPE VARIATIONS • • • •

Homemade Wing Sauce: The simplest (and most authentic) wing sauce is this: Heat 1 stick of butter in a saucepan until just melted, then whisk in one 12-ounce bottle of hot pepper sauce. That's it. From there you can customize it with garlic (fresh or powdered), onion, black pepper, honey, etc. For thicker sauce, whisk 1 or more teaspoons corn starch into the hot sauce first, then simmer briefly.

BBQ Tuna with Onion: Here's a zesty idea for your grill: Mix ½ cup Texas-style barbecue sauce with 1 tablespoon of dried chives and a teaspoon of hot sauce. Marinate the tuna 20 minutes, and fill with 1 package of softened cream cheese mixed with ¼ cup chopped onion. Grill over medium heat (to prevent the sauce from burning) 4 to 6 minutes per side.

Stringing Celery

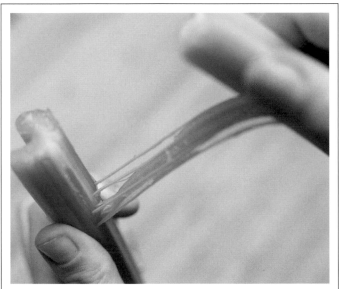

- When purchasing celery, look for solid, rigid stalks with a glossy surface of light to medium green.

- With a sharp knife, remove the base end of the celery and trim the leaves from each stalk.

- Remove strings of celery if necessary by hand. Snap off the top or bottom inch from a celery stalk, and slowly pull off any attached strings.

- Then slice, dice, or julienne the celery as directed in the recipe.

Cutting the Pockets

- Thick fish steaks can easily be cut into to form pockets that can be stuffed with various mixtures.

- One trick that makes this an easy task is to place the fish steaks in the freezer until they are semi-frozen.

- In a semi-frozen state, the steaks are firm but not frozen solid.

- Use a small and very sharp knife to carefully cut a deep pocket into each steak. Be careful not to cut all the way through.

BEER-BATTERED ONION COD

This version of Britain's famous dish adds new ingredients and new levels of flavor

When traveling in the British Isles, you'll find that even the tiniest hamlets have a fish and chips shop—or "chippie"—whose enticing fragrance will electrify your appetite.

In this version, meaty cod loins are thickly coated with a batter that features a favorite British flavor combination: cheddar and onions. The result is a decadent mix of crunchy, creamy goodness. Pacific cod is perfect for this dish (Atlantic cod is overfished); haddock is also excellent.

Use fresh, neutral oil for frying (like canola) and make sure to scoop out any onion pieces or batter bits from the oil between batches. *Yield: 4 servings*

Ingredients:

1 cup all-purpose flour

¹/₂ cup shredded cheddar cheese

¹/₂ cup chopped onions

1¹/₂ teaspoons baking powder

1 teaspoon Old Bay or other seafood seasoning

¹/₂ teaspoon salt

¹/₂ teaspoon black pepper

¹/₄ teaspoon cayenne

¹/₂ cup beer (plus additional if needed)

Oil for frying

2 pounds cod loin fillets

Beer-battered Onion Cod

- Combine the first 8 ingredients in a bowl. Slowly add beer until a thick batter is formed.

- Heat 2 inches of oil in a Dutch oven or heavy stockpot to 375°F. Rinse and dry fillets. Dip in batter and carefully lay fillets in oil.

- Fry a few pieces at a time, maintaining temperature, until golden.

- Drain on a rack and keep warm in a 200°F oven until all pieces are done. Serve with malt vinegar or lemon.

Spicy Oven Chips: Preheat oven to 450°F. Cut 4 large Idaho potatoes into ¼-inch thick lengthwise slices, then cut each slice into ¾-inch wide strips (like steak fries). Rub the inside of a large bowl with a crushed garlic clove; discard garlic. Gently toss the potatoes with 2 to 3 tablespoons canola oil and 2 teaspoons Old Bay. Place on a cookie sheet and bake until golden and crisp, turning occasionally.

Lemony Tarragon Vinegar: In a non-reactive saucepan, combine 1 cup of white wine vinegar with ⅛ cup of crushed fresh tarragon leaves. Heat slowly until just below a simmer. Remove from heat and let cool. Add the juice of 1 large lemon and squeeze the rind into the pot to extract the oils. Stir in ¼ teaspoon each of salt and sugar (or more to taste). Strain and bottle.

Mixing the Batter

- Coating fish with a batter ensures that the fish will retain its natural flavor and juiciness, without absorbing a lot of oil when fried.

- In a large bowl, combine the flour, shredded cheese, chopped onions, baking powder, seafood seasoning, salt, pepper, and cayenne.

- Slowly add the beer until a thick batter forms.

- Add more beer if needed.

Frying the Cod Fillets

- Canola oil is good for frying fish fillets such as these.

- The right temperature is essential. Use a thermometer to ensure that 375°F is maintained.

- When the fillets are golden brown, use a slotted spatula to lift the cooked fish out of the oil.

- Drain on paper towels. Keep the fish warm in a 200°F oven.

COD WITH RED PEPPER SAUCE

Foil cooking seals in the savory goodness in this easy and impressive cod dish

There are many benefits to cooking fish in foil: The fish stays perfectly moist while becoming deeply infused with flavor, it can be cooked with almost no oils or fats, and cleanup is an absolute breeze. The majestic rise of aromatic steam when the foil is opened always inspires ooo's and ahhh's.

The cod cooks up tender and flaky in its own juices, flavored by a sauce, based on a Spanish *romesco,* that features toasty almonds and fragrant tarragon wedded to the smokiness of roasted sweet red pepper.

Roasting peppers is quite easy and worth the effort for the unique flavor. Use fresh tarragon if possible; dried tarragon lacks a certain brightness. *Yield: 2 servings*

Ingredients:

3 large cloves garlic, minced

2 tablespoons olive oil

2 tablespoons white wine

1 large red bell pepper, roasted, seeded, and coarsely chopped

2 tablespoons fresh tarragon, minced (or 1 tablespoon dried)

¹/₄ teaspoon salt

¹/₄ cup chopped toasted almonds

2 (8-ounce) cod fillets

Salt and pepper

Chopped parsley for garnish (optional)

Cod with Red Pepper Sauce

- Sauté the garlic in olive oil until softened; add the wine, red pepper, tarragon, and salt. Cook 3 minutes; let cool.

- In a food processor or blender, pulse the almonds until finely ground. Add red pepper mixture; pulse until nearly smooth.

- Rinse and dry fillets; season with salt and pepper. Place each fillet in the center of an oiled 12-inch square of heavy aluminum foil.

- Top fillets with pepper mixture and seal foil. Bake at 375°F for 20 minutes.

•••• RECIPE VARIATION ••••

Cod with Poblanos and Queso: Oil two 12-inch squares of heavy aluminum foil. Rinse and pat dry 4 canned poblano peppers. Open 1 pepper on each square; sprinkle with 1 tablespoon quesadilla cheese. Dry two 8-ounce fillets, sprinkle with seasoned salt, and place on cheese. Top fish with 2 more tablespoons cheese and remaining pepper. Tent and seal foil. Bake at 375°F for 20 minutes.

ZOOM

Cod, in all its guises, has a long history, beginning with early American colonists. Cod helped turn many seaports into very profitable salted cod export centers. Cape Cod in Massachusetts was named for its connection to what had become the state's biggest business. There are more than 20 types of cod. The best known is Atlantic cod, which has been overfished in recent years.

Roasting Peppers

- Peppers can be roasted over the flame in a gas burner, or in the oven under the broiler.

- When the skin on the peppers blackens and puffs up like a balloon, it can easily be lifted off in whole sections.

- Roasted peppers should be allowed to cool before handling.

- Allowing the peppers to steam for 15 minutes in a paper bag makes it even easier to remove the charred skin.

Sealing the Foil Packets

- Place each fish fillet in the center of a 12-inch square of heavy-duty aluminum foil that's been oiled.

- Top each fillet with the pepper mixture.

- Fold each square of foil in half.

- Starting at 1 end, fold over the ends of the foil, crimping the edge again and again until a completely sealed packet is formed.

CRUNCHY BROILED HAKE FILLET

With its delightful mix of flavors and textures, this dish is sure to please

When you need something that's easy enough to make for a weekday meal, yet impressive enough for even the most special of occasions, this dish is it. Hake is less popular than cod, but it's a juicy and fine-tasting white-fleshed fish.

The pistachio crust in this dish is bound with mayonnaise, which adds flavor, keeps the fish moist, and aids in browning (don't use fat-free mayo for this as it will just separate).

You can substitute toasted chopped hazelnuts for pistachios. Use either panko crumbs or coarse, dry white bread crumbs. Regular bread crumbs are too finely ground and will just form a paste. Watch the fillets carefully during broiling so the topping doesn't burn. *Yield: 4 servings*

Ingredients:

1 cup shelled unsalted pistachio kernels

¼ cup mayonnaise

¼ cup panko crumbs

1 tablespoon minced parsley

⅛ teaspoon cayenne pepper

¼ teaspoon salt

¼ teaspoon black pepper

4 (6- to 8-ounce) hake fillets (or steaks)

Olive oil

Fresh lemon juice

Crunchy Broiled Hake Fillet

- In a food processor or blender, pulse the pistachios until finely chopped.

- In a bowl, combine the pistachios with the mayonnaise, panko crumbs, parsley, cayenne, salt, and pepper.

- Preheat broiler. Season fillets lightly with salt and pepper and place in an oiled, oven-proof skillet over medium heat. Top fillets with pistachio mixture and cook 4 to 5 minutes.

- Transfer pan to broiler. Broil until golden and bubbly, 3 to 4 minutes. Sprinkle with lemon juice.

Broiled Hake with Cashew Taratoor: In a food processor, grind together 1 cup cashew pieces, 2 cloves garlic, $\frac{1}{2}$ teaspoon dried thyme, and 1 tablespoon extra virgin olive oil until smooth. Add 2 tablespoons each fresh lemon juice and water a little at a time and process until emulsified. Adjust salt. Season hake with salt, pepper, and cumin; top with taratoor and broil until golden and bubbly.

Hake Cotija: In a shallow pan, combine $\frac{3}{4}$ cup panko crumbs with $\frac{3}{4}$ cup grated Cotija cheese and 2 tablespoons finely minced cilantro. Dry two 8-ounce hake fillets or steaks well. Brush fillets with 2 tablespoons melted butter. Sprinkle with chili powder and dredge in panko/Cotija mixture. Chill in refrigerator 5 to 10 minutes to set crust. Broil for 6 to 8 minutes until evenly browned.

Making the Nut Crust

- When pulsing the pistachios in the food processor, don't overdo the pulsing. You do not want the pistachios to be completely ground.

- Be sure to mix the combined pistachio mixture well, so that it will provide an even crust on the filet.

- Top each fish fillet with an even layer of the pistachio nut crust.

Toasting the Crust

- When broiling, keep an eye on the clock as well as on the fish fillets.

- Often the cooking time cited in the recipe might be completed, but the fish may not yet have the desired color.

- Continue to broil the fish fillets until they are golden brown, making a visual check every 30 seconds.

SAVORY GARLIC HAKE STEAK

Exotic fried capers and an unusual coating give this hake dish its exciting flavor

The city of Madrid is known for its graceful architecture, sunny squares, and broad avenues. But its side streets are home to many small neighborhood restaurants serving outstanding food, like this hake dish. A pair of clever techniques make these simple ingredients sing.

First, you infuse the olive oil by briefly sautéing a crushed garlic clove and bay leaf. Second, you dredge the fish in flour and egg—and put it directly into the oil: no second dredging in flour. This creates a puffy, golden crust that seals in the sweet fish flavor. This recipe adds mellow fried capers and lemon zest as a finishing touch. *Yield: 2 servings*

KNACK FISH & SEAFOOD COOKBOOK

Ingredients:

Olive oil for frying

2 tablespoons small capers, well dried on paper towels

1 large clove garlic, lightly crushed

1 large bay leaf

2 (6- to 8-ounce) hake steaks (approximately 1 inch thick)

Salt and pepper

$1/2$ cup flour

2 eggs, beaten

$1/2$ teaspoon lemon zest

Savory Garlic Hake Steak

- Pour ½ inch of oil in a deep skillet, add the capers, and bring to medium heat. Cook until capers begin to color. Drain on paper towels.

- Cook garlic and bay leaf until garlic is golden; remove garlic and bay leaf.

- Lightly season hake with salt and pepper. Dredge in flour; shake off excess. Dip in beaten egg and place immediately into oil.

- Cook until golden, turning once (6 to 8 minutes total). Top with fried capers and lemon zest.

•••• RECIPE VARIATION ••••

Cream-poached Hake Steaks: Bring 2 cups low-sodium chicken broth and 2 sprigs of fresh rosemary to a simmer, covered 5 to 7 minutes. Remove rosemary and stir in 1 cup light cream and $1/4$ teaspoon white pepper. Place hake steaks or fillets in pan; poach just below a simmer for 6 to 8 minutes. Remove fish and keep warm. Strain off 1 cup of liquid and reduce until thickened. Pour over fish.

MAKE IT EASY

Citrus zest—from lemons, limes, oranges, tangerines, or grapefruits—is an easy way to add bright sophisticated flavor to your dishes. If you don't own a zester, you can use a microplane or fine hole grater to remove just the very top, colored layer of the peel where the essential oils reside. Take care not to grate into the white pith, which is usually bitter.

Seasoning the Oil

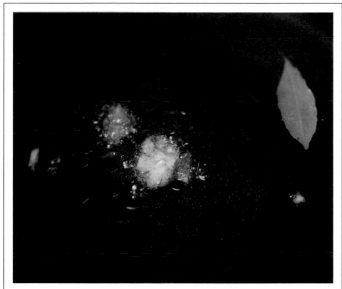

- In a deep skillet, heat $1/2$ inch of oil over medium heat.

- Add the capers and cook until they start to brown. With a slotted spoon, remove the capers from the oil and drain them on a paper towel.

- Add the garlic and bay leaf to the hot oil. Cook until the garlic is golden.

- Remove the garlic and bay leaf from the oil, which is now infused with flavor.

Dip in Egg Batter

- The surface of the hake must be completely dry for the batter to stick to the outer surface.

- The layer of flour forms a moisture barrier that absorbs moisture from the food as it cooks.

- Water in the batter produces a lighter crust than milk.

- A separated egg, with the beaten white folded in, produces a puffer coating.

79

EASY VENETIAN FISH STEW

The flavors of Italy's legendary city of canals flow together in this aromatic dish

For centuries, as a center of finance and trade, Venice received visitors from all corners of the known world. With them came new foods, spices, and techniques. Consequently, Venetian dishes often have as much in common with North Africa and the Near East as they do with traditional Italian food.

Spices have long been some of the most important and valuable commodities. For many years, saffron was worth more than its weight in gold, and highly spiced dishes were a mark of wealth and prestige.

This dish incorporates several of those prestigious and formerly exotic flavors into a simple, graceful stew that captures some of the diversity of Venetian cuisine. *Yield: 4 servings*

Ingredients:

2 tablespoons olive oil

2 medium sweet onions, peeled, halved, and sliced (about 2$^1/_2$ cups)

1 cup baby carrots, ends trimmed, cut in half

1 cup white wine

1 cup chicken stock

Juice of 1 orange

1 teaspoon dried ginger

$^1/_2$ teaspoon saffron threads, crushed (optional)

Pinch of nutmeg

2 pounds skinless, boneless haddock, cut into 1-inch pieces

$^1/_4$ cup pine nuts

1 teaspoon orange zest

Easy Venetian Fish Stew

- Heat oil in a large covered pot. Sauté onions and carrots over medium heat 5 minutes.

- Add wine, stock, juice, ginger, saffron (if using), and nutmeg. Bring to a boil; reduce heat, cover, and simmer 10 minutes.

- Add fish and simmer 5 to 7 minutes more until cooked through.

- Lightly toast the pine nuts in a dry pan until just beginning to color. Stir the orange zest into the stew; ladle stew into bowls and garnish with pine nuts.

Haddock with Peas and Rice: Briefly sauté 2 cloves minced garlic in 2 tablespoons olive oil. Add 1 pound haddock cut into pieces and toss to coat. Add 1¼ cup short-grain rice, 1 teaspoon marjoram, ½ teaspoon salt, and 2 cups water. Stir in 1½ cup frozen peas. Bring to simmer, cover, and reduce heat. Cook 15 minutes; adjust seasonings.

Haddock with Oil-cured Olives: Drain 1 can of cannellini beans; simmer with ¼ cup chicken broth until almost absorbed. Remove from heat; add 1 clove finely minced garlic. Puree with immersion blender. Heat 2 tablespoons olive oil with a sprig of fresh rosemary and ½ cup oil-cured olives; add two 8-ounce fillets to pan. Cook 3 to 4 minutes per side. Serve fish over puree; top with olives.

Saffron Colors and Flavors

- Saffron is the most expensive spice in the world.

- It has a distinctive aroma and a penetrating, bitter, and highly aromatic taste.

- Saffron threads are red-orange in color and sometimes yellow. The more vibrant the color, the higher the quality. Ground saffron is also available.

- Saffron is a key ingredient in the fish and rice dishes of Spain, France, and Italy.

Add Zest for Brightness

- A zester is a tool used to extract thin strips of the rind from oranges and lemons.

- A fine zest of orange or lemon can be obtained by using a microplane, rasp, or a very small hole grater.

- Constantly turn the fruit as it is rubbed against the grater; the zest falls onto the work surface.

- A small amount of zest is added to dishes at the end of the cooking process for a bright citrus flavor.

81

GREEK-STYLE SEAFOOD BITES

These delicate Greek seafood appetizers have a creamy texture and a bold, garlicky flavor

Sometimes, appetizers can be a bit, well, boring. There's a dull certainty in the old familiar "stuff-on-crackers" or "stuff-on-toothpicks" ideas that some folks probably find comforting, but my question is this: If the appetizers are dull, what's the party going to be like? Which is why we like these so much—1 bite of their garlicky goodness and your guests will know they came to the right place!

Use a firm white bread for these. If you use the very soft kind, cut back a bit on the liquids. Don't be afraid to use so much garlic; it won't overwhelm the end result and really gives these bites a wonderful aroma. Handle these gently as they have a delicate texture. *Yield: about 36 appetizers*

Ingredients:

3 slices white bread, crusts removed

3 large cloves garlic, coarsely chopped

1 tablespoon chopped parsley

4 ounces haddock, cut in small chunks

4 ounces small shrimp, peeled and deveined

2 tablespoons white wine vinegar

1 tablespoon olive oil

1/4 teaspoon salt

1/4 teaspoon white pepper

1/4 teaspoon cayenne

Oil for frying

1 cup panko crumbs

1 tablespoon dried oregano, crushed

Greek-style Seafood Bites

- In a food processor bowl, process the bread, garlic, and parsley until finely chopped. Remove.

- Pulse the haddock, shrimp, vinegar, olive oil, and seasonings until smooth. Fold in the bread and garlic mixture and mix gently but thoroughly.

- Heat 1/2 inch of oil in a deep skillet. Combine the panko and oregano and spread on a plate.

- Form the seafood mixture into small balls, roll in panko crumbs, and fry, turning, until golden brown. Drain on paper towels.

Spicy Seafood Sausage: Pulse $^1/_2$ pound haddock in food processor until smooth. In a bowl, mix haddock with $^1/_2$ pound peeled salad shrimp, $^1/_2$ pound small bay scallops, 2 lightly beaten egg whites, 2 tablespoons cracker crumbs, 1 teaspoon Old Bay, and $^1/_2$ teaspoon red pepper flakes. Divide in 4; form each into sausage shape on plastic wrap, roll up tightly, and twist ends. Simmer 5 to 7 minutes until firm.

Dilled Tzatziki Sauce: Combine 2 cups thick Greek-style yogurt (unflavored) with 4 cloves of finely minced garlic, $^1/_2$ cup grated seedless cucumber (squeezed dry), 2 teaspoons of fresh lemon juice, and $1^1/_2$ tablespoons chopped fresh dill. Mix thoroughly and chill at least 1 hour. Excellent as a sauce or dip for seafood, grilled meats, steamed vegetables, etc.

Folding the Mixture

- The ingredients in this recipe must be folded together so they will retain their volume and lightness.

- Folding incorporates light and heavy ingredients without deflating pockets of air.

- Using a rubber spatula, cut through the ingredients in the bowl and turn them over, rotating the bowl.

- Repeat this technique until the ingredients are thoroughly but gently mixed.

Forming the Seafood Bites

- It's important that these seafood bites are all the same size. Each seafood bite should be the size of a grape.

- Take about a tablespoon of the seafood mixture and form a ball.

- Roll each ball in the palms of your hands until firm and well packed.

- Then roll the balls in the panko mixture, coating them well.

SOUTHERN CATFISH CRUNCH

Don't be surprised if these are the best catfish fillets you have ever tasted

In the South, pork is revered (and consumed) in all its varied forms. Few people here wrinkle their noses at pork rinds, though elsewhere some are positively horrified at eating what they think of as pure fat.

In truth, pork rinds are mostly air. What they do have a lot of, though, is a meaty flavor similar to bacon. Added to cornmeal and seasoned with black pepper, they make a delicious coating for catfish fillets, chicken, or just about anything.

Use large, firm fillets for this recipe. Dry them well and remove any red or dark flesh along the center. Keep the fried fillets on a rack in the oven so they don't get soggy while you make the gravy. *Yield: 3 servings*

Ingredients:

1¹/₂ cups finely crushed pork rinds

¹/₂ cup yellow cornmeal

1 teaspoon dried thyme

¹/₂ teaspoon black pepper

1 large egg

1 teaspoon milk

Oil for frying

6 skinless catfish fillets

Pecan Gravy:

1 tablespoon butter

¹/₃ cup chopped pecans

1 tablespoon flour

1¹/₄ cups milk

¹/₄ teaspoon salt

¹/₄ teaspoon black pepper

¹/₄ teaspoon onion powder

Southern Catfish Crunch

- Preheat oven to 200°F. Combine first 4 ingredients; spread mixture on a plate.

- Beat together the egg and milk. Heat ½ inch of oil in a deep skillet to 350°F. Dip fillets in egg, dredge in breading; press to coat.

- Fry until golden brown, turning once (about 5 minutes total). Keep warm in the oven.

- Make gravy (see Technique). Spoon gravy on to the plate and plate the fish. Garnish with parsley, if desired.

84

Miz Patty's Catfish Bites: Cut 2 pounds of catfish nuggets into bite-size pieces. Dry well and season with salt and cayenne. Mix 1 cup of flour with $1/2$ teaspoon lemon pepper and additional cayenne in a zip-top bag. Shake catfish in flour; place pieces on foil-lined baking sheet skin side down. Lightly coat with plain cooking spray and bake at 475°F until golden brown and crunchy.

Smothered Catfish: Fry catfish as for main recipe (without sauce) and keep warm in oven. Heat one 15-ounce can stewed tomatoes with 1 can corn (drained) and 1 tablespoon each Worcestershire and hot sauce. Add $1/2$ pound frozen cut okra and 1 teaspoon dried thyme; cover and simmer 20 minutes. Adjust seasonings; spoon over fish on serving plates. Garnish with chopped parsley.

Crush the Pork Rinds

- Using a food processor or blender, crush pork rinds in batches until you have 1 $1/2$ cups.

- In a bowl, combine the crushed pork rinds with the yellow cornmeal, dried thyme, and black pepper. Mix well.

- Spread the crushed pork rind mixture on a large plate.

- Use this mixture as a coating on the catfish.

Make the Pecan Gravy

- In a sauté pan over medium heat, melt the butter.

- Add the chopped pecans and sauté them for 2 minutes. Stir in the flour, and cook for 1 additional minute.

- Add the milk gradually, stirring constantly with a wooden spoon or whisk, until it thickens.

- Add salt, black pepper, and onion powder for flavor.

CAJUN CATFISH BAKE

This easy-to-make casserole has lots of flavor and could well become your family's favorite

Once considered a strictly regional fish and an acquired taste, catfish has gone on to become one of the most popular fish in the United States in a remarkably short time. Why? In a word: aquaculture.

Farm-raised catfish from states like Alabama and Mississippi are of consistent quality and have none of the "muddy" flavor

often found in wild-caught catfish. They're low in fat, and their texture holds up to everything from steaming to grilling.

This casserole takes very little time to prepare features a crunchy corn bread topping, tender and well-seasoned catfish fillets, and a bottom layer of roasted Yukon Gold potatoes that soak up the flavorful juices. *Yield: 4–6 servings*

Ingredients:

1 1/2 pounds Yukon Gold potatoes, cut in 1/4-inch slices

1 large yellow onion, sliced

2 cloves garlic, chopped

2 tablespoons olive oil

1/4 teaspoon salt

1/8 teaspoon cayenne

4 (6- to 8-ounce) skinless catfish fillets

1 tablespoon oil

1 teaspoon each paprika, garlic powder, onion powder, and black pepper

1/2 teaspoon each oregano, thyme, and salt

1/4 teaspoon cayenne

1 box (6 ounces) Stove Top–type corn bread stuffing mix

1/4 cup melted butter

Cajun Catfish Bake

- Preheat the oven to 375°F. Combine the first 6 ingredients and spread in an oiled casserole dish. Bake 20 minutes, stirring twice.

- Rinse and dry the fillets; rub with oil. Mix all the seasonings together (paprika through cayenne) and dust fillets with mixture (you

  may have some left over).

- Place fillets on potatoes. Spread the corn bread stuffing over fillets and pat down. Drizzle butter evenly over top.

- Bake for 20 to 25 minutes until fish flakes easily and potatoes are tender.

Cat 'n' Crawfish Bake: Dry four 8-ounce catfish fillets and brush with melted butter, dust with seasonings from main recipe (paprika through cayenne), and place in a baking dish. Sauté ¼ cup each onion, celery, and green pepper in butter; add 1½ cups crawfish tail meat and 2 tablespoons brandy. Cook briefly; adjust seasonings and pour over catfish. Bake 20 minutes at 350°F.

Quick Catfish Gumbo: Cut up and fry ½ pound smoked sausage (preferably andouille) in 2 tablespoons olive oil; remove sausage. Cut 1 pound catfish into pieces, fry in the oil; remove. Stir in 1 cup chicken broth until thickened. Add 1 tablespoon garlic and ½ pound frozen gumbo vegetables. Heat through; return sausage, cover and cook 20 minutes. Return catfish and cook 10 more minutes.

Combine the Seasonings

- In a bowl, combine the paprika, garlic powder, onion powder, black pepper, oregano, thyme, salt, and cayenne, mixing well.

- This is a basic combination of spices that can be used in many Cajun recipes.

- You might want to double up on the quantities, and keep half in a sealed container for future use.

- Dust the catfish fillets with the Cajun spice mixture.

Assemble the Casserole

- Combine potatoes (peeled or not, as you prefer), onion, garlic, olive oil, salt, and cayenne making sure the olive oil thoroughly coats the mixture.

- Evenly distribute mixture on the bottom of the casserole dish so that potatoes and onions cook evenly.

- Place the seasoned fillets on top of the mixture.

- The corn bread stuffing makes up the top layer giving the casserole its crunchy texture.

- The melted butter adds flavor and moisture to the dish.

SWEET BOURBON-GLAZED CATFISH

A bourbon glaze made with brown sugar and a hint of lime adorns these fillets

You won't get drunk from eating these catfish fillets, but your mouth will be dizzy with pleasure! The savory shallots, hints of lime and ginger, and sweet brown sugar combine with the complex flavors of the bourbon to produce a glaze that perfectly complements the tender catfish.

This dish is also very easy to make and leaves you with just one saucepan to clean if you line your broiling pan with aluminum foil. Be careful not to cook the glaze over high heat or it might darken and burn. Allow it to cool before pouring it over the catfish fillets.

Serve this with the Minted Vegetable Medley and steamed white rice for an easy and delicious dinner. *Yield: 4 servings*

Ingredients:

2 tablespoons butter

1 tablespoon minced shallots or finely minced onion

1 teaspoon lime juice

1/4 teaspoon dried ginger

1/4 teaspoon salt

1/4 teaspoon black pepper

1/4 cup bourbon

1/2 cup brown sugar

4 (6- to 8-ounce) catfish fillets

Sweet Bourbon-glazed Catfish

- Melt the butter in a saucepan. Cook the shallots until softened; add the lime juice, seasonings, and bourbon. Cook 2 minutes.

- Add the brown sugar, stir until dissolved, and remove from heat. Let cool.

- Pour the glaze over the catfish in a zip-top bag. Refrigerate 20 minutes.

- Preheat broiler. Place catfish on an oiled pan; broil until fish is cooked through (about 7 minutes). Serve with Minted Vegetable Medley (see Variations).

Minted Vegetable Medley: Sauté 1 minced clove of garlic in 1 tablespoon light olive oil; add ³/₄ pound fresh green beans (ends removed). Cook 3 to 5 minutes until beans are crisp-tender. Add 1 medium yellow squash, cut into ¹/₄-inch strips ("french fry" cut), 1 teaspoon minced fresh mint leaves, ¹/₄ teaspoon each salt and pepper; sauté 2 to 3 minutes longer. Serve as a side dish.

Southern Comfort Catfish: In a small saucepan, heat ³/₄ cup of Southern Comfort whiskey with 1 tablespoon minced jalapeño pepper, 1 teaspoon crushed coriander seeds, ¹/₄ teaspoon salt, and 8–10 mint leaves to a bare simmer for 5 minutes. Let cool. Brush 6 catfish fillets and refrigerate. Preheat grill; add pecan smoking chips to hot coals. Grill catfish 5 to 7 minutes, basting with glaze, until golden.

Cooking the Glaze

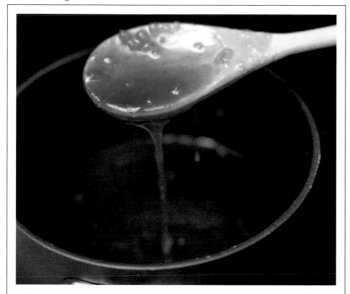

Broiling the Catfish

- In a saucepan, melt the butter. Add the minced shallots and cook until softened.

- Add the lime juice, ginger, salt, black pepper, and bourbon. Cook for 2 minutes.

- Add the brown sugar. Stir until the sugar dissolves. Remove the saucepan from the heat.

- Allow the glaze to cool before pouring it over the catfish.

- Broiling involves cooking with radiant heat with the food being cooked under the heat source.

- It's best to place the food 3 to 4 inches below the heat source.

- As the food cooks, it gives off moisture as steam, which can toughen the food.

- Leaving the oven door ajar while broiling allows some of the steam to escape.

TILAPIA & ASPARAGUS STIR-FRY

Delicate golden pieces of tilapia grace this flavor-rich and colorful stir-fried meal

Stir-fried meals are a great way to get more servings of a wider variety of vegetables into family meals. Kids can help with the setup, and after all the ingredients are prepped and assembled the cooking goes very quickly and the finished dish can be on the table in minutes.

Tilapia, like catfish, is almost always farm-raised. Though some tilapia is farmed in the U.S., most is imported and can vary in quality. Tilapia fillets should be firm and moist, with almost no scent. When shopping for frozen fillets, look for ones that are IQF (Individually Quick Frozen) and preferably individually vacuum sealed. This locks in the freshness and prevents deterioration from freezer burn. *Yield: 2 servings*

Ingredients:

- ¹/₂ cup canola or peanut oil
- ¹/₂ cup corn starch
- ¹/₄ teaspoon dried ginger
- ¹/₄ teaspoon salt
- 1 pound tilapia fillet, cut into approx. 1-inch pieces
- 2 cloves garlic, minced
- ¹/₂ pound asparagus spears, cut into 1-inch pieces
- 3–4 shiitake mushrooms, sliced
- ¹/₂ of a medium red bell pepper, cut into strips
- ¹/₄ pound snow pea pods, ends trimmed
- 1–2 scallions, chopped
- 1 jalapeño pepper, seeded, cut into thin strips
- 1 tablespoon oyster sauce
- ¹/₂ teaspoon light soy sauce
- Toasted sesame seeds

Tilapia and Asparagus Stir-fry

- Heat the oil in a wok. Mix the corn starch, ginger, and salt; dredge the fish pieces and fry until golden. Keep warm.

- Pour off all but 1 tablespoon of the oil. Stir-fry the next 4 ingredients for 2 to 3 minutes. Add the snow peas, scallions, and jalapeño. Cook for 1 to 2 minutes more.

- Mix the oyster and soy sauces. Toss the vegetables with the sauce and remove to a bowl or platter.

- Top with the tilapia pieces, sprinkle with sesame seeds, and serve immediately.

Tilapia is considered the world's first cultivated fish. Hieroglyphic paintings depict King Tut and other Egyptian pharaohs raising and catching tilapia. Historians believe that tilapia was the fish Jesus fed to the multitudes and the fish Jesus is said to have miraculously filled St. Peter's nets with. Today tilapia is farm raised in California. The boneless, skinless white fillets are mild, moist, and slightly firm.

• • • • RECIPE VARIATION • • • •

Tilapia with Sweet Corn Batter: Combine 1 cup of flour, $1/2$ teaspoon each salt and white pepper, and 1 can cream-style corn with enough club soda to make a thick batter. Cut $1^1/2$ pounds tilapia fillets into $1/2$-inch strips and dry well. Heat 2 inches of peanut oil in a wok; batter tilapia and fry in batches until golden and puffed.

Wok-frying the Tilapia

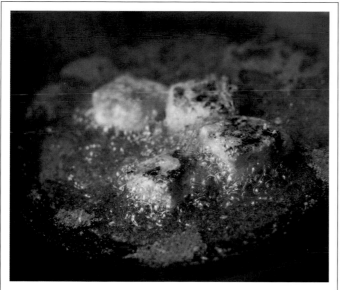

- Woks are excellent for frying small pieces of food because the food can be browned evenly in a small amount of oil.

- Dredge the pieces of tilapia in a mixture of corn starch, ginger, and salt.

- Heat the oil in the wok.

- Fry the tilapia in batches until the pieces are golden brown. Keep the fried pieces warm until all the tilapia is cooked.

Stir-frying the Vegetables

- Stir-frying is the most common method of cooking Chinese food.

- It's a simple, quick and healthy way to prepare vegetables.

- If possible, all the vegetables should be cut into uniform shapes and sizes to ensure even cooking.

- Ingredients that take the longest to cook should be added to the wok first.

CRAB-STUFFED TILAPIA FILLETS

Flaky tilapia and sweet crabmeat pair beautifully in this flavorful dish

There are few word pairings that go together quite so well as "'crab" and "stuffed." In either order, they usually indicate something that's going to be briny-sweet and at least a little decadent.

But so much depends on quality when it comes to crab. Those ersatz "krab" constructions—whether "flakes" or "legs"—are okay for some applications, but not for dishes where real crabmeat will be co-starring.

In this recipe, the crabmeat is enfolded by sweet flaky tilapia fillets. The tilapia is then lightly seasoned and broiled. Only use quality crabmeat for this recipe, as the flavor will be prominent. You can use any of the different grades of freshly picked or refrigerated cans of crabmeat (not the shelf-stable kind). *Yield: 4 servings*

Ingredients:

2 slices white bread (crusts removed), torn into small pieces

8 ounces crabmeat, shell bits and cartilage removed

1 teaspoon minced fresh chives

1 tablespoon prepared horseradish

Mayonnaise (approximately 1 tablespoon)

Salt and pepper to taste

12 thin lemon slices

4 (4- to 6-ounce) tilapia fillets

1 tablespoon light olive oil

Lemon pepper

Crab-stuffed Tilapia Fillets

- Pulse bread in a food processor until fine. Mix the bread crumbs with the crabmeat, chives, and horseradish. Add mayonnaise to bind; season with salt and pepper.

- On an oiled baking pan, lay the lemon slices in 4 rows of 3. Divide the stuffing and mound on the middle slice of each row.

- Mold the fillets over the stuffing; secure with toothpicks. Brush with oil, season with lemon pepper.

- Broil until fish is cooked through and golden, about 5 to 7 minutes.

Kathy's Crab Casserole: Pick over 1 pound of crabmeat to remove shell bits and cartilage. Remove crusts from 4 slices white bread; pulse bread in food processor until fine. Combine crab and bread crumbs with 1½ cups chopped onion, 1 cup mayonnaise, ¼ teaspoon cayenne, salt and pepper to taste. Spread in a small buttered casserole and bake at 350°F 30 to 45 minutes until golden and bubbly.

Tilapia Caprese: Cut 1 large ripe tomato and 1 ball (about 8 ounces) fresh mozzarella into ¼-inch slices. Place two 8-ounce tilapia fillets in an oiled baking pan and brush tops with balsamic vinegar. Sprinkle with salt and pepper. Top with alternating slices of tomato and mozzarella, separated by fresh basil leaves. Drizzle with olive oil, season with salt and pepper; bake at 375°F for 8 to 12 minutes.

Mounding the Stuffing

- In an oiled baking pan, preferably one with low sides, lay the thin lemon slices in 4 rows of 3 each, with no overlap.

- This will help keep the crab-stuffed tilapia fillets together when served.

- Divide the stuffing into 4 equal portions.

- Mound 1 portion of stuffing on each of the 4 middle slices of lemon.

Forming the Stuffed Fillets

- Mold a tilapia fillet over each mound of stuffing.

- A toothpick can be inserted at the point where the 2 ends of the tilapia fillet meet.

- This will hold the stuffed fillets together while they broil in the oven.

- Brush the fillets with light olive oil. Season with lemon pepper.

CATFISH & TILAPIA

STEAMED GINGER BASIL TILAPIA

This classic Asian preparation brings out the natural sweetness and juiciness of whole tilapia

Whole fish can seem intimidating, but it is actually quite easy to prepare. Cooking fish whole produces the absolute best, most natural flavor by sealing the moisture inside.

You don't have to be an expert on skinning or filleting, either: After cooking, the skin slips right off and the meat will come off the bones easily with a fork or chopsticks.

You can also use a wide turner or spatula to lift the cooked meat in large sections right off the bones. Then you simply turn the fish over and do the same to the other side.

And don't worry about neatness—the process is inherently messy regardless of your level of expertise. Just relax and enjoy the superior flavor. *Yield: 2 servings*

Ingredients:

1 whole tilapia (approximately 2 pounds), cleaned and scaled, fins trimmed

2 tablespoons Chinese cooking wine (or dry sherry)

Juice of ¹/₂ lemon

1 tablespoon finely shredded fresh ginger

2 tablespoons finely shredded basil leaves

¹/₂ teaspoon white pepper

4 cups water

2 tablespoons soy sauce

1 teaspoon sugar

2 tablespoons vegetable oil

1 tablespoon finely shredded fresh basil

2 scallions (green parts only) cut on the diagonal into fine shreds

1 teaspoon lemon zest

1 small hot pepper, seeded and thinly sliced (optional)

Additional finely shredded fresh ginger (optional)

Steamed Ginger Basil Tilapia

- Rinse and dry fish; check for stray scales. Make 3 diagonal cuts, about an inch apart, on both sides of fish.

- Place fish on an oval plate; coat with next 5 ingredients.

- Bring water to a boil in a wok. Put plate on a wire rack inside wok; cover. Steam for 15 to 20 minutes until thickest part of fish is cooked. Remove; pour liquid from plate.

- Heat soy, sugar, and oil in a saucepan; pour over fish. Garnish with remaining ingredients.

MAKE IT EASY

A fresh whole fish should be stiff, not floppy. When you press the flesh with your finger, it should feel firm and spring back, leaving no indentation. The skin should be shiny and moist, but not slimy, with the scales still attached. The gills should be a deep red. The eyes should be bright and bulging. There should be no "fishy" odor. Fresh fish has the mild, pleasant smell of the sea.

• • • • RECIPE VARIATION • • • •

Tilapia with Salted Black Beans: Combine 2 tablespoons salted black beans (available at Asian groceries), 1 tablespoon each minced garlic and grated ginger, and 1 teaspoon sesame oil in a bowl. Spread onto two 8-ounce tilapia fillets on a plate. Top with fine strips of jalapeño pepper and thin slices of scallion cut at an angle. Place plate in bamboo steamer; cook 8 to 10 minutes.

Preparing the Tilapia

- Rinse and dry the fish. If the scales are still on the fish, use a metal spoon or knife to scrape them off. This is best done with the fish underwater to contain the scales.

- Make 3 diagonal cuts about 1 inch apart on both sides of the fish.

- Place the fish on an oval plate. In a bowl, combine the wine, lemon juice, ginger, basil, and white pepper.

- Coat the fish with the wine mixture.

Steaming Whole Fish

- In steaming, food is cooked over rather than in boiling water. It is often a preliminary step before smoking or frying food.

- Steamed foods can be reheated in the steamer.

- Rice can also be reheated in the steamer.

- Leftover steamed food items can be sealed in a plastic bag and frozen for up to one month.

95

CRUNCHY FLOUNDER FINGERS

Fun for kids of any age, these crunchy, lowfat "fingers" are long on flavor

If you're looking for a recipe that gives you all the flavor and crunch of fried fish without the frying, look no further.

Boxed stuffing mix has savory seasonings built right in, and you can't beat corn bread crumbs when it comes to crunch.

Trim away any very thin edges from the flounder, and then cut them into long strips about the same shape and size of chicken tenders. In this recipe, the zucchini still retains a bit of firmness when done. If you prefer it tender, bake it for 7 minutes more than the fish pieces.

You can also use reduced fat mayo and dressing, or try smooth salsa or bottled chili sauce as a dip instead. *Yield: 4 servings*

Ingredients:

1 (6-ounce) box Stove Top-type corn bread stuffing mix

1 cup all-purpose flour

1/4 teaspoon celery salt (or plain salt)

1/4 teaspoon black pepper

1 pound small zucchini, ends trimmed

2 eggs, beaten

1 1/2 pounds flounder fillets, cut into "finger" strips

Cooking spray

1/2 cup bottled ranch dressing

1/4 cup mayonnaise

1 tablespoon sweet pickle relish

Pinch of cayenne (optional)

Crunchy Flounder Fingers

- Pulse stuffing in a food processor until coarsely chopped; spread on a plate. Mix flour, salt, and pepper. Preheat oven to 400°F.

- Cut the zucchini into long thin wedges. Rinse and drain. Dip zucchini into flour mixture, then egg, then corn bread crumbs.

- Place on a nonstick baking pan. Repeat with fish. Lightly coat zucchini and fish with cooking spray. Bake 15 minutes. Turn pieces, coat with cooking spray; bake until golden.

- Combine remaining ingredients. Serve alongside fish and zucchini.

Cut the Flounder Fingers

- Rinse the flounder fillets under cold running water and pat them dry with paper towels. Place fillets on a clean cutting board.

- Cut each fillet in half lengthwise to make the "fingers."

- If the fillets are rather large, cut them into thirds to make the fingers.

- The flounder fingers should be about the same size as chicken tenders.

Coat with Cooking Spray

- A cooking spray is applied to food and/or frying pans to prevent the food from sticking to the pan.

- This is done in place of butter, shortening or oils to grease a pan.

- A cooking spray contains a type of oil combined with an emulsifier and a propellant.

- Food prepared with cooking sprays has fewer calories than food prepared with the traditional butter, shortening, or oils.

EASY FLOUNDER CREPES

Pre-made crepes from the supermarket are the secret to this impressive brunch or dinner treat

Homemade crepes, while time consuming, are not all that difficult to make—once you get the hang of it. Until then, you'll be making more mistakes than you will crepes. And if you don't make them regularly, you'll soon lose the knack.

The solution is to either make a ton of them at once and freeze them, or to buy them pre-made. Since the supermarket ones are uniformly excellent, the decision is actually simple!

Look for flounder fillets that are light in color and moist, but not waterlogged. Avoid gray fillets or those with dried edges. Trim away any dark spots before cooking.

Use a quality white wine, and remember to squeeze the spinach dry before cooking. *Yield: 4 servings*

KNACK FISH & SEAFOOD COOKBOOK

Ingredients:

1 pound flounder fillets

Salt and pepper

4 tablespoons butter, divided

8 ounces sliced cremini ("Baby Bella") or white mushrooms

1 tablespoon minced shallots (or white part of scallion)

1 cup white wine

10-ounce box frozen chopped spinach, defrosted

$1/2$ cup heavy cream

$1/4$ teaspoon nutmeg

Salt and pepper to taste

8 ounces grated Asiago cheese

8 large pre-made crepes at room temperature

Easy Flounder Crepes

- Lightly season flounder with salt and pepper. Cook in 2 tablespoons butter over medium heat until lightly firm. Remove from pan. Sauté mushrooms and shallots until softened; remove.

- Deglaze pan with wine, add remaining butter. Add spinach and cook 5 minutes;

stir in cream. Remove from heat. Season with nutmeg, salt, and pepper.

- Cut flounder into strips. Divide fish, mushrooms, and cheese between crepes; roll up. Place in a buttered casserole, top with spinach; bake 15 to 20 minutes at 400°F.

Flounder with Green Peppercorn Sauce: Preheat broiler. Season flounder fillets with salt and pepper. Broil 2 to 3 minutes per side, or until fish becomes opaque and flaky. In saucepan over medium heat, reduce ½ cup white wine mixed with crushed pickled green peppercorns to 1 tablespoon. Add 3 tablespoons heavy cream, minced parsley, tarragon, salt, and pepper. Simmer to thicken.

MAKE IT EASY

Easy Crepes: In bowl, beat 2 eggs, add 1 cup milk, ½ teaspoon salt, 1 cup flour, and 2 tablespoons melted butter. Cover 30 minutes. Heat pan; coat with butter. Ladle in 3 tablespoons of batter. Quickly tilt pan so batter spreads evenly in thin layer. Cook until bottom is lightly browned and edges lift easily. Flip crepe over. Cook for a few minutes. Freeze stacked and wrapped in foil or plastic wrap.

Deglazing the Pan

Folding the Crepes

- Deglazing is a method to remove the natural glaze that accumulates in a cooking pan.

- Simply add a liquid, such as wine, to the hot pan in which the fish has been cooked. Scrape up any bits of food in the pan.

- This will produce a small amount of sauce.

- Butter can be added, as in this recipe.

- Divide the fish, mushrooms, and cheese into 8 equal portions. Place a portion of the filling across the center of each crepe, leaving about ¾ of an inch on either side.

- Fold the bottom of the crepe up over the filling.

- Fold in both sides of the crepe, and then fold the top of the crepe down to make a neat little bundle.

- This is the same technique used to make burritos and spring rolls.

SOLE PRIMAVERA WITH BOWTIES

Sole fillets are rolled around colorful vegetables and served with creamy pasta and shrimp

This is a dish that sings with flavor. At a glance, it might seem complicated, but it's actually not. First you do a bit of poaching, then you make a simple sauce, and then you're done. And for your effort you've got a wonderful, colorful meal that will make you think of springtime in any season.

Buy sole fillets that are nearly white, fresh-smelling, and not mushy. Sole is a delicate fish and needs to be handled carefully as flat fillets, but it's more durable when rolled.

The vegetables will still have a bit of crispness when done; you can poach them briefly in the stock before rolling them in the fillets if you prefer them tender. *Yield: 4 servings*

Ingredients:

1 (16-ounce) box bowtie pasta, cooked in salted water according to package directions

4 sugar snap peas

4 strips red bell pepper (about 1/4 by 3 inches)

4 strips yellow squash (about 1/4 by 3 inches)

4 strips carrot (about 1/8 by 3 inches)

4 (4- to 5-ounce) sole fillets

3 cups low-sodium chicken stock

1/2 cup dry vermouth or white wine

2 teaspoons Old Bay or other seafood seasoning

2 bay leaves

8 black peppercorns (optional)

1 pound uncooked small shrimp, peeled and deveined

2 large cloves garlic, minced

3 scallions, thinly sliced

2 tablespoons full-flavored olive oil

1 tablespoon all-purpose flour

Salt and pepper to taste

Chopped parsley for garnish (optional)

Sole Primavera with Bowties

- Cook pasta as directed. Divide vegetables (one of each) among fillets. Roll; secure with toothpicks.

- Bring stock, wine, and seasonings to a simmer in a 2- to 3-quart saucepan; simmer shrimp until opaque; remove.

- Simmer rolled fillets in stock 5 to 7 minutes until fish flakes. Remove; keep warm.

- In a deep skillet or pot, briefly sauté garlic and scallions in oil. Stir in flour; cook 2 minutes. Gradually whisk in 1 cup stock, stirring until thickened. Add pasta and shrimp; toss to coat; reheat.

Sole with Hazelnut Butter: Season the sole fillets with salt and pepper, and dust with flour. In a frying pan, cook the fillets in butter over medium heat. Add $\frac{1}{2}$ cup chopped hazelnuts to the pan. Cook until the butter and nuts are lightly browned. Deglaze the pan with $\frac{1}{2}$ cup of white wine or chicken broth. Allow the ingredients to simmer and thicken.

Sole with Arugula and Citrus Fruit Salad: Brush sole fillets lightly with olive oil and season with lemon pepper. Layer sole with de-stemmed arugula leaves, overlapping slightly, in steamer. After steaming sole, let cool slightly. Serve the sole barely warm with a salad of orange and grapefruit segments and slivered sweet onions dressed with sweetened lime juice and a pinch of cayenne pepper.

Rolling the Fillets

- Spread the sole fillets on a clean work surface.

- Place a sugar snap pea and strips of red bell pepper, yellow squash, and carrots in the center of each fillet.

- If you prefer the vegetables to be more tender, they can be par-cooked in advance.

- Roll up each fillet into a tidy bundle, and secure with a toothpick.

Poaching the Primavera Rolls

- In a 2- or 3-quart saucepan, combine the chicken stock, wine, seafood seasoning, bay leaves, and peppercorns. Bring this poaching liquid barely to a boil.

- Add the shrimp and simmer until the shrimp are opaque. Remove the shrimp.

- Add the rolled-up fillets to the poaching liquid. Simmer for 5 to 7 minutes, or until the fish flakes.

- Remove the rolled-up fillets and keep warm.

CREAMY BAKED SOLE

This creamy rice and sole casserole features almonds, tomatoes, and a Parmesan cheese sauce

This easy to make recipe is designed to make 6 servings, but it's oh so good you might plan on serving 3—because everyone will want seconds!

One of the best things about this casserole is that you can put it together in advance and bake it when you're ready. Just let the sauce cool before pouring it over the fish and rice,

then cover tightly and refrigerate. Take it out about 15 to 20 minutes before you put it in the oven, or add about 7 to 10 minutes to the cooking time.

You can use larger sole fillets, and you can substitute thin flounder fillets for the sole. Use ripe Roma (aka plum) tomatoes and use freshly grated Parmesan cheese. *Yield: 6 servings*

Ingredients:

4 cups cooked rice

1/2 cup slivered almonds

1 teaspoon lemon pepper (use less if rice was cooked with salt)

6 thick slices Roma tomato

6 teaspoons grated Parmesan cheese

6 (4- to 5-ounce) sole fillets

3 tablespoons butter

3 tablespoons flour

2 1/2 cups milk

2 tablespoons finely minced parsley

1/4 teaspoon celery salt (or plain salt)

1/4 teaspoon white pepper

Creamy Baked Sole

- Mix rice, almonds, and lemon pepper. Spread in bottom of a buttered casserole or baking dish.

- Lay 1 slice of tomato topped with a teaspoon of Parmesan on bottom half of each fillet; fold top over. Place folded fillets in casserole, slightly overlapping.

- Melt butter in a deep skillet or saucepan. Add flour; stir 3–4 minutes. Gradually whisk in milk, stirring until thickened. Add parsley and seasonings; pour over casserole.

- Bake at 350°F for 25 minutes.

Baked Sole with Pesto: Place sole fillets in a single layer in a buttered baking dish. Gently spread pesto (available already made in jars at the supermarket) over the tops of the fillets. Bake the fillets in a 350°F oven for 20 minutes. Cover with foil to prevent fish from drying out. Optional: The sole can be baked on a bed of thickly sliced tomatoes or precooked gnocchi.

Easy Seafood Lasagna: In baking dish, layer no-boil–type lasagna noodles with a thinned-out alfredo sauce (combine 1 jar sauce with ¼ to ½ cup milk). In each layer, include tiny salad shrimp, bay scallops, and/or sole fillets that were lightly sautéed in butter and garlic, and dabs of ricotta cheese. Finish top layer with a layer of sauce and bread crumbs. Bake according to directions on the package.

Filling the Sole Fillets

- Rinse the sole fillets under cold running water. Pat them dry with paper towels. Place the fillets on a clean working surface.

- Lay a thick slice of Roma tomato on the bottom half of each fillet.

- Top each tomato slice with 1 teaspoon of Parmesan cheese.

- Fold the top half of the fillet over the bottom half.

Assembling the Dish

- This dish begins with a layer of rice, almonds, and lemon pepper in the bottom of a buttered casserole or baking dish.

- The folded fish fillets are placed on top of the rice mixture, slightly overlapping one another.

- A sauce is made with the butter, flour, milk, parsley, salt, and pepper.

- The sauce is poured over the fish fillets in the casserole.

FLOUNDER/SOLE/HALIBUT

MEXICAN HALIBUT WITH VEGGIES

This tasty, tangy entree is a novel way to enjoy some very familiar ingredients

Escabeche is a dish enjoyed in many Latin countries. Like another marinated fish specialty, ceviche, it is built around the freshest ingredients, often incorporating whatever the day's catch might be.

Escabeche often has savory herbs and intriguing hints of spice in the vinegar-based marinade. Here, we use marjoram (sweeter and more delicate than oregano) and allspice berries. Traditionally, the fish is allowed to marinate in the sauce and is then served at room temperature, which allows the flavors to fully combine. *Yield: 4 servings*

Ingredients:

2 tablespoons full-flavored olive oil

2 cloves garlic, cut into thin slices

2 medium carrots, cut into thin slices

1 large onion, halved and cut into thin slices

1 large red or yellow bell pepper, cut into strips

2 large bay leaves

6 allspice berries

1 teaspoon dried marjoram

1/2 teaspoon dried thyme

1/4 teaspoon each of salt, black pepper, and sugar

1/2 cup white wine vinegar

1/2 cup chicken stock

1/4 cup pickled jalapeño strips (or slices)

Olive oil for frying

4 (6- to 8-ounce) halibut steaks

Salt and pepper

1/2 cup flour

Mexican Halibut with Veggies

- Heat oil on medium heat; sauté next 4 ingredients until softened. Add seasonings, vinegar, and stock; simmer uncovered for 15 minutes. Add jalapeños.

- While sauce is simmering, heat ¼ inch of olive oil in a skillet over medium-high heat. Season halibut with salt and pepper, dust lightly with flour; cook until nicely browned, 3 to 4 minutes per side. Keep warm.

- Place fish in a shallow bowl. Strain sauce and spoon over fish. Discard bay and allspice; top fish with the marinated vegetables.

Curried Halibut Escabeche: Simmer 1 cup apple juice, ¼ cup apple cider vinegar, juice of 1 lime, 4 allspice berries, and 4 crushed cardamom pods for 15 minutes. Strain. In remaining sauce, simmer chopped apples, sliced sweet onions, and golden raisins. Set aside. Prepare halibut as directed in main recipe, with 1 teaspoon of mild curry powder added to the flour. Pour sauce over fish. Serve at room temperature.

Grilled Cumin-scented Halibut: In a large baking dish, marinate the halibut steaks in a mixture of 1 cup lime juice, chopped cilantro, ground coriander, and lightly crushed toasted cumin seeds for at least 30 minutes. Remove the fish from the marinade. Brush the fish with olive oil. Grill the halibut over high heat. It is recommended that this dish be grilled outdoors.

Making the Vinegar Sauce

- In a saucepan, heat the olive oil over medium heat. Sauté the sliced garlic, carrots, onion, and peppers until softened.

- Add the bay leaves, allspice berries, dried marjoram, dried thyme, salt, black pepper, sugar, white wine vinegar, and chicken stock.

- Simmer uncovered for 15 minutes.

- Add the pickled jalapeño. Strain the sauce, reserving the vegetables and liquid in separate bowls. Discard the bay leaves and allspice berries.

Serving the Fish

- In 4 shallow soup bowls, place the cooked halibut steaks.

- Using a ladle, pour the strained sauce over the fish in each bowl.

- An equal amount of the marinated vegetables that were strained from the sauce should be placed on top of each halibut steak.

- Traditionally this dish is served at room temperature.

FLOUNDER/SOLE/HALIBUT

ORANGE HALIBUT SKEWERS

An unusual and sophisticated flavor combo gives these skewers their delightful aroma and taste

If you've never tried the combination of orange, caraway, and vanilla before, you're missing out on something special. Together, they create an aromatic flavor that's as exotic as it is familiar.

Halibut are a very large flat fish that can weigh several hundred pounds. Its flesh is white and very lean, so take care not to overcook it or it will dry out. Choose halibut that is translucent white and fresh smelling.

Serve these skewers with lime wedges to add a spritz of bright citrus flavor. *Yield: 4–5 servings*

Ingredients:

¹/₂ cup orange liqueur (such as Cointreau, Triple Sec, or Gran Marnier)

¹/₄ cup water

¹/₂ teaspoon caraway seeds, crushed

¹/₄ teaspoon pure vanilla extract

Pinch of salt

Pinch of cayenne

2 pounds halibut steak, cut into ³/₄-inch pieces

8–10 wooden skewers

Lime wedges

Orange Halibut Skewers

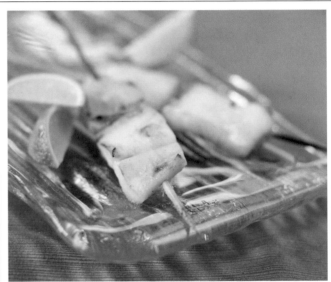

- In a small saucepan, slowly bring the orange liqueur, water, and caraway to a simmer for 3 to 5 minutes. Remove from heat; add vanilla, salt, and cayenne. Let cool.

- Place the halibut pieces in a bowl or zip-top bag; pour glaze over fish and mix thoroughly. Marinate 20 to 30 minutes. While fish is marinating, soak skewers in water.

- Preheat broiler or grill. Thread the halibut pieces on the skewers and broil or grill, turning occasionally, until cooked through (about 7 to 10 minutes).

• • • • RECIPE VARIATIONS • • • •

Halibut with Sweet Mustard Barbecue Sauce: In a bowl, combine ¼ cup of yellow mustard, 2 tablespoons of honey, 1 tablespoon of steak sauce, 1 teaspoon of tomato paste, 1 teaspoon of fresh lemon juice and ¼ teaspoon of ground allspice. Mix well. Brush 4 halibut steaks with the sauce. Broil 2 to 4 minutes per side, turning the fish only once. Baste fish regularly during the cooking time.

Broccoli Rice: Over medium-high heat, sauté 1 cup chopped onion and 2 cups small broccoli florets in 2 tablespoons olive oil until they just begin to color. Stir in 1½ cups rice, ½ teaspoon salt, 1 cup water, 1 cup chicken or vegetable broth, and ¼ cup white wine. Bring to a boil; cover and simmer over very low heat 15 minutes. Garnish with toasted slivered almonds. Serve as a side dish.

Simmer the Glaze

Marinate the Halibut

- In a small saucepan, combine the orange liqueur, water, and caraway seeds. Slowly bring this mixture to a simmer, and cook for 3 to 5 minutes.

- Remove the saucepan from the heat.

- Add the vanilla extract, salt, and cayenne pepper. Mix well.

- Allow this glaze to cool before using it on the halibut steak.

- With a very sharp knife, cut the halibut steak into ¾-inch pieces.

- Place the halibut pieces in a bowl or plastic bag.

- Pour the glaze over the halibut. Mix thoroughly. Cover the bowl, or seal the bag tightly.

- Allow the halibut to marinate in the glaze for 20 to 30 minutes before broiling or grilling the fish.

FLOUNDER/SOLE/HALIBUT

CRISPY BROILED SNAPPER

A fun and tasty broiled fish that will have your guests angling for your recipe

This recipe brings the crunch in a big way by using both saltines and potato chips in the coating. Before dredging, the fillets are spread with a kicked-up mayo mixture that helps the coating adhere and seals in the natural juices of the fish.

Snapper has fine, white flesh and a sweet taste. Because of its low-to-medium oil content, it takes to almost any method of cooking and is a perfect fish for spicy, textured preparations like this one.

You can use dried chives in this (¹/₂ tablespoon) and add a bit more garlic powder if you like. The hot sauce is optional, but it is highly recommended as it adds a hint of tangy zing.
Yield: 4 servings

Ingredients:

³/₄ cup coarsely crushed saltines

³/₄ cup coarsely crushed potato chips

¹/₂ cup mayonnaise

1 tablespoon minced fresh chives

¹/₄ teaspoon garlic powder

¹/₄ teaspoon black pepper

¹/₂ teaspoon hot pepper sauce (optional)

4 (6- to 8-ounce) skinless snapper fillets

Lemon wedges

Crispy Broiled Snapper

- Thoroughly combine the saltines and potato chips on a plate or in a pie pan.

- In a small bowl, mix together the mayonnaise, chives, garlic powder, black pepper, and hot sauce.

- Preheat the broiler. Pat fillets dry with paper towels.

- Spread the mayonnaise mixture evenly on both sides of fillets.

- Coat thoroughly with the cracker/chip mixture and place fillets on a broiling pan. Broil 3 to 4 minutes per side until fish is cooked and topping is golden. Serve with lemon wedges.

There are several hundred species of snapper, the most common one being red snapper. Snapper is usually sold in fillet form. Make sure the skin is still on so you can be sure you are buying snapper, which has pink to red markings. When pan-fried, the skin turns crispy and retains its reddish color. If you can buy a whole snapper, leave the scales on so it won't stick to the grill.

• • • • RECIPE VARIATION • • • •

Broiled Snapper with Pepper Jelly: Rinse and dry the snapper fillets. Spread red or green jalapeño pepper jelly (available in jars at the supermarket) over the fillets. Refrigerate uncovered for 20 minutes. Broil 2 to 3 minutes per side, or until the fish starts to flake. Serve over stewed posole (1 can of posole rinsed well and cooked with chopped onions, canned tomatoes, and green chiles).

Crushing Crackers and Chips

- It's very easy to crush potato chips, saltines or other crackers to use as a coating on fish.

- Place the potato chips or crackers in a large plastic bag that you can seal tight.

- Squeeze out the air inside the bag, then seal it closed.

- Pound the plastic bag with the smooth side of a meat mallet, a rolling pin, a heavy soup can, or empty wine bottle.

Coating the Fillets

- In a small bowl, combine the mayonnaise, chives, garlic powder, black pepper, and hot sauce.

- This will act as the "glue" that keeps the crumbs on the fish.

- Pat the fish fillets dry with a paper towel. Spread the mayonnaise mixture on both sides of the fillets.

- Coat the fillets thoroughly with the mixture of crushed potato chips and crackers.

MARINATED SNAPPER SALAD

Ceviche, made with fresh fish and citrus juices, is a refreshing seafood salad idea

A popular appetizer in Latin America, ceviche (also spelled *seviche* or *cebiche*) is a salad of very fresh raw fish and/or shellfish marinated in citrus juices. The acids in the juice "cook" the fish, firming it and turning it opaque while imparting a refreshing flavor. This recipe uses a combination of juices for a tropical flavor. Because of the acid, be sure to marinate the

fish in a non-metallic bowl, preferably glass or high-quality glazed ceramic. Let it marinate at least 2 hours; you want the snapper pieces to be opaque all the way through.

If you can, have your purveyor cut the fillets from fresh, whole fish or buy firm white fillets with a clean scent. *Yield: 4–6 servings*

Ingredients:

1 ¹/₂ pounds very fresh skinless snapper fillets

1 cup fresh lime juice

¹/₄ cup fresh lemon juice

¹/₄ cup orange juice

¹/₄ teaspoon sea salt

1 medium green bell pepper, seeded and diced

¹/₄ cup diced red (or white) onion

4 plum tomatoes, seeded and diced

1–2 jalapeño peppers, seeded and thinly sliced

¹/₄ cup chopped fresh cilantro leaves

2–3 tablespoons extra virgin olive oil

¹/₄ teaspoon white pepper

Additional sea salt to taste

Lime slices for garnish

Saltines

Marinated Snapper Salad

- Cut fillets into short, ¼ inch thick strips. Gently toss strips with lime, lemon, and orange juices, and salt in a glass bowl (or other non-metallic bowl).

- Cover and refrigerate, stirring occasionally, until fish is fully opaque (2 to 3 hours).

- Pour off marinade and discard. Gently combine the snapper with the next 7 ingredients; cover and chill 1 hour.

- Serve in martini glasses or individual ramekins (garnished with a slice of lime) and saltines or other plain crackers on the side.

Slicing the Fillets

- Rinse the snapper fillets under cold running water, and pat them dry with a paper towel.

- Place the fillets on a clean work surface.

- Using a very sharp knife, cut each fillet into strips that are ¼ inch by 1½ inches in size.

- This is easier to do if the fish fillets are in a semi-frozen state. Simply put them in the freezer for 30 minutes before slicing.

Preparing the Snapper

- Marinating not only moistens and tenderizes fish. It also creates a variety of interesting flavors.

- Marinades usually consist of oil, an acid, and herbs or spices for flavoring.

- It's best to marinate in a glass bowl or plastic bag.

- Delicate seafood actually starts to cook while in a marinade so be careful not to marinate the fish for too long.

SNAPPER/BASS/MAHI

GARLIC-ROASTED SEA BASS

This sea bass dish—with garlic in, on, and over—is a garlic lover's dream

Yes, this dish uses over 4 full heads of garlic, but no, it's not overpowering at all. All of the garlic inside the fish mellows in the roasting process and deeply infuses the flesh with flavor.

The roasted garlic heads add yet another layer of mellow garlicky goodness. Each diner can squeeze out the soft, sweet cloves onto their fish or onto a piece of crusty bread.

Sea bass are firm and lean, with a mild flavor that takes seasoning well. Whole sea bass should have clear moist eyes and resilient flesh; avoid any that feel mushy or limp. Take care to remove the spiny dorsal fin before prepping the fish, as it is quite sharp. *Yield: 4 servings*

Ingredients:

4 whole heads fresh garlic (stems trimmed), plus 4 large garlic cloves, peeled and crushed

Full-flavored olive oil

Coarse sea salt or kosher salt

4- to 5-pound (scaled and cleaned) whole sea bass, rinsed and well dried

Black pepper

1 lemon (1 half cut into thin slices, other half juiced)

Garlic-roasted Sea Bass

- Cut the top ¼ inch off the whole heads of garlic, exposing the cloves. Drizzle with olive oil; sprinkle with salt.

- Preheat oven to 375°F. Season the fish with olive oil, crushed garlic; lemon juice, salt, and pepper.

- Place lemon slices and crushed garlic cloves inside fish. Roast fish and whole garlic heads in a roasting pan (with rack), uncovered, 30 to 40 minutes, basting often.

Chipotle Sea Bass: Prepare the whole sea bass as directed in the main recipe. Rub the inside of the fish with a mixture of minced garlic, ground cumin, salt, pepper, and lemon juice. Rub the outside of the fish with a paste made of chipotle pepper sauce, mayonnaise, sweet paprika, and onion powder. Let sit at room temperature for 20 minutes before roasting in the oven.

ZOOM

The bass family consists of many kinds of fish, but they all have one thing in common—a very sharp, pointed dorsal fin, which must be removed before cooking. Saltwater bass include black sea bass, giant sea bass, grouper, striped bass, and white sea bass. All have very tender, moist white flesh that separates into large flakes. Sea bass can be baked, broiled, or sautéed.

Cutting the Garlic Heads

Seasoning the Fish

- Preheat the oven to 375°F.

- Slice the top ¼ inch from each whole head of garlic. Remove some of the papery skin from the outside, but be careful not to separate the cloves.

- Place the garlic heads in the roasting pan. Pour olive oil over each head. Sprinkle with salt.

- Some cooks also sprinkle the garlic heads with pepper and thyme leaves.

- To season the fish, make 3 shallow diagonal cuts in both sides of the whole sea bass. This will allow the seasonings to penetrate the fish.

- Coat the entire fish with olive oil. Rub the entire fish with crushed garlic.

- Sprinkle lemon juice, salt, and pepper over the entire fish for even flavoring.

- Place lemon slices and crushed garlic cloves inside the fish.

SNAPPER/BASS/MAHI

PAN-FRIED SEA BASS

Aromatic spices, fresh ginger, and tangy yogurt infuse these fillets with Indian savor

This dish is deeply flavored with the fragrant seeds and spices of classic Indian cooking. Sea bass is an excellent choice for this treatment because its lean, firm flesh takes up flavor readily. The yogurt marinade not only draws the flavor into the fish, but the acids "cook" the surface slightly and help the fish retain its juices while forming a golden crust. Be sure to use a glass, high-quality ceramic, or other non-metal bowl when marinating the fish.

The carrot rice features crunchy peanuts, aromatic seeds, and fragrant basmati rice in addition to the sweetness of shredded carrots. Purchase the very best basmati rice you can find for an aroma like no other. *Yield: 4 servings*

Ingredients:

4 (6- to 8-ounce) skinless sea bass fillets (cut each fillet in 2)

1 cup plain yogurt

1 teaspoon ground coriander

1 teaspoon mild curry powder or garam masala

1/2 teaspoon paprika

1 clove garlic, finely minced

1 teaspoon freshly grated ginger

1/2 teaspoon salt

1 small onion, chopped

1/2 cup shelled roasted peanuts

1/2 teaspoon each coriander seed and mustard seed

1 clove garlic minced

2 tablespoons butter

2 large carrots, grated

2 cups basmati rice, rinsed and drained

1 teaspoon salt

3 1/2 cups water

Chopped cilantro for garnish

Pan-fried Sea Bass

- Rinse the fillets and dry well with paper towels.

- Combine the yogurt and next 6 ingredients in a bowl. Fold in the sea bass; cover and refrigerate for 45–60 minutes.

- Sauté the onions, peanuts, seeds, and garlic in butter.

Stir in carrots, rice, and salt; add water. Cover; simmer on low heat 15 minutes.

- Remove fish and pat lightly with paper towels. Fry the fish in an oiled pan, 3 to 4 minutes per side, until well crusted. Serve over carrot rice. Garnish with cilantro.

Marinate the Sea Bass

Making the Carrot Rico

- Sea bass is a very tender, moist, white-flesh fish fillet that only improves when marinated.

- The right seasonings will allow the flavor of this fish to shine through.

- Curry powder is the most popular spice blend in south Indian cooking.

- Garam masala is a spicy blend of highly aromatic spices from northern India.

- In a large skillet over medium-high heat, sauté the onions, peanuts, seeds, and garlic in butter.

- Stir in carrots, basmati rice, and salt. Add the water and cover.

- Simmer for 15 minutes on low heat.

- For best results, finely grate the carrots and chop onion into small pieces to ensure balanced cooking.

- Stir rice mixture thoroughly before serving to evenly distribute the flavors and textures.

CHIMICHURRI MAHIMAHI

Flavorful chimichurri sauce, a South American favorite, makes a delicious marinade for fish

Popular in Argentina and Uruguay as a topping for grilled meats, chimichurri sauce is so tasty and versatile that once you try it you'll find yourself reaching for it often. Once you make this dish, you'll never want to have mahimahi any other way!

You can find excellent quality bottled chimichurri sauce in the Latin or international foods aisles of many supermarkets, but making your own is quick, easy, and allows you to customize the proportions to your taste.

Mahimahi fillets can vary in color, often appearing grayish with streaks of red. The texture should be fine and the flesh should have a clean sea smell. Avoid fillets that are brownish or mushy. *Yield: 4 servings*

Ingredients:

¹/₄ cup olive oil

¹/₂ cup red wine

2 tablespoons lemon juice

1 tablespoon balsamic vinegar

¹/₂ cup minced parsley

2 teaspoons dried oregano

¹/₂ teaspoon salt

¹/₂ teaspoon white pepper

¹/₄ teaspoon red pepper flakes (optional)

4 (6-ounce) mahimahi fillets

Chimichurri Mahimahi

- Thoroughly combine the first 9 ingredients. Place the fillets in a bowl and cover with marinade.

- Or, place the fillets in a large zip-top bag, pour the marinade over, press out the air, and seal the bag. Refrigerate for 30 to 45 minutes.

- Preheat the broiler; place the fillets in a broiling pan and broil 3 to 4 minutes.

- Turn fillets over, spoon some additional marinade on top. Broil 2 to 3 minutes more until lightly firm.

Pan-roasted Garlic Potatoes: Cut 4 medium potatoes into ¼-inch slices. Heat 1 tablespoon olive oil in skillet. Add potatoes in layers, sprinkle with salt, pepper, and more oil. Turn to coat well. Cover; cook over medium-high heat until tender (25 minutes). Turn potatoes occasionally. Stir in 1 minced garlic clove and 1 tablespoon minced parsley, turn off heat, and let rest before serving.

If you prefer an Asian flavor, you can serve mahimahi in a simple teriyaki broth. Sauté the fillets in canola oil in a hot pan for 3 to 4 minutes per side. Set the cooked fish aside. In the same pan, combine 2 tablespoons soy sauce, 2 tablespoons sake, 2 tablespoons mirin, and ¾ cup dashi. Simmer for 30 seconds. Pour this broth over the fish in a bowl. Garnish with chopped scallions.

Making Chimichurri Sauce

Broiling the Mahimahi

- In a glass bowl, combine the olive oil, red wine, lemon juice, balsamic vinegar, parsley, dried oregano, salt, white pepper, and red pepper flakes (if desired).

- Whisk the ingredients together to blend well.

- A green version of chimichurri can be made by using chopped parsley and white wine vinegar instead of the red wine and balsamic vinegar.

- Chimichurri can also be used as a marinade for grilled meat.

- Mahimahi is the Hawaiian name for dolphinfish, which has nothing to do with the mammal of the same name.

- Mahimahi means "strong-strong," in reference to the fight this fish puts up once caught on a line.

- Most mahimahi comes from Hawaii or even further west.

- The skin should be removed before broiling.

SNAPPER/BASS/MAHI

COCONUT-CRUSTED MAHIMAHI

If you like coconut-crusted shrimp, this mahimahi dish will really shake your tree!

Believe it or not, there are some people out there who suffer from Fish Indifference. They could take it or leave it, but they just can't get excited about it. If you know anyone who suffers from this syndrome, you now have the cure right in your hands. This dish will make them jump up and rejoice!

Hawaiians gave this tasty fish the name mahimahi, and this recipe is inspired by the flavors of those islands. The creamy, nutty batter is the perfect base for the sesame coconut crust, which seals in the juicy flavor of this versatile fish.

Be sure to use an oil thermometer to measure the temperature, and skim the oil between batches. *Yield: 4 servings*

Ingredients:

1 cup self-rising flour

1/4 cup ground macadamia nuts

1/4 cup ground almonds

1 tablespoon ground ginger

1 teaspoon salt

1/4 teaspoon white pepper

2 eggs, beaten

1 cup milk

1 1/2 cups sweetened shredded coconut

4 tablespoons sesame seeds

Canola or peanut oil for frying

4 (6-ounce) mahimahi fillets

Coconut-crusted Mahimahi

- Combine the first 6 ingredients in a large bowl. Stir in the eggs and milk, mix well.

- Mix together the shredded coconut and sesame seeds; spread on a plate.

- Heat 1/4 to 1/2 inch of oil in a deep skillet to 360°F. Dry the fillets well; dip fillets in batter, then dredge in the coconut mixture.

- Fry fillets until golden, turning once (approx. 6 minutes total); drain on paper towels or cooling rack.

Mexican Mahi-stuffed Poblanos: Rinse whole poblanos from a can and stuff with strips of mahimahi, sautéed onions and garlic, and slices of quesadilla cheese. Place the stuffed peppers in a casserole. Moisten with half-and-half or light cream. Top with a layer of Cotija or Asiago cheese and minced cilantro. Bake at 350°F for 45 minutes, or until cheese is bubbly.

Mahimahi with Avocado Salsa: Brush the mahimahi fillets with butter, dust them with smoked paprika, and broil them 2 to 3 minutes per side, or until the fish starts to flake. Serve the mahimahi with a "dry" salsa of chopped avocado, cubanelle peppers, green olives, and scallions, lightly dressed with lime juice, coarse salt, and a pinch of oregano.

Grinding the Nuts

- Ideally the almonds and macadamia nuts should be ground in an electric spice grinder.

- Most nuts can also be ground in a blender or food processor.

- Nuts can be ground in a coffee grinder, but only one that has been dedicated to grinding nuts and is no longer used to grind coffee beans.

- Nuts can also be ground by hand using a mortar and pestle.

Dredging the Mahimahi

- On a large flat plate, combine the sweetened shredded coconut and sesame seeds. Mix to blend well.

- Rinse the mahimahi fillets under cold running water. Pat them dry with a paper towel.

- Dip each fish fillet into the batter.

- Then dip each fillet in the coconut mixture, making sure to coat both sides well for frying.

SNACKS

CRISPY BAJA PERCH TACOS

This lower-fat alternative to the fried fish taco uses crushed tortilla chips for crunch

Baja fish tacos originated on the beaches of northern Mexico and made their way over the border into Southern California. While they are often made with shark, this version uses ocean perch, which has a more tender texture, a fine flavor, and is more readily available.

While the original calls for battering the fish and frying in oil, in this version the fish is marinated, then rolled in crushed white corn chips and baked to give it a crunchy, lower-fat coating. You can also use reduced fat mayo in the topping.

Perch fillets can be slightly grayish, but lighten as they cook. Look for fresh smelling fillets and remove any dark lines for a milder flavor. *Yield: 4 servings*

Ingredients:

Juice of 2 limes

1 large clove garlic, minced

1/2 teaspoon dried oregano

1/4 teaspoon salt

1 teaspoon chipotle hot sauce

1 pound boneless, skinless perch, cut into 8 long pieces

2 eggs, beaten

1 1/2 cups coarsely crushed white corn tortilla chips

1 1/2 cups very finely shredded cabbage

1 cup finely shredded lettuce

1 tablespoon finely shredded cilantro leaves

1 large jalapeño pepper, seeded and cut in thin shreds (optional)

3 tablespoons mayonnaise

...lk

...pper

...n tortillas

...acamole

PPER/BASS/MAHI

Crispy Baja Perch Tacos

- Mix the lime juice, garlic, oregano, salt, and chipotle sauce. Fold in the fish; refrigerate 15 minutes.

- Blot fish with paper towels. Dip in egg, roll in chips; bake on a nonstick pan 15 minutes at 375°F or until crisp. Keep warm.

- Combine the next 7 ingredients in a bowl. Warm the tortillas in the oven.

- To serve, spread a little guacamole in the bottom of a tortilla. Add a piece of fish, and top with the cabbage mix.

Ocean perch is actually a rockfish, with the best being caught along the Baja California coast all the way north to the Bering Sea. If whole, it's best to steam, deep-fry, or bake this fish. Fillets are good braised, poached, in soups, and in stews. Avoid grilling for this fish tends to stick. When cooked, this fish is white with a fine flake. Its flavor is delicate and mildly pronounced.

YELLOW ● LIGHT

The tacos in the United States are different from those served in Mexico, where they are sold in little taco stands, along with ice-cold beer. Inland, the Mexican tacos are made with meats cooked over mesquite. Along the coast, the fish tacos are topped with chopped cabbage, white onions, and cilantro. Different, yes, and aficionados would argue tacos are much better in Mexico.

Baking the Crispy Perch

Assembling the Fish Tacos

- There are two varieties of ocean perch: Atlantic perch and Pacific perch.

- They are not to be confused with lake perch, which is usually not available commercially.

- Allow ⅓ to ½ pound of perch fillets per serving.

- Perch fillets can easily be baked in a greased baking dish in a 350°F oven for 15 to 18 minutes, or until the fish is flaky and tender.

- In Mexico, especially in the Baja region, almost any kind of breaded fish is used in tacos.

- In North Baja, red snapper fillets is used in making Tacos de Pescado.

- Tacos de Camarones, or shrimp tacos, are also popular.

- Fish tacos can also be made with scallops or oysters, Usually the fish is fried.

SAVORY CREOLE-STYLE PERCH

Sauce picante, a New Orleans favorite, jazzes up this easy simmered dish

Sauce picante is just so tasty that you might find yourself pouring it over everything from grilled chicken breasts to your morning pancakes. Okay, maybe not pancakes, but it can even make alligator taste good—and that's saying something!

It's a wonderful simmering sauce for fish, because it both adds and receives flavor in the cooking process. The acids in the tomatoes and pepper sauce firm up the ocean perch fillets and help them hold together better.

The resulting sauce, when served with the fish over white rice or grits, is "slap your mama" good. Sprinkle each serving with some thinly sliced green onion tops and a sprinkle of fresh lemon juice. Let the good times roll! *Yield: 4 servings*

Ingredients:

2 tablespoons olive oil

1 cup each diced onion, celery, green pepper

3 large cloves garlic, minced

1 jalapeño pepper, seeded and diced

2 (15-ounce) cans petite diced tomatoes

1 cup water

2 tablespoons tomato paste

1 tablespoon hot sauce

1/2 teaspoon each salt and black pepper

1 lemon (1 half juiced; other half thinly sliced)

2 pounds skinless perch fillets, cut into 2-inch chunks

2 tablespoons chiffonaded parsley

2 scallions (green parts only), sliced thin on the diagonal

Savory Creole-style Perch

- Heat oil in a large skillet. Sauté onion, celery, green pepper, garlic, and jalapeño for 5 minutes.

- Add tomatoes and water; bring to a simmer and stir in tomato paste, hot sauce, salt, pepper, and lemon juice (reserve slices for the garnish).

- Simmer 20 minutes. Fold fish into sauce; simmer 15 minutes or until fish flakes.

- Garnish with parsley, scallions, and lemon slices.

If you are intrigued by this recipe but can't find perch in your local fish market, you can substitute tautog, black sea bass, scup, pollack, grouper, or red snapper for the perch. Perch does well when paired with cucumber or asparagus, or with a simple basil butter sauce poured over the baked fish. Perch can also be used in a seafood version of the classic Italian dish known as saltimbocca, using mozzarella cheese for added flavor.

· · · · RECIPE VARIATION · · · ·

Dirty Rice: Cook 1 cup long-grain rice in 2 cups water with a pinch of salt. In a food processor, chop 1 pound of chicken livers, 1 celery stalk, 1 green pepper (seeded), and 2 medium onions. Heat 2 tablespoons oil in a large frying pan. Cook the liver mixture over moderate heat, stirring gently. Reduce heat to low and cook 30 to 40 minutes. Stir in the rice. Heat through. Season to taste.

Cut the Fish

- Rinse the perch under cold running water. Pat the fish dry with paper towels.

- Lay the skinless fish down on a clean cutting board.

- Using a very sharp knife, cut the fish lengthwise so you have long pieces about 2 inches wide. Then cut these long strips into chunks that are about 2 inches in size.

- This is even easier to do if the fish is semi-frozen.

Making Parsley Chiffonade

- You can sharpen your knife skills by making a chiffonade of parsley.

- Roll up the parsley into a tight ball on a cutting board.

- Hold the parsley with your thumb tucked in and your fingertips turned under, knuckles perpendicular to the cutting board.

- With a very sharp chef's knife in your other hand, make repeated cuts into the parsley, resulting in minced parsley.

CREAMY PARMESAN WHITING BAKE

A layer of Italian cheeses, fresh tomato, and basil leaves top buttery whiting fillets

Whiting is a delicious, economical, readily available, but often overlooked fish. It is an affordable alternative for a large-grained white fish like cod. With the skin removed, the flavor of whiting fillets is very mild and sweet. They can handle just about any cooking method short of grilling.

IQF (Individually Quick Frozen) whiting fillets are fine for this casserole. Make sure to thaw them completely in the refrigerator and dry them well before you begin.

Use a good-quality, fresh-grated Parmesan cheese. Also, use whole milk or part skim ricotta in this recipe; the nonfat kind will separate. You can substitute Roma tomatoes with additional basil for the regular tomatoes. *Yield: 4 servings*

Ingredients:

1 1/2 pounds skinless whiting fillets

3/4 cup bottled creamy Italian dressing

1 cup grated Parmesan cheese, divided

3 cups ricotta cheese

2 large eggs, beaten

1/4 cup coarsely chopped parsley leaves

1/4 teaspoon white pepper

1 cup Italian-style seasoned bread crumbs

Cooking spray

4 large tomato slices

4 large parsley or basil leaves

Creamy Parmesan Whiting Bake

- Combine fish and Italian dressing in a zip-top bag; refrigerate 30 minutes.

- Mix ¾ cup of Parmesan with next 4 ingredients. Refrigerate.

- Dredge fillets in bread crumbs mixed with remaining Parmesan. Place in a well-buttered baking dish; lightly coat fish with cooking spray. Bake at 375°F for 20 minutes.

- Spread cheese mixture over fish. Lay tomatoes evenly over top; bake 10 minutes. Place a leaf on each tomato. Place the dish under the broiler for a minute or two.

ZOOM

IQF stands for Individually Quick Frozen. IQF fish fillets are all processed and frozen within hours of catch. Most of these fillets are frozen in nitrogen tunnels to maintain optimum freshness and to ensure the highest quality. Each fillet is inspected for quality and then sized carefully for packaging.

Baking the Whiting Fillets

- This dish is baked in two separate stages.

- The first stage involves baking the fish fillets after they have been dredged in the Parmesan-bread mixture.

- The second stage takes place after the fish has been topped with the cheese and tomatoes.

- This ensures thorough cooking of the fish fillets without overbrowning the delicate topping.

Browning the Cheese Topping

- When you place the baking dish back in the oven for the second stage of cooking, the aroma of melting cheese and fresh herbs will fill the air.

- Check fish fillets after 10 minutes.

- The fish fillets are perfectly done when the topping starts to brown in spots.

- Be very careful when broiling delicate fish. A minute too long under the broiler can ruin the dish.

BRAISED WHITING WITH PANCETTA

A delicious whiting dish with the flavors of the Andalusia region of Spain

The Moorish invaders of Spain brought with them the ingredients and culinary techniques of their homelands, and their influence on the food traditions of Spain is still felt to this day.

This dish uses sweet pitted dates—a gift of the desert—and aromatic ground coriander seeds to create a depth of flavor that complements the fine sweet taste of the whiting fillets. Pancetta adds a meaty, salty note to the sauce, and the garlic draws them all together.

You can use frozen whiting fillets, properly defrosted, in this dish, though fresh is better if they are available. If you buy whole pitted dates, you can chop them easily by using a wet knife or scissors. *Yield: 4 servings*

Ingredients:

1/4 pound pancetta, diced or cut in small strips

2 cloves garlic, minced

2 medium zucchini, diced

1/4 cup chopped dates

Olive oil

2 teaspoons ground coriander

1/4 teaspoon black pepper

1 cup chicken stock

1 tablespoon tomato paste

1 teaspoon paprika

1 1/2 pounds whiting fillets

Braised Whiting with Pancetta

- Fry the pancetta over medium heat until crisp. Remove the pancetta from the pan and set aside.

- Add the garlic, zucchini, and dates to the pan; sauté 5 minutes, adding a little olive oil if needed.

- Stir in the coriander, black pepper, chicken stock, tomato paste, paprika, and reserved pancetta. Bring to a boil; lay the fish in the pan and cover with sauce.

- Reduce heat and simmer, covered, for 15 minutes or until fish is firm.

ZOOM

A staple in Italian cooking, pancetta is the salt-cured pork from the belly of the pig. It is rolled and sometimes spiced with pepper, cloves, nutmeg, fennel, hot peppers, and garlic. Some varieties are much like American bacon. Pancetta rigatino is a lean pancetta from the region of Tuscany in Italy. You can find pancetta in the deli section of Italian food markets.

• • • • RECIPE VARIATION • • • •

Venetian Rice: In skillet over medium heat, cook 4 bacon slices until crisp. Set bacon aside on paper towels. In same pan, cook 1 large sliced onion until tender crisp. Add 1 1/2 cups uncooked rice, 1 (10-ounce) package frozen peas, 3 cups chicken broth, 1/4 cup sherry, and 1/2 teaspoon ground turmeric. Bring to a boil, stir, reduce heat, cover, simmer 15 minutes. Add cooked bacon. Toss lightly; serve.

Frying the Pancetta

- If you are unable to find pancetta in your supermarket or in an Italian grocery store, you can substitute bacon.

- Dice the bacon, or cut it into small strips.

- Fry the bacon just as you would fry the pancetta in a skillet over medium heat.

- You will get the best results when cooking bacon if you cook it low and slow.

Making the Braising Sauce

- Braising usually takes a long time, but fish can be braised in as little as 15 minutes, as in this dish.

- Braising done properly will result in a concentrated blend of flavors.

- All the ingredients in the braising liquid not only contribute flavor and moisture to the dish.

- They also serve as a protective bed on which the fish is placed, shielding it from the source of direct heat.

EASY POLLACK STEW WITH BISCUITS

Easy to make and delightful to eat, the whole family will enjoy this pollack casserole

Pollack is another often overlooked fish with fine qualities similar to the more expensive cod. It is sometimes found fresh but more often as frozen fillets, which are quite good, especially in this tasty casserole. One of the best things about this dish is that it requires very little in the way of seasonings. The various ingredients add their flavors to the mix and the whole becomes more than the sum of its parts.

When the fish is just cooked and the vegetables have softened, biscuit dough is placed on top and baked. When it's done, the tops of the biscuits are golden brown and crisp, while the bottoms have the flavor and appealing texture of steamed dumplings. *Yield: 6 servings*

Ingredients:

2 pounds russet potatoes, peeled and cut in $1/4$-inch slices

$1/2$ teaspoon garlic powder

Salt and pepper as needed

2 pounds skinless pollack fillets, cut into large pieces

1 stick butter, melted

1 large or 2 medium yellow onions, thinly sliced

1 (16-ounce) bag mixed frozen vegetables, thawed and drained

1 (15-ounce) can stewed tomatoes

$1/4$ cup chopped parsley leaves

1 can refrigerated "Grands!" (type of biscuit dough)

Easy Pollack Stew with Biscuits

- Spread potatoes in the bottom of a large, buttered casserole, overlapping slightly if necessary. Sprinkle with the garlic powder, plus a little salt and pepper.

- Dip each fish piece in melted butter and place evenly on potatoes. Spread onions over fish, spread mixed vegetables over onions; pour stewed tomatoes (with juice) over all.

- Sprinkle with parsley. Bake, covered, at 375°F for 25 minutes.

- Top evenly with biscuits. Bake uncovered 15 minutes or until biscuits are golden.

A member of the cod family, Atlantic pollack is also called blue cod and Boston bluefish. In England, it is used to make traditional fish and chips. A distant cousin, Alaskan pollack is mostly converted in Japan into surimi, which is used to make imitation crab sticks and commercially prepared foods such as fish sticks.

• • • • RECIPE VARIATION • • • •

New England Fish Chowder: Pollack, haddock, or cod can be used to make a traditional fish chowder, in combination with the usual onions, bacon, potatoes, heavy cream, salt, pepper, and bouquet garni (fresh thyme sprigs, a bunch of parsley, and bay leaves tied up in cheesecloth). Use 1 large potato for every pound of fish in your chowder. Garnish with freshly chopped chives.

Layering the Casserole

- In a large buttered casserole, layer the following ingredients to make this stew.

- First, the potato slices, overlapping if necessary, sprinkled with garlic powder, salt, and pepper.

- Next, the pollack fillets that have been dipped in butter, followed by the sliced onions and mixed vegetables.

- Next, the stewed tomatoes with juice, and a sprinkle of chopped parsley.

Top with Biscuits

- After the stew goes through an initial baking, it is removed from the oven and topped with biscuit dough.

- Biscuit dough is available in the refrigerator section of your supermarket.

- The dough should be spread evenly over the stew, even if that means it must be stretched slightly.

- The stew is then baked uncovered for another 15 minutes, or until the biscuits are golden.

FIESTA FISH CAKES

These cakes are full of Tex-Mex flavor and make a deliciously different lunch or dinner

Fish cakes can be dry, dull, lifeless things—or they can be the life of the party like these Southwest-inspired treats. Inside, they're big on flavor, and they have a satisfyingly crunchy exterior made from finely crushed tortilla chips. Served with salsa verde and a dab of sour cream, they'll have you heading back for seconds.

Frozen pollack is fine for this recipe. Let it defrost fully and dry it well with paper towels. If you're using frozen corn, let it revive in cool water for 15 to 20 minutes beforehand to plump it up. You can use parsley instead of cilantro for a milder flavor and plain Monterey Jack cheese to turn down the heat if you prefer. *Yield: 4 servings*

Ingredients:

1 pound skinless pollack fillets, cut into large pieces

1 cup cooked black beans, rinsed and drained

1 cup canned (or thawed frozen) yellow niblet corn

$^1/_2$ cup fresh bread crumbs

$^1/_4$ cup minced yellow onion

4 ounces pepperjack cheese, cut into approx. $^1/_4$-inch cubes

1 tablespoon finely minced cilantro leaves

2 large cloves garlic, minced

1 egg, beaten

1 small (4-ounce) can fire-roasted green chiles, drained

$^3/_4$ cup finely crushed tortilla chips (white or yellow)

Oil for frying

Fiesta Fish Cakes

- Pulse pollack in food processor until finely minced. Place in mixing bowl, add next 8 ingredients, and stir well to combine. Fold in green chiles until just mixed through.

- Form into 8 cakes, roll in tortilla crumbs; cover and refrigerate 15 minutes.

- Heat ¼ inch of oil in a heavy skillet over medium-high heat. Fry the cakes in hot oil until golden brown (about 2 minutes per side).

- Drain on paper towels or on a wire cooling rack.

Making Fresh Bread Crumbs

- The easiest way to make your own bread crumbs is to pulverize small pieces of bread in a food processor or blender.

- Use unsweetened white bread with the crusts cut off to make fresh crumbs.

- Do not use bread that is stale because the crumbs will have a stale taste.

- It's best to store leftover fresh bread crumbs in the freezer to prevent mold.

Resting Foods before Frying

- There is some debate as to whether or not freshly breaded fish should rest before frying.

- Some cooks say the breaded fish will hold together better during frying if allowed to rest.

- Others believe the breading will get soggy and separate from the fish.

- This recipe recommends that you form 8 fish cakes, roll them in tortilla crumbs, cover, and refrigerate for 15 minutes before frying.

SWORDFISH WITH MUSTARD CREAM

This elegant, classic preparation brings out the very best of this magnificent fish

A fresh swordfish steak, properly prepared, is one of life's great pleasures. This recipe uses classical French techniques and ingredients to prepare a sauce that coats the swordfish in wonderfully complex flavors that linger on the palate. Swordfish steaks can vary in color from creamy white to pink to nearly orange. The flesh should be firm and resilient, and should smell clean with just a hint of the sea. Any dark spots in the flesh should be reddish, not brown, and there shouldn't be any iridescent shine on the surface (brown spots and iridescence indicate age). Frozen swordfish fillets should be defrosted slowly and completely in the refrigerator and patted dry before cooking. *Yield: 2 servings*

Ingredients:

2 (6- to 8-ounce) swordfish steaks (about $1/2$ inch thick)

2 tablespoons butter, melted

Coarse sea salt

Freshly ground black pepper

2 tablespoons Herbes de Provence (or combine 2 teaspoons each dried thyme and marjoram with 1 teaspoon each crushed dried rosemary and ground fennel seeds)

2 tablespoons cognac or brandy

1 teaspoon small capers

1 tablespoon coarse-ground Dijon mustard

2 tablespoons heavy cream

Salt and pepper to taste

Swordfish with Mustard Cream

- Heat a skillet over medium-high heat. Remove any skin and dark flesh from steaks.

- Brush steaks with melted butter, season all sides with salt and pepper; sprinkle top and bottom evenly with Herbes de Provence.

- Cook the steaks 3 to 4 minutes; turn and cook 2 to 3 minutes more; remove and keep warm.

- Deglaze pan with cognac, stirring well. Add capers and mustard; cook 1 minute. Turn off heat; stir in cream. Adjust salt and pepper. Spoon sauce over steaks.

Lemon Butter Sauce: In a small saucepan over low heat, melt 1 stick of unsalted butter. Whisk in 2 tablespoons of heavy cream and heat through. Remove the saucepan from the heat. Whisk in the juice from 1 lemon and 2 teaspoons of freshly minced parsley. Season to taste with salt and white pepper. Capers can also be added to this sauce. Makes about 1 cup.

Provençale Sauce: In a skillet, heat 2 tablespoons of olive oil. Sauté 2 minced garlic cloves and 1 large chopped onion. Add ¼ cup of dry red wine and reduce it slightly. Add 3 large tomatoes that you've chopped along with ½ teaspoon of dried thyme, a bay leaf, and 2 chopped parsley sprigs. Cook over medium heat for 10 minutes. Remove the bay leaf before serving.

Removing Dark Spots

- Swordfish steaks have dark red areas much like tuna steaks. These should be dark red and not brown.

- Avoid buying swordfish steaks that show signs of browning, which changes the flavor of the fish.

- Trim the swordfish steaks of any bits of skin and dark spots before cooking.

- Use a very sharp paring knife to cut away the dark flesh.

Making the Mustard Cream

- After cooking the swordfish steaks in the skillet, remove the steaks and keep them warm.

- Deglaze skillet with cognac, stirring to scrape up any brown bits in the pan.

- Add the capers and mustard. Cook over medium heat for 1 minute.

- Turn off the heat. Stir the cream into the skillet. Season to taste with salt and pepper.

SUPER GROUPER SANDWICH

Chipotle sauce and homemade mango chutney make this grouper sandwich a super experience

This sandwich is not shy about asserting itself. It's got smoky chipotle pepper sauce, a corn chip crust, and it's topped with a spiced homemade mango-jalapeño chutney. It's served on a buttered, toasted kaiser roll and will make your taste buds sing.

Grouper, a relative of the sea bass, is a highly prized food fish. The flesh is dense, sweet, and quite flaky in texture. Look for grouper fillets that are fresh smelling, firm (not mushy), and pinkish-white. Frozen fillets are available and are very good.

Use crushed Frito-style corn chips for the coating. You can use less or more jalapeño peppers in the chutney, or eliminate them completely if you want to turn down the heat a bit. *Yield: 4 servings*

Ingredients:

4 (6-ounce) skinless grouper fillets

Flour for dusting

1/2 cup bottled chipotle pepper sauce (such as Tabasco brand chipotle sauce)

1 1/2 cups finely crushed corn chips

1 (15-ounce) can of mangos in syrup

1 piece cinnamon stick (about 2 inches)

6 whole cloves

1 tablespoon white vinegar

2 large jalapeño peppers, seeded and diced (about 3 tablespoons)

Pinch of salt

4 buttered, toasted kaiser rolls

2 cups shredded romaine or green leaf lettuce

Super Grouper Sandwich

- Pat fish dry. Dust fillets with flour; shake off excess. Coat with chipotle pepper sauce and dredge in corn chip crumbs. Refrigerate at least 15 minutes.

- Drain mangos and cut into chunks. Add mango and next 5 ingredients to saucepan; cook over medium-low heat, stirring, 5 to 7 minutes. Remove spices.

- Preheat oven to 375°F. Bake fish for 10 to 12 minutes or until fish flakes and coating is crunchy.

- Serve fish on rolls with lettuce and mango-jalapeño chutney.

It is very hard to note the differences in the taste or texture of the many groupers being caught these days. All are white fleshed and lean. Giant groupers weighing at least 300 pounds usually end up in a chowder. Large groupers, 25 to 50 pounds, are best when cut into fingers and fried. The smaller groupers are ideal for the home cook and can be broiled, fried, or steamed.

• • • • RECIPE VARIATION • • • •

Crunchy Grouper: Dip 4 grouper fillets (around 6 ounces each) into a glass bowl containing 2 beaten eggs and $1/2$ cup milk. Dredge the fillets in a mixture of $1/2$ cup flavored bread crumbs, $1/2$ cup Special K cereal, and $1/2$ cup corn flakes. In a large skillet, sauté the fillets in oil 4 to 5 minutes per side, more or less depending on the thickness of the fish.

Making the Mango Chutney

- Drain the canned mangos well, and cut them into bite-size chunks.

- In a saucepan, combine the mango chunks with the cinnamon stick, whole cloves, white vinegar, jalapeño peppers, and salt.

- Cook over medium-low heat for 5 to 7 minutes, stirring occasionally.

- Strain the mixture to remove the whole spices. Place the chutney in a glass serving bowl.

Baking the Grouper Fillets

- Preheat the oven to 375°F.

- Rinse the grouper fillets under cold running water. Pat them dry with a paper towel.

- Dust the fillets with flour, shaking off the excess. Coat each fillet with the chipotle pepper sauce. Dredge each fillet in the crushed corn chips. Refrigerate the fillets at least 15 minutes.

- Bake the fillets for 10 to 12 minutes, or until the fish flakes and the coating is crunchy.

SESAME-CRUSTED CALAMARI

If you've never tried calamari, this recipe is an easy and delicious introduction

A lot of people who've never tried it swear they wouldn't enjoy squid—and then find themselves pleasantly surprised by calamari. Some are put off by tentacles, but you can easily enjoy squid without ever touching a tentacle. Frozen squid rings are already cleaned, de-tentacled, sliced, and ready to cook. They require nothing more than defrosting in the refrigerator. A simple coating and a short stay in hot oil is all they need to be delicious.

But there's an important rule to follow: never fry calamari longer than 2 minutes. More than that will produce inedible rubber bands. Deep-fry rings just long enough to cook the coating and your calamari will be perfect. *Yield: 2–4 servings*

Ingredients:

³/₄ cup white sesame seeds, divided

1 sheet sushi nori (Japanese sushi roll sheet)

¹/₄ cup all-purpose flour

¹/₂ teaspoon salt

¹/₄ teaspoon white pepper

¹/₄ teaspoon cayenne

1 pound frozen calamari rings, defrosted

2 egg whites, beaten

Canola or peanut oil for frying

Sesame-crusted Calamari

- Lightly toast the sesame seeds in a dry frying pan, 2 to 3 minutes. Set aside to cool.

- Briefly toast nori sheet over a gas flame until dry. Break into small pieces and pulse in blender or food processor with ¼ cup of sesame seeds until powdered; mix with flour and seasonings.

- Dredge calamari in sesame/flour/nori mix, then egg white, then in whole sesame seeds.

- Fry in ½ inch of oil until light golden, 1 to 2 minutes. Drain on a wire cooling rack.

Ginger-soy Dipping Sauce: In glass bowl, combine ½ cup of soy sauce, 2 tablespoons of rice wine vinegar, 2 tablespoons of sugar, 3 shots of hot pepper sauce, 1 tablespoon of freshly minced ginger, and 2 teaspoons of thinly sliced scallions. (You can use white wine vinegar in place of the rice wine vinegar.) Serve the dipping sauce in individual bowls for your guests.

Orange-cilantro Dipping Sauce: In glass bowl, combine 1 sliced orange and 1 tablespoon freshly chopped cilantro with 4 tablespoons rice wine vinegar, 1 tablespoon peanut oil, dash of sesame oil, 1 tablespoon freshly minced ginger, and black pepper to taste. (White wine vinegar can be substituted for rice wine vinegar.) Allow to stand at room temperature for 15 minutes before serving in individual bowls.

Toasting the Nori

- Sushi nori are flat sheets of seaweed specially prepared for making sushi. They can be purchased in Asian markets.

- Briefly toast the sushi nori over a medium gas flame until dry.

- If you have an electric stove, toast the sushi nori over a very hot burner until dry.

- To do this safely, hold the sushi nori with metal tongs that have an insulated handle.

Frying the Calamari

- Dredge the calamari in the powdered mixture of toasted sesame seeds, sushi nori, flour, salt, white pepper, and cayenne.

- Dip the calamari in the beaten egg whites.

- Dip the calamari in the remaining toasted sesame seeds.

- In a deep frying pan, heat ½ inch of canola or peanut oil. Fry the calamari in batches until lightly golden, 1 to 2 minutes. Drain the calamari on a wire cooling rack lined with paper towels.

BRAISED SPICED MONKFISH

Monkfish gets an unusual but classic preparation in this variation on an historic Italian recipe

Many people have heard of osso buco, the famous veal shank dish, but there is a less well-known recipe—osso buco bianco—that may be older. This "white" osso buco uses exotic spices to lend a special aroma to the dish.

In this version, flavorful monkfish takes the place of veal. Monkfish is a relative newcomer to the world of food fish. For years it was considered a "trash" fish with no market value, probably due to its very unpleasant appearance and the fact that only the tail is edible. But the unique texture and flavor of monkfish have become widely appreciated. This dish brings out those unique qualities and enhances them with a perfect balance of flavors. *Yield: 4 servings*

Ingredients:

1–1 1/2 pounds skinless whole monkfish tail or fillets

1 medium onion, chopped

1 celery rib (strings removed), diced

1/2 cup of thinly sliced leeks (white part only)

1 tablespoon fresh thyme leaves

2 teaspoons minced garlic, divided

2 tablespoons full-flavored olive oil

1 1/2 cups white wine

1 1/2 cups chicken stock

1 large bay leaf

1/4 teaspoon allspice

1/4 teaspoon cinnamon

1/4 teaspoon dried ginger

Salt and pepper to taste

2 tablespoons minced parsley

Zest from 1/2 medium lemon

Braised Spiced Monkfish

- Peel off membrane, if any; cut fish in 1-inch segments.

- Sauté onion, celery, leeks, thyme, and 1 teaspoon garlic in olive oil until softened. Add wine, simmer 5 minutes. Add stock, bay leaf, and spices; simmer 15 minutes.

- Remove bay leaf; add fish to sauce, simmer 10 to 15 minutes until fish is opaque and tender.

- Make gremolata by combining the parsley, lemon zest, and remaining garlic. Place fish in shallow bowls and spoon sauce over fish; top with gremolata.

Cutting the Monkfish Tail

- Monkfish is usually sold as a whole tail, but sometimes the tails are sold already cut into fillets.

- If your monkfish tail still has the skin attached, use a paring knife or a boning knife to peel off the outer black skin.

- You also should remove the thin membrane with small black spots beneath the skin.

- The fillets can be removed by slicing next to the bone on each side of the central backbone.

Zesting Citrus Fruits

- Gremolata is a mixture of garlic, lemon peel, and finely chopped parsley that is commonly sprinkled over osso buco in Italian cooking.

- You can zest a lemon with a zester, kitchen rasp, small hole grater, or microplane.

- The microplane is held at an angle over the work surface, and the lemon is rubbed against the rough surface and constantly turned.

- The zest falls from under the microplane into a small pile.

CARIBBEAN-STYLE SKATE WING

Based on a French classic, this skate wing dish has a spicy island flair

Sole meunière is a classic French brown butter and lemon preparation. This recipe uses the same techniques on skate wing, but adds fun, spicy Caribbean elements like allspice, hot peppers, and lime juice for a deliciously different taste.

Skate, a relative of the stingray, is not like other fish. It consists of 2 large "wings" around a smallish central body. Only the wings, which are essentially 2 flat muscles on either side of a central cartilage, are edible. The flesh is arranged in long parallel lines and has a taste similar to scallops.

You can use small whole wings or sections of a larger wing. In either case, have them skinned and filleted, as it's somewhat difficult. *Yield: 2 servings*

Ingredients:

¼ cup all-purpose flour

¼ teaspoon allspice

¼ teaspoon coriander

Pinch of cayenne (optional)

2 (8-ounce) boneless skate wings

Sea salt

White pepper

4 tablespoons butter

1 small jalapeño pepper, unseeded, cut into paper-thin slices

1 teaspoon finely minced sweet red pepper

Juice of 1 lime (cut and reserve 2 thin center slices for garnish before juicing)

1 teaspoon finely minced cilantro leaves

Caribbean-style Skate Wing

- Combine the flour, allspice, coriander, and cayenne in a shallow bowl or plate. Lightly season wings with salt and white pepper. Dust with flour; shake off excess.

- Melt half the butter over medium-high heat. Fry until surface is golden and flesh is creamy white (about 5 minutes total); remove and keep warm.

- Add peppers and remaining butter to pan. Stir in lime juice and remove from heat.

- Stir in cilantro and spoon sauce over skate wings. Serve immediately.

• • • • RECIPE VARIATION • • • •

Traditional Sole Meunière: Season sole fillets with salt and white pepper. Dredge lightly in flour. Melt 3 tablespoons butter. Sauté fish until golden brown, 2 to 3 minutes per side. Remove; keep warm. Add 3 more tablespoons butter to skillet. Allow butter to foam and turn light brown. Whisk in lemon juice. Cook for another minute, or until foaming subsides. Pour sauce over sole.

ZOOM

Skate eat mollusks (which includes clams, mussels, and oysters), and that results in skate having a wonderful flavor, often compared to scallops. Skate wings become more tender if they are stored in the refrigerator for a few days before cooking. Skate wings should also be soaked in water with a little vinegar or lemon juice for several hours before cooking.

Turning the Skate Wings

- An extra-wide spatula called a fish slice is needed when cooking skate wings.

- This wide turner allows you to remove the cooked skate wing from the pan without the fish falling into pieces.

- If you don't have a fish slice, you can use 2 spatulas next to each other when you lift the skate wing.

- With either method, carefully lift the delicate fish out of the pan for plating.

Finishing the Meunière Sauce

- In the same skillet that you cooked the skate wings, add the remaining butter, jalapeño pepper slices, and finely minced sweet red pepper.

- Stir in the lime juice. Remove the pan from the heat.

- Stir in the finely minced cilantro leaves. Mix well.

- Spoon the sauce over the cooked skate wings.

GRILLED BASA VIETNAMESE-STYLE

A very popular fish abroad, tasty basa is beginning to catch on in the U.S.

Basa, a large, meaty farm-raised fish similar to catfish, is becoming increasingly available in the United States as individually quick frozen (IQF) fillets. The fillets are large, white, and tender, and they take to almost any cooking method from steaming in foil to pan-frying to grilling.

Basa is particularly good when paired with the assertive flavors and textures of Southeast Asian cuisines. This recipe incorporates the flavors of Vietnamese culinary traditions and shows off the best qualities of this up-and-coming fish.

Fresh lemongrass is best for this dish, but frozen minced lemongrass can be substituted. Avoid dried lemongrass; it has none of the aromatic flavor of fresh. *Yield: 2 servings*

Ingredients:

2 (6- to 8-ounce) skinless basa fillets, each fillet cut into 3 pieces

1 1/2 cups canned coconut milk

2 scallions, chopped

1 tablespoon grated ginger

1 tablespoon finely chopped lemongrass

1–2 small green chiles, chopped

Canola or peanut oil

1/4 cup thinly sliced shallots

1 tablespoon all-purpose flour

2 tablespoons chopped peanuts

Salt and pepper

Mixed baby greens

1 tablespoon coarsely chopped basil leaves

1 tablespoon coarsely chopped cilantro leaves

1/2 cup bean sprouts

1/4 cup very thinly sliced red pepper strips

Lime wedges for garnish

Grilled Basa Vietnamese-style

- Marinate fish 1 hour in coconut milk with next 4 ingredients.

- Heat 1/4 inch oil in a pan. Toss shallots with flour and fry until crispy; remove. Fry peanuts 15 seconds. Drain on paper towels.

- Remove fish; dry well. Rub with oil; season with salt and pepper. Cook on a hot grill or grill pan, 3 to 4 minutes per side.

- Serve fish on baby greens; top with basil, cilantro, sprouts, and pepper strips. Sprinkle with shallots and peanuts. Garnish with lime wedges.

Fresh ginger has become more widely available in recent years because of growing interest in Asian cooking. When shopping for fresh ginger, look for rock-hard ginger that is noticeably weighty. The color of the skin can be beige or light tan, while the flesh ranges from cream to pale golden. Fresh ginger will keep in the refrigerator for 2 to 3 weeks.

MAKE IT EASY

Fresh ginger can be peeled, sliced, shredded, minced, grated, smashed, juiced, and pounded. This recipe calls for grated ginger. Ideally, use a Japanese grater made specifically for ginger, available in gourmet shops carrying Japanese cookware. Or you can use the chopping blade of a food processor, which will give better results than your all-purpose Western grater.

Using Fresh Lemongrass

- Fresh lemongrass is available in some supermarkets, and Asian food shops stock the dried and powdered variety.

- A lemongrass stalk is fleshy and fibrous even after cooking, so avoid chewing it. It can be cut in small pieces and added directly to a dish being prepared.

- Lemongrass is often used whole or sliced in soups.

- It can also be pounded into a paste with other ingredients and added to stews.

Making the Crispy Shallots

- In a large skillet over medium-high heat, heat ¼ inch of canola or peanut oil.

- In a large bowl, toss the thinly sliced shallots with the flour.

- Shake off the excess flour.

- Fry the shallots in the hot oil. Remove the fried shallots from the skillet. Allow them to drain on paper towels.

143

GOLDEN PAN-FRIED SHRIMP

An amusing coating gives these shrimp their deep golden color and addictive crunch

Those tasty little Goldfish crackers are the secret of this crowd-pleasing dish. They impart a rich cheddar flavor that complements the sweetness of the shrimp.

Butterflying, an easy and very useful technique, gives the shrimp more surface area for the tasty coating and it speeds up the cooking time as well. Make sure the shrimp have plenty of room in the pan to prevent greasiness. Keep batches warm in the oven as you're frying. Drain on a cooling or roasting rack to keep the undersides from getting soggy.

Incidentally, butterflying is a great technique for battered shrimp too; dust with a little corn starch or plain flour before dipping and batter will adhere perfectly. *Yield: 3–4 servings*

Ingredients:

2 large eggs

1 tablespoon milk

1 teaspoon hot pepper sauce (optional)

1 1/2 pounds extra large (26-30) raw shrimp, peeled and deveined

2 cups Goldfish or other small cheddar crackers

1/2 teaspoon black pepper

1/2 teaspoon garlic powder

1/2 teaspoon onion powder

Oil for frying

Golden Pan-fried Shrimp

- Beat together the eggs, milk, and pepper sauce, if using. Butterfly the shrimp by cutting along the back almost completely through.

- Fold the shrimp into the egg mixture, coating thoroughly.

- In a blender or food processor, crush the crackers to a fine powder. Add the spices, mix well, and spread on a plate.

- Heat ½ inch of oil in a skillet to 365°F. Dredge shrimp in the cracker mix and fry in batches 2 to 3 minutes until golden.

Shrimp come in a variety of sizes with names to match. There are about 70 tiny shrimp in 1 pound. Small shrimp are 43 to 50 per pound; medium shrimp are 31 to 35; large shrimp are 16 to 20; and extra large shrimp are 10 to 15 per pound. Jumbo shrimp are very big; expect to get 10 or less per pound.

MAKE IT EASY

The easiest shrimp dish to make is boiled shrimp. Bring 3 cups of salted water to a boil. Add the shrimp. Reduce the heat, cover, and simmer for 3 to 5 minutes, depending on the size of the shrimp. Shrimp is cooked when it turns pink and its center is opaque. Test 1 shrimp by cutting it in half. Drain the shrimp and rinse thoroughly under cold running water. Chill.

Butterfly the Shrimp

Fry Shrimp in Batches

- Peel and devein all the shrimp.

- Using a very sharp paring knife, butterfly the shrimp by cutting each one along its back almost all the way through.

- This enables you to spread the shrimp out, giving the shrimp more surface area for the coating.

- Shrimp that have been butterflied will cook faster so plan accordingly.

- In a skillet or heavy frying pan, heat ½ inch of oil to 365°F. Use a frying thermometer for accuracy.

- Dredge the butterflied shrimp in the crushed cracker mixture.

- Fry the shrimp in small batches. Do not fill the skillet more than half full with the shrimp.

- After frying for 2 to 3 minutes, the shrimp should be golden.

SPANISH-STYLE GARLIC SHRIMP

The flavors of sunny Spain combine in this easy and very enticing dish

Many people who try Spanish-style Garlic Shrimp say it's one of the best shrimp dishes ever. We say they're right! Best of all, you can make it in minutes and serve it as an appetizer, main course, or as a stunning brunch dish.

Make sure you serve this with lots of warm, crusty bread (the sauce is ambrosial) and a crisp, chilled white or blush wine. Serve cheese and fruit for dessert for the full Spanish meal experience.

You can use any size shrimp for this dish; make sure to fully defrost frozen shrimp in the fridge, then drain and dry them well. The flavor of the olive oil is important here, so use the best you can find. *Yield: 2 servings*

Ingredients:

3 tablespoons olive oil (a full-flavored Spanish olive oil is best)

1 large bay leaf

4-6 cloves garlic, minced

¹/₂ teaspoon red pepper flakes

1 tablespoon small capers

1 tablespoon brandy (or white wine with a pinch of brown sugar)

1 pound extra large (26-30) raw shrimp, peeled and deveined (dry well on paper towels)

1 teaspoon smoked paprika

2 tablespoons minced parsley

Salt

Spanish-style Garlic Shrimp

- In a heavy skillet, heat the olive oil and bay leaf over medium heat. Add the garlic and sauté, stirring for a minute until just softened.

- Add the pepper flakes, capers, and brandy, and cook off the alcohol for a minute.

- Bring heat to medium-high and toss in the shrimp, stirring quickly to cook them evenly. Cook shrimp until opaque and just firm.

- Remove from heat; stir in the paprika and the parsley. Taste for salt. Serve immediately.

Cook Off the Alcohol

Stir in the Seasonings

- This recipe calls for cooking off the alcohol in the sauce made with brandy.

- The amount of alcohol retained in food can range from 5 to 85 percent, depending on the preparation method.

- A dessert flambéed with orange liqueur will retain more alcohol than a stew made with red wine that has been cooked for several hours.

- Simply heating the alcohol will not make it all evaporate.

- A wooden spoon or silicone-type spatula comes in handy when making sauces.

- Use the spoon to stir the shrimp in the pan containing the olive oil, bay leaf, minced garlic, red pepper flakes, and capers.

- Remove the pan from the heat. Stir in the paprika and parsley.

- Season to taste with additional salt, if needed.

SHRIMP

SHRIMP CHORIZO BURGERS

Flavorful chorizo and sweet shrimp are a perfect pair in this very tasty burger

Mexican-style chorizo sausage is garlicky and delicious. This recipe combines the warm, deep spicing of Mexican chorizo with shrimp and adds a touch of smoky heat from chipotle peppers.

Canned chipotles (which are deeply smoked jalapeño peppers) come packed in a dark red adobo sauce, which is a

taste treat on its own. A small can goes a long, long way and keeps well, so they are well worth the effort to find.

Use any size shrimp for this dish, but the smaller ones are less expensive and often more flavorful. Use ground pork that isn't too lean, as a little fat will help burgers stay nice and juicy. And don't forget the fresh lime! *Yield: 4 servings*

Ingredients:

8 ounces small (51–60) or medium (41–50) raw shrimp

8 ounces ground pork

2 cloves garlic, minced

2 tablespoons minced Spanish olives (with pimento)

2 teaspoons sweet paprika

1 medium chipotle pepper (in adobo), plus 1 teaspoon of adobo sauce

2 scallions, chopped

2 teaspoons red wine vinegar

$1/2$ teaspoon salt

$1/4$ teaspoon sugar

2 tablespoons olive oil

4 soft French rolls

Garnishes: lettuce, mayonnaise, chopped cilantro, lime juice

Shrimp Chorizo Burgers

- In a food processor, pulse the shrimp until coarsely chopped.

- Mix the shrimp gently but thoroughly with the next 9 ingredients. Chill mixture about 15 minutes to meld the flavors.

- Divide into patties and fry over medium heat.

- Serve the shrimp burgers on soft French rolls with lettuce, mayo, cilantro, and a sprinkle of lime juice.

Chipotle is a hot flavor trend in more ways than one. The chipotle chile is a dried, peat-smoked jalapeño pepper. It looks almost leathery with its deep brown color, and it measures about 3 inches long. Its flavor is unmistakable---mildly sweet, hot, and smoky, an absolute must for Mexican cooking. The chipotle is readily available canned in adobo sauce.

Spanish chorizo gets its deep red color from the dried smoked red peppers used to make the sausage. Mexican chorizo has a higher chile and spice content, which results in a drier sausage with the consistency of ground beef. Both have a distinctively smoky flavor. Chorizo can be used as a replacement for ground pork or beef in recipes.

Chop the Shrimp

- Place the raw shrimp in the bowl of a food processor.

- Pulse the shrimp until coarsely chopped.

- Gently but thoroughly, combine the chopped shrimp in a large glass bowl with the ground pork,

minced garlic, Spanish olives, sweet paprika, chipotle pepper, adobo sauce, chopped scallions, red wine vinegar, salt, and sugar.

- Refrigerate the mixture for 15 minutes.

Pan-fry the Patties

- Divide the chopped shrimp mixture into 4 patties of equal size.

- In a large skillet over medium heat, fry the patties in olive oil for 3 to 4 minutes per side.

- The patties are done when they are cooked through and firm.

- If in doubt, cut one of the patties open to make sure it is cooked through.

SHRIMP & BROCCOLI CASSEROLE

You can use pre-cut vegetables and cooked shrimp in this easy timesaving recipe

This dish has something for everyone: sweet shrimp, colorful veggies, a creamy cheese sauce, and a buttery toasted topping. It's a real crowd pleaser and a great way to stretch a pound of shrimp to feed 4 or more.

Though the recipe calls for raw shrimp, you can easily use cooked shrimp instead; just add them in with the cooked veggies and noodles and pour the sauce over them.

You can also save time by buying pre-cut onions and broccoli crowns in the produce section. Baby carrots are a great ingredient for quickie meals since they require no preparation at all. You can also add other veggies, such as peas or diced red and green peppers to this dish. *Yield: 4–6 servings*

Ingredients:

1 package (12 ounces) egg noodles

1 pound fresh (or thawed frozen) broccoli crowns

1 cup baby carrots

1 small onion, chopped

2 tablespoons olive oil

1 pound medium-large (36–40) raw shrimp, peeled and deveined

1 can condensed cheddar cheese soup

$1/2$ cup chicken broth

2 tablespoons minced parsley

1 cup panko or plain bread crumbs

$1/4$ cup melted butter

Shrimp and Broccoli Casserole

- Cook noodles according to package directions; drain well.

- Over medium-high heat, sauté broccoli, carrots, and onions in oil; add shrimp. Cook until shrimp turn pink.

- Combine shrimp and vegetable mix with noodles and pour into buttered casserole dish. Heat cheese soup, broth, and parsley together; pour over casserole and mix gently.

- Top with bread crumbs, drizzle with melted butter, and bake at 350°F for 20 to 25 minutes. Allow to stand 5 minutes before serving.

For best results, cook fresh shrimp within 1 or 2 days of purchase. Store cooked shrimp in refrigerator up to 3 days. Raw shrimp frozen in the shell maintain quality longer than frozen cooked shrimp. Thaw frozen shrimp in refrigerator, allowing 24 hours for pound of shrimp. For quicker thawing, place under cold running water. Never thaw at room temperature, and never refreeze shrimp.

Baked Stuffed Shrimp: In a saucepan, melt $1/2$ cup of butter. Add 2 teaspoons of minced garlic. Sauté until soft. Add $1/4$ pound of chopped scallops and cook for 1 minute. Add 1 sleeve of Ritz crackers that you've crushed, $1/4$ cup chopped parsley, and 2 tablespoons of lemon juice. Mix well. Allow to cool. Stuff 12 jumbo shrimp. Bake in a 350°F oven for 10 to 12 minutes.

Sauté Shrimp until Pink

- Raw shrimp will be tough if cooked too long.

- Depending on their size, shrimp are best when they are pan-fried for only 2 to 3 minutes. Shrimp can be cooked with or without their shells.

- Perfectly cooked shrimp should be orange, with curled tails and firm opaque flesh.

- Pan-fried shrimp work well in combination with other ingredients, especially vegetables.

Add Toppings to Casserole

- Make sure to butter the casserole dish before pouring in the cooked noodle mixture for baking.

- The bread crumbs will form a slightly crunchy surface on the finished dish.

- The melted butter will help to moisten the bread crumbs.

- The butter will also add another level of flavor to this dish.

SHRIMP AVOCADO SOUP

Multiple layers of flavor and texture make this soup a fiesta in a bowl

Don't be fooled by the cool, creamy color of this soup. It's actually a bowl of barely contained excitement, with its rich depth of flavor matched with tender shrimp, refreshing lime, and crunchy tostadas topped with melted cheese.

You can use any size shrimp here, though the smaller sizes are better in soups. Prepared guacamole is terrific stuff; it's rich in real avocado flavor enhanced by just a few simple ingredients. It's also very convenient, since it requires no preparation or messy cleanup. Most often used as a dip, it also makes a wonderful ingredient—try using it as the "sauce" next time you make pizza.

Garnish this soup with a variety of goodies for a fun, festive look. *Yield: 4 servings*

Ingredients:

1 large white or Vidalia onion, chopped

1 Anaheim pepper, chopped

1 large jalapeño pepper (seeds removed), minced

1 large clove garlic, minced

2 tablespoons olive oil

1 (15-ounce) can chicken broth

1 1/2 cups water

1 tablespoon lime juice

4 tostadas (or 4 small corn tortillas fried until crisp)

4 ounces pepperjack cheese

2 ounces grated Cotija cheese (or substitute Parmesan)

1 pound large cooked shrimp, peeled and deveined (reserve 12 for garnish)

2 (7-ounce) packages prepared guacamole

Garnish Options: chopped tomato, sliced black olives, shelled pumpkin or sunflower seeds, chopped cilantro or parsley, chopped pimento, sour cream

Shrimp Avocado Soup

- In a large saucepan, sauté onions, peppers, and garlic in oil over medium heat for 7 minutes. Add broth, water, and lime juice. Bring to a simmer.

- Place tostadas on a cookie sheet; sprinkle with cheeses. Broil briefly until cheese melts. Keep warm.

- Add shrimp to the soup; stir until just warmed. Remove soup from the heat and stir in guacamole.

- Ladle into wide, flat bowls and place a tostada on each; top with reserved shrimp and your choice of garnishes.

Fresh guacamole is simple to make. The secret is to fold the ingredients together, starting with 2 ripe avocados that have been peeled, seeded, and chopped into chunks. Add $1/2$ finely chopped white onion, 1 chopped Roma tomato, 1 finely chopped jalapeño chile, 2 minced garlic cloves, the juice of 1 key lime, celery salt, and black pepper to taste. Serve with tortilla chips and ice-cold margaritas.

Another secret to really good Mexican food is the use of key limes, which are different from the Persian limes commonly seen in the supermarket. Persians are larger and greener than a key lime, and their flavor is stronger and more acidic. Once you experience the delicate taste of the key lime, you'll appreciate the difference. It is also known as the Mexican lime.

SHRIMP

Broil the Tostadas

Stir in the Guacamole

- Tostada is the Spanish word for "toasted." In Mexico, it refers to a tortilla that is toasted or fried.

- If you can't find tostadas at the supermarket, you can use small corn tortillas that have been fried until crisp.

- Place the tostadas on a cookie sheet. Sprinkle with cheeses.

- Broil the tostadas briefly in the oven until the cheeses melt. Cover them with aluminum foil to keep them warm.

- The soup is almost done. It's simmering on the stove, and you add the large cooked shrimp. Stir to help the shrimp heat through.

- Remove the saucepan containing the soup from the heat.

- Gradually stir the prepared guacamole into the hot soup.

- It's a good idea to let the guacamole come to room temperature before adding it to the soup.

LOWCOUNTRY SHRIMP & GRITS

This simple, yet extraordinary shrimp dish brings you a taste of the Carolina coast

The Carolinas are blessed with an abundance of wonderful seafood, including some of the best tasting shrimp anywhere.

Originally a breakfast dish for the early-rising shrimp boat crews, shrimp and grits are now a favorite in the humblest homes and the fanciest restaurants, and are served for lunch, dinner, brunch—or whenever.

There are almost as many ways to make shrimp and grits as there are good cooks in the Carolina Lowcountry! Some like it made with a dark, flour-based sauce while others like it as simple as possible. This recipe leans toward the latter; it lets the ingredients create a sauce of their own natural flavors enhanced with butter and a little lemon juice. *Yield: 4 servings*

KNACK FISH & SEAFOOD COOKBOOK

Ingredients:

1 cup regular or quick-cooking (not "instant") grits

3 cups water

1 cup milk

2 tablespoons butter

1/4 teaspoon salt

6 slices thick-cut bacon

1/2 cup finely diced green peppers

3 scallions, chopped

2 cloves garlic, minced

1 pound extra large (26–30) raw shrimp, peeled and deveined

1 tablespoon minced parsley

1 teaspoon fresh lemon juice

1/4 teaspoon black pepper

Additional butter (optional)

Lowcountry Shrimp and Grits

- Combine first 5 ingredients in a heavy saucepan. Stir very well and bring to a boil over medium heat, stirring often.

- Reduce heat; cover. Simmer 20 to 25 minutes until thickened, stirring regularly.

- Cook bacon until crisp; remove from pan and crumble. Drain off all but 2 tablespoons of bacon fat; add peppers, scallions, and garlic. Sauté until softened.

- Add shrimp to pan and cook until just firm. Stir in bacon, parsley, lemon juice, and black pepper. Serve over hot buttered grits.

A simple recipe for shrimp and grits begins with 2 cups of raw medium shrimp that have been peeled and deveined. Cook the shrimp in a large skillet with 3 tablespoons of butter for 5 to 10 minutes over medium heat. Season to taste with salt, pepper, and a dash of garlic powder. Serve over hot grits, cooked according to package directions.

Lowcountry Sauce: Bring 1 pound crab meat, 1 pound tiny shrimp, and 1 pound chopped scallops to a boil in 1½ quarts water. Cook for 4 minutes. Sauté 1 chopped onion, 1 chopped celery stalk, and 2 chopped bell peppers in 1 stick of butter. Add this to seafood mixture. Add 3 tablespoons tomato paste and let simmer. This is a delectable sauce to pour over baked red snapper.

Stir the Grits

- In a heavy saucepan over medium heat, combine the grits with the water, milk, butter, and salt. Regular or quick-cooking grits may be used, but do not use instant grits in this recipe.

- Bring to a boil, stirring often.

- Reduce the heat. Cover the pan. Simmer for 20 to 25 minutes until thickened.

- Stir the grits regularly while it simmers.

Season the Shrimp

SHRIMP

- Some seafood experts consider shrimp to be the single most important shellfish in the world.

- Southeast and Gulf Coast white shrimp are considered by many to have the best flavor.

- Shrimp should be rich, flavorful, and firm. Do not use shrimp that is bitter or mushy.

- Frozen shrimp offers the most flexibility, while fresh shrimp has the best flavor.

SHRIMP SCAMPI & RICE SKILLET

So simple and so delicious, this one-pot meal is perfect for weeknights or anytime

Shrimp scampi, the well-loved Italian classic that pairs succulent shrimp with garlic, lemon, parsley, and white wine, is usually served on a bed of pasta. This version uses rice instead, and uses the shrimp and other ingredients to flavor the rice as it cooks, resulting in a wonderfully savory and fragrant meal that cooks quickly and only uses 1 pan.

Fresh lemon juice, real butter, and fresh parsley are absolutely essential here for the flavor they provide. Use larger shrimp for this dish, if you prefer. A dry white wine is very good, but dry white vermouth has a more complex flavor profile and adds a certain something to the result. It's a worthwhile addition to your pantry. *Yield: 4 servings*

Ingredients:

2 tablespoons olive oil

3 cloves garlic, minced

2 cups medium- or long-grain rice

1/2 cup white wine or dry vermouth

1/2 tablespoon Worcestershire sauce

Juice of 1 lemon (about 3 tablespoons)

2 1/2 cups chicken stock

1 pound large (31–35) raw shrimp, peeled and deveined

2 tablespoons butter

1/4 teaspoon black pepper

2 teaspoons lemon zest

2 tablespoons minced parsley

Shrimp Scampi and Rice Skillet

- In a large fry pan or skillet, sauté the garlic in oil over medium heat for about 1 minute. Add the rice and stir to coat.

- Pour in the wine, Worcestershire, lemon juice, and stock; bring to a boil. Stir in the shrimp and return to a simmer.

- Cover and cook over very low heat 15 minutes or until liquid is absorbed. Stir in butter and black pepper.

- Sprinkle with lemon zest and parsley before serving.

Basic Shrimp Scampi: Preheat broiler. Use a baking pan large enough to hold 2 pounds shrimp in 1 layer. In a saucepan, melt 1 stick of butter. Stir in ¹/₂ cup olive oil, 1 tablespoon lemon juice, ¹/₄ cup minced shallots, 1 tablespoon minced garlic, salt, and pepper to taste. Pour over shrimp in pan, coating completely, Broil 5 minutes, then turn shrimp and broil 4 to 10 minutes longer.

ZOOM

When buying fresh shrimp, make sure they are firm with their shells well attached. Look for a sweet smell. Old shrimp will have a mild ammonia odor. If the heads are still attached, plan on cooking the shrimp on the same day you buy them for they deteriorate more quickly than shrimp that have had their heads removed.

Peeling and Deveining Shrimp

Stir Rice to Coat

- With a very sharp, small knife, make a shallow incision along the back of each shrimp from head to tail.

- Strip off the shell and legs.

- Rinse the shrimp under cold running water to remove the vein. The tip of your knife can help remove stubborn bits of the vein.

- This is called a fantail shrimp. Kitchen shears or a shrimp deveiner may also be used for this task.

- In a large frying pan or skillet, heat the olive oil over medium heat.

- Sauté the minced garlic in the oil for about 1 minute.

- Add the medium- or long-grain rice.

- Stir to coat all the rice well with the olive oil and garlic mixture. This will give the rice more depth of flavor, and the rice will be fluffier.

MORE SHRIMP & PRAWNS

CKEN & SHRIMP NOODLE BOWL

...omatic flavors and appealing textures give this meatball ... Asian flair

Asian noodle soups often combine simple but flavorful broths with colorful, crunchy, thinly cut vegetables. This version adds tender meatballs made from chicken and shrimp to the mix for a truly satisfying meal-in-a-bowl.

Any size shrimp will do, but it's more economical to use the smaller sizes since it will be chopped. White meat ground chicken produces paler meatballs, but the less expensive mixed ground chicken is juicier and more flavorful. Either choice is fine. Precut matchstick carrots are widely available and are a timesaver. Add them to salads, soups, and cooked dishes for a quick dash of color and crunch. Use freshly grated ginger for its flavor and fragrance. *Yield: 4 servings*

KNACK FISH & SEAFOOD COOKBOOK

Ingredients:

8 ounces small (51–60) or medium (41–50) raw shrimp, peeled and deveined

8 ounces ground chicken

1 egg white

1 scallion, minced

1 tablespoon soy sauce

1/4 cup fresh bread crumbs

12 ounces lo mein noodles (or substitute linguine)

2 cups chicken stock

2 cups water

1 tablespoon grated ginger

2 cloves garlic, minced

1 cup bean sprouts

1/2 cup matchstick carrots

12 snow pea pods

1 tablespoon chopped cilantro

Chicken and Shrimp Noodle Bowl

- In a food processor, pulse the shrimp until coarsely chopped. Mix shrimp with next 5 ingredients; refrigerate.

- Cook the noodles according to package directions. While noodles are cooking, bring stock, water, ginger, and garlic to a boil.

- Form chicken/shrimp mixture into small meatballs. Gently simmer meatballs in broth until cooked through (about 7 minutes).

- Divide noodles between 4 bowls. Top with bean sprouts, carrots, and snow peas. Ladle soup into bowls; sprinkle with cilantro.

Treat family or friends to an Asian feast. Serve the Chicken and Shrimp Noodle Bowl as the first course, followed by a whole steamed fish served with a variety of dipping sauces. The dipping sauces might feature a vinegar-soy sauce. Other accompaniments could be Chinese rice noodles with bok choy and Chinese green beans with sesame seeds.

Vinegar-Soy Sauce: In a glass bowl, combine 3 tablespoons of cider vinegar with 1 tablespoon of soy sauce. Add 1 tablespoon of chopped scallions and a dash of white pepper. If you don't mind the heat, add a pinch of cayenne pepper. Or a little chili oil could be drizzled into the sauce. Mix well. Serve this sauce in individual dipping bowls.

Form the Meatballs

- It's important that these shrimp and chicken meatballs be uniform in size.

- Use a tablespoon to measure out the shrimp and chicken mixture.

- The egg white and breadcrumbs will act as a binder, holding the meatballs together.

- Using the palms of your hands, roll each meatball until firmly compacted. Each meatball should be about the size of a grape.

Serving the Soup

- Presentation is everything when it comes to food, especially with Asian dishes.

- If possible, serve this Chicken & Shrimp Noodle Bowl in an Asian-inspired tureen with matching individual soup bowls and spoons.

- Asian cookware is available in Asian markets and gourmet shops.

- All white soup bowls also lend themselves nicely to the proper serving of Asian cuisine.

MORE SHRIMP & PRAWNS

OVEN-BARBECUED SHRIMP
This Big Easy shrimp dish is a buttery, peppery, spicy delight to eat

Can shrimp be finger lickin' good? Oh, yes! First served by the famous Pascal's Manale Restaurant in New Orleans, Oven-barbecued Shrimp isn't made on the barbecue, nor is it covered in barbecue sauce. It's actually made in a sauté pan or the oven (or both) and is coated with melted butter and heavily seasoned with black pepper, garlic, herbs, and other goodies.

Eating a bowl of barbecued shrimp should be a messy, raucous, spicy good time. Provide lots of napkins or paper towels, lots of crusty French bread, and lots of ice cold beer—the perfect antidote for barbecued tongue!

This dish is meant to be very boldly flavored, but you can reduce the amounts of spice to your taste. *Yield: 4–6 servings*

Ingredients:

2 pounds jumbo (21–25) or extra jumbo (16–20) raw shrimp, shell on

4 tablespoons butter or margarine

2 tablespoons full-flavored olive oil

1 tablespoon minced garlic

1 tablespoon Worcestershire sauce

1 teaspoon hot pepper sauce

1 tablespoon coarse ground black pepper

$1^1/_2$ teaspoons dried Italian seasoning (or $^1/_2$ teaspoon each dried oregano, basil, and rosemary)

$^1/_2$ teaspoon paprika

$^1/_8$ teaspoon cayenne pepper

$^1/_2$ lemon, sliced thin

Salt to taste

Oven-barbecued Shrimp

- Dry the shrimp and place them in a large baking dish. In a saucepan, melt the butter and oil and add the next 7 ingredients.

- Pour the seasoned butter over the shrimp, add the lemon slices, and stir thoroughly to coat.

- Bake in a preheated oven at 400°F for 15 to 20 minutes, stirring occasionally, until shrimp are pink and tails are curled.

- Serve in shallow bowls with warm, crusty French bread for dipping.

Stovetop Barbecue Shrimp: In skillet, melt $1/2$ cup butter. Add 1 teaspoon each white, black, and cayenne pepper, chopped fresh thyme, rosemary, and marjoram, and 1 crushed garlic clove. Add 1 teaspoon Worcestershire sauce, $1/2$ cup fish stock and 4 tablespoons dry white wine. Bring to boil. Cook 3 minutes to reduce. Add 1 pound large shrimp, cooked and unpeeled. Toss to coat and heat through.

Mango-lime Mayonnaise: You might also want to try grilled shrimp with this cool combination of $1/3$ cup of mayonnaise, $1/2$ of a ripe mango that's been grated, the juice from a fresh lime, and a dash of sea salt. Mix well and set aside. Serve grilled shrimp with this mayo on the side for dipping.

Pour Seasoning over Shrimp

Bake Shrimp until Pink

- If using frozen shrimp, rinse the shrimp under cold running water in a colander for five minutes, or until thawed. Pat dry with a paper towel.

- It is very important to make sure the shrimp is evenly coated with the olive oil and seasonings.

- If you do not have all the necessary seasonings, you could substitute 2 tablespoons of Cajun spice mix.

- Combine the Cajun spice mix with the olive oil, minced garlic, Worcestershire sauce, and hot pepper sauce.

- Shrimp generally will be done in 2 to 5 minutes when stir-fried, sautéed, broiled, grilled, or deep-fried.

- Shrimp can also be baked or roasted for a short time on high heat.

- The shrimp will be more tender and flavorful if coated with melted butter or olive oil.

- In this recipe, bake the shrimp in a 400°F oven, stirring occasionally, until the shrimp are pink and their tails are curled, about 15 to 20 minutes.

MARINATED SPICED SHRIMP

A refreshingly different take on shrimp salad, perfect for a summertime lunch or brunch

In the South, pickled shrimp are a longtime favorite. These chilled shrimp have a satisfying bite and a pleasantly sweet and sour marinade that makes a tasty dressing.

White vinegar is traditional, but you can use a gentler white wine vinegar or champagne vinegar if you prefer. Fresh lemon juice is essential, as are perfectly fresh garlic and fully ripe tomatoes. If using frozen shrimp, let them thaw slowly and completely in the fridge and drain them well before adding them.

Use a tightly sealing glass or other non-metallic container for this (and any) acidic dish. *Yield: 4 servings*

Ingredients:

1/2 cup white vinegar

1/4 olive oil

Juice of 2 lemons

1 teaspoon sugar

4 large garlic cloves, thinly sliced

1 small onion, thinly sliced

1 teaspoon dried rosemary

1/2 teaspoon red pepper flakes

1 tablespoon black peppercorns

1 teaspoon fennel seeds

1/2 teaspoon salt (kosher or non-iodized)

1 pound large (31-35) raw shrimp, peeled and deveined

Romaine leaves or assorted baby greens

4 slices toasted Italian bread

3-4 small Roma tomatoes, sliced

4 hard-boiled eggs, sliced

1 tablespoon chopped parsley

Marinated Spiced Shrimp

- In a large saucepan, combine the first 11 ingredients and simmer, covered, for 10 minutes. Add the shrimp and cook just until shrimp turn pink.

- Pour shrimp and marinade into a non-reactive container. Refrigerate until cool, stirring occasionally.

- Just before serving, arrange some of the greens on 4 plates. Place a slice of Italian bread in the center; arrange the tomatoes and sliced egg around the bread.

- Spoon the shrimp and marinade onto the bread; sprinkle with chopped parsley.

A very simple shrimp salad can be made with 1 pound of cooked shrimp that's been chopped, combined in a glass bowl with 1 cup of finely chopped celery, 2 chopped hard-boiled eggs, $1/2$ cup of mayonnaise, salt, and pepper to taste. Mix well. Serve on lettuce leaves or stuffed into hollowed-out tomatoes. Since it's chopped, you can use smaller, less expensive shrimp.

Grilled Shrimp and Tomato Salad: Grill 16 large shrimp. Lightly grill 1 large tomato that's been cut into $1/4$-inch slices. On each salad plate, place a mound of mesclun greens. Top with tomatoes and then 4 shrimp per plate. Drizzle with orange-basil vinaigrette, made by reducing 2 cups orange juice to $1/4$ cup. Cool. Stir in freshly chopped basil. Whisk in $1/4$ cup olive oil. Season to taste.

Marinate the Shrimp

- It's essential to marinate ingredients in a glass container or plastic bag rather than in a metal bowl.

- This will ensure you avoid the chemical interactions that can occur when the metal bowl comes into contact with the acid in the marinade.

- It's also important to turn the shrimp several times for an even absorption of flavors.

- This is most easily done when the shrimp are placed in a plastic bag.

Arrange the Salad Elements

- This is what a professional chef would call a composed salad.

- Rather than simply tossing together the various ingredients, the salad is artfully plated.

- Beginning with the bed of lettuce, the salad is built in stages just before serving.

- If possible, chill the salad plates—and even the salad forks—in advance in the refrigerator.

MORE SHRIMP & PRAWNS

ORANGE GINGER PRAWNS

A light citrus glaze and toasted sesame seeds bring out the flavor of these prawns

Prawns, a very close relative of shrimp, are becoming more available in the U.S. as "prawn farming" continues to grow.

The most popular farmed variety are freshwater Malaysian prawns, which can grow quite large. Their flavor is sweet and mild and they are quite tender. They're delicious in any recipe that calls for shrimp, but this recipe was specifically developed to accentuate the flavor of jumbo freshwater prawns. You can substitute an equivalent size of raw shrimp.

If you're lucky enough to find fresh, live prawns you may be shocked at the size of their pincers, which can often exceed their body length! But don't worry: Even if they do "bite," you probably won't even feel it. *Yield: 3 servings*

Ingredients:

12 (or 24) long bamboo skewers

36 Jumbo raw prawns (or shrimp), peeled and deveined

1 large or 2 small cans mandarin orange segments, well drained

¼ cup orange juice concentrate

1 teaspoon light soy sauce

2 teaspoons ginger powder

½ cup toasted sesame seeds

Orange Ginger Prawns

- Soak skewers in water for 20 to 30 minutes. Pat prawns dry with paper towels and thread 3 prawns on each skewer, alternating with orange segments.

- Mix the orange juice concentrate, light soy, and ginger powder together in a small bowl. Lay the skewers on a rack set on a baking sheet.

- Brush orange glaze onto 1 side of skewers. Broil until nicely colored.

- Turn, brush other side, and broil until just cooked through. Sprinkle both sides with sesame seeds.

What is the difference between shrimp and prawns? Shrimp are found in the ocean, while prawns live in fresh water. But to confuse the situation, jumbo shrimp are often called prawns. Prawns, which come from Hawaii and parts of Asia, are considered to be sweeter than shrimp and more perishable. Prawns are often available in fish markets in the Chinatown section of major cities.

• • • • RECIPE VARIATION • • • •

Coconut Curry Sauce: Cook 1 tablespoon butter, 1 tablespoon curry powder, 1 teaspoon freshly minced ginger, 1 minced garlic clove, and $1/4$ teaspoon ground cardamom over low heat 3 minutes. In another pan, reduce 1 cup heavy cream to $3/4$ of a cup. Add $1/4$ cup coconut milk, 1 tablespoon coconut flakes, 4 fresh mint leaves, and curry mixture. Simmer 5 minutes. Serve with grilled prawns.

Thread the Skewers

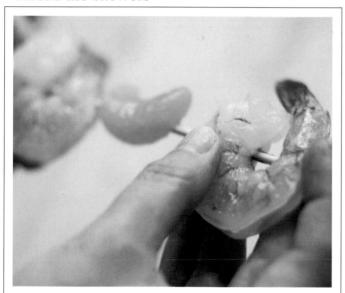

- Whenever you plan to use bamboo or wooden skewers, you must soak them in water for at least 20 minutes prior to use. This will prevent the skewers from catching on fire or burning while under the broiler or on the grill.

- Insert the skewer through the thickest part of each prawn.

- Thread 3 prawns on each skewer, alternating with 3 orange segments.

- Use jumbo shrimp and the largest orange segments possible.

Brush on the Glaze

- In a glass bowl, combine the defrosted orange juice concentrate with the soy sauce and ginger. Mix well.

- Brush this orange glaze onto 1 side of the shrimp and orange skewers.

- Broil until shrimp is pink. Remove skewers from oven. Turn skewers over. Brush the other side with glaze. Return the skewers to the oven to broil until just cooked through.

- Sprinkle the skewers with sesame seeds.

PRAWNS WITH SALTED PEPPER

Based on a Chinese culinary classic, this recipe spices up sweet jumbo prawns

Restaurants in New York's Chinatown often have large tanks with live fish, eels, crabs, lobster, etc., and they draw on them for the freshest possible ingredients for their wonderful seafood dishes. Some restaurants even have huge tanks with hundreds of live (and very lively) prawns.

The signature dish of one of these restaurants is Prawns with Salted Pepper: crunchy deep-fried prawns (still in the shell) along with strips of deep-fried hot peppers glistening with crystals of coarse salt. You eat the prawns, crunchy shell and all, as you enjoy the savory heat of the salted peppers.

This recipe duplicates the flavor—without the shell—of this exciting dish. *Yield: 2 servings*

Ingredients:

1 pound jumbo (21–25) raw prawns (or shrimp), peeled and deveined

$1/4$ cup corn starch

3 tablespoons peanut or canola oil

2 large jalapeño peppers, seeds removed, cut into matchsticks

$1/2$ of a large red bell pepper, seeds removed, cut into matchsticks

$1/4$ teaspoon black pepper

$1/4$ teaspoon white pepper

$1/4$ teaspoon coarse ground or kosher salt (plus more to taste)

Prawns with Salted Pepper

- Dry the prawns very well with paper towels. Place the prawns in a large plastic bag and sprinkle the corn starch over them.

- Close the bag and shake well to coat thoroughly. Remove prawns and shake off excess corn starch.

- Heat the oil in a wok or large sauté pan over high heat. Add the prawns and toss for 1 to 2 minutes.

- Add the remaining ingredients and toss until prawns are cooked through (about 3 to 4 minutes); serve immediately.

Deseeding and Deveining Hot Peppers

- Jalapeño peppers should be deseeded and deveined before use in cooking.

- Be careful to wash your hands, or wear gloves and don't rub your eyes when handling hot peppers.

- With a very sharp paring knife, cut off both ends of the pepper, then cut the pepper in half lengthwise.

- Spread open each half of the pepper. Use the blade of the knife to scrape out bitter seeds and ribs of the pepper.

Dust Prawns with Corn Starch

- Using paper towels, make sure the jumbo prawns are completely dry, otherwise the corn starch will not stick.

- Place the prawns in a large plastic bag. Using a large spoon or small measuring cup, sprinkle the corn starch over the prawns.

- Close the bag and shake well to coat the prawns thoroughly.

- Remove the prawns from the bag. Shake off any excess corn starch.

MORE SHRIMP & PRAWNS

CLASSIC CHESAPEAKE CRAB CAKES

Sweet crabmeat and classic seasonings are the reason these crab cakes are so satisfying

The Chesapeake Bay is famous for its seafood, especially the blue crab, whose Latin name translates to "savory beautiful swimmer."

These tender cakes combine crabmeat with flavorful and aromatic seasonings that enhance the sweet crab flavor rather than overwhelming it.

You can use blue or Dungeness crab here—they're both delicious—and any grade from the most expensive jumbo lump to economical claw meat. Just be sure to buy the freshest you can find. Don't use the shelf stable canned crab (it lacks flavor); use the refrigerated kind. And don't forget to gently pick through crab for shell bits, etc. *Yield: 4 servings*

Ingredients:

- ³/₄ cup fresh white bread crumbs
- ¹/₄ cup finely crushed saltines
- ¹/₄ cup mayonnaise
- 2 tablespoons finely diced celery
- 2 tablespoons finely diced onion
- 1 tablespoon diced red pepper
- 1 tablespoon finely minced parsley
- 1¹/₂ teaspoon Old Bay or seafood seasoning
- 1 teaspoon dry mustard
- 1 teaspoon dried marjoram
- ¹/₂ teaspoon Worcestershire sauce
- 1 large egg, beaten
- 1 pound crabmeat, shell bits and cartilage removed
- 2 tablespoons butter
- 2 tablespoons canola oil

Classic Chesapeake Crab Cakes

- Combine first 12 ingredients in a mixing bowl. Gently fold in the crabmeat.

- Form the mixture into cakes.

- Melt the butter with the oil over medium heat and fry the cakes, turning once, until golden brown and heated through (about 3 to 4 minutes per side).

- Alternately, you can bake them at 400°F for 20 minutes or until golden.

Sun-dried Tomato-basil Mayonnaise: Turn these crab cakes into sandwiches with just a little of this mayo on your roll. In a glass bowl, combine ³/₄ cup mayonnaise with 6 sun-dried tomatoes (in oil, finely chopped), 2 tablespoons lemon juice, 2 tablespoons freshly chopped basil, 1 teaspoon minced garlic, salt and pepper to taste. Mix well. Store leftover mayo in the refrigerator.

Tarragon-mustard Sauce: For a zesty spread on your bread, combine the following in a glass bowl: 2 tablespoons tarragon vinegar, 2 tablespoons Dijon mustard, 1 teaspoon dried tarragon, ¹/₄ cup plus 2 tablespoons plain lowfat yogurt, and ¹/₄ cup light mayonnaise. Stir mixture until well blended. This sauce can also be used on grilled fish.

Form the Crab Cakes

- Once you create your mixture, you'll have to form the crab cakes.

- Being firm yet gentle, form 12 crab cakes of equal size.

- Place the crab cakes on waxed paper or other non-stick surface. Cover and chill in the refrigerator for 15 to 20 minutes before frying.

Fry Cakes until Golden

- Fry the crab cakes in small batches. Do not crowd pan.

- Overcrowding will cause a drop in the temperature of the pan and the fats in the pan.

- Pan-frying should be done slowly in a small to medium amount of moderately hot fat.

- When the bottom surface of the crab cakes is golden brown, they should be turned over carefully.

CRABS & CRABMEAT

169

CRAB & ZUCCHINI CHOWDER

An easy-to-make soup with extraordinary flavor that's both comforting and nourishing

This is the perfect soup for a rainy day, or any day when you just need to feel warm and comforted. It's got tender Red Bliss potatoes and zucchini in a savory seafood and tomato broth, topped with a soft dollop of tarragon cream.

Cutting the vegetables in small cubes allows them to cook quickly and by sautéing them with the garlic, they become infused with flavor. Clamato combines clam juice with seasoned tomato juice and is a great timesaver when making seafood soups and chowders.

You can use a cheaper flaked grade of crabmeat here as it should be spread somewhat evenly throughout the soup and texture isn't crucial. *Yield: 2 servings*

Ingredients:

1 small clove garlic, minced

1 tablespoon olive oil

2 medium Red Bliss potatoes, cut in 1/4-inch pieces

2 whole scallions, diced

2 medium zucchini, cut in 1/4-inch pieces

2 cups Clamato juice

1 cup water

1 cup (about 6 ounces) crabmeat, shell bits and cartilage removed

1/4 teaspoon pepper

1/4 cup whipping cream

1 teaspoon dried tarragon leaves, crushed

Crab and Zucchini Chowder

- In a large saucepan over medium heat, sauté the garlic briefly in the olive oil. Add the potatoes and scallions; cook over medium heat 3 minutes.

- Add the zucchini, cook 3 to 5 minutes more. Pour in the Clamato juice and water; bring to a simmer and cook until vegetables are tender.

- Stir in crabmeat and heat through. Adjust pepper (no salt needed).

- Whisk together the cream and tarragon until thickened. Serve chowder in shallow bowls with a dollop of tarragon cream.

The blue crab has long been considered a delectable and flavorful crustacean. This crab is usually 3 to 8 inches wide. The rock crab and the Jonah crab have a shell width of about 4 inches. They are less sought after and less expensive, but still flavorful. These crabs are usually steamed in combination with other shellfish.

Crab and Corn Chowder: Give this recipe a sweet twist with the use of corn instead of zucchini. One (15-ounce) can of whole-kernel corn, with its liquid, is all that you will need. You can also substitute $1/4$ cup of butter for the olive oil, and a dash of cayenne pepper in place of the tarragon for a completely different tasting chowder.

Sauté the Vegetables

Fold in the Crabmeat

- In a large saucepan over medium heat, heat the olive oil. Sauté the minced garlic until golden.

- Add the cut-up potatoes and diced scallions. Cook for 3 minutes, stirring occasionally.

- Add the zucchini pieces to the saucepan. Cook for another 3 to 5 minutes.

- Pour in the Clamato juice and water. Bring to a simmer. Cook until the vegetables are tender.

- When the vegetables are tender, gently stir in the crabmeat.

- In soups, the texture of the crabmeat isn't crucial so you can use a less expensive grade of crabmeat in this recipe.

- Season the soup to taste with pepper. No salt should be needed.

- Finish the soup with the addition of whipping cream and tarragon leaves. Make sure the soup is heated thoroughly.

CRAB & TOMATO BAKE

Tomato pie, a Southern culinary favorite, gets a boost with savory crabmeat and Vidalia onions

No springtime brunch or garden party in the South would be complete without tomato pie, an appetizing dish made with sweet ripe tomatoes, cheese, onion, and a little gentle seasoning in a flaky crust. The tomatoes melt into the other ingredients until the flavors combine, and once you've had it, the mere sight of tomato pie will perk up your appetite.

This version adds sweet crabmeat and Georgia's famed Vidalia onions, drawn together with a hint of garlic and basil that accents the tomato flavor beautifully. The lush cheese topping is baked until bubbly; the result is a pie you'll savor from first bite to last. Use a good grade of lump crabmeat here for the best result. *Yield: 4–6 servings*

Ingredients:

2 or 3 large ripe tomatoes, cored

1 large (9-inch) deep-dish frozen pie crust

8 ounces shredded mild cheddar cheese, divided

1 medium Vidalia or other sweet onion, very thinly sliced

8 ounces crabmeat, shell bits and cartilage removed

1 cup mayonnaise

1/2 cup grated Parmesan cheese

1 small clove garlic, minced

1 teaspoon dried basil

Crab and Tomato Bake

- Cut tomatoes in half, scoop out seeds, and slice; lay slices on paper towels to drain. Bake the pie shell at 375°F until lightly browned.

- Spread half the cheddar in the bottom of crust, add half of tomato slices, then onion slices, then crabmeat, then remaining tomatoes.

- Mix the mayonnaise, remaining cheddar, Parmesan, garlic, and basil; spread evenly over top.

- Bake at 375°F for 30 to 40 minutes until cheese is melted and nicely browned.

A simple baked crab dish can be made by combining 1 chopped onion, 1 chopped green pepper, 1 cup chopped celery, 1 pound crabmeat, 1 cup mayonnaise, and ½ teaspoon Worcestershire sauce in a buttered baking dish. Mix well. Combine 1 cup fresh bread crumbs with 4 tablespoons melted butter. Sprinkle over top of casserole. Bake in a 350°F oven for 30 minutes, or until golden brown.

ZOOM

To go with this Crab and Tomato Bake, serve a refreshing salad with a lemon-caper dressing. In a bowl, combine ½ cup light mayonnaise with 1 tablespoon drained capers, 1 tablespoon lemon juice, 1 teaspoon Worcestershire sauce, ½ teaspoon mustard, and as much hot pepper sauce as you desire. Use this dressing on a salad of mixed greens garnished with tender asparagus spears.

Layering the Ingredients

Spreading the Topping

- In the baked pie shell, start layering the ingredients, first with half of the shredded mild cheddar cheese spread evenly over the base of the pie shell.

- Next, spread an even layer of the sliced ripe tomatoes.

- Next, add an even layer of very thin onion slices, then the crabmeat.

- Top with the remaining tomato slices.

- In a medium-size glass bowl, combine the mayonnaise with the cheddar cheese, grated Parmesan cheese, minced garlic, and dried basil.

- Mix thoroughly.

- Using a flexible spreader or spatula, carefully spread the mayonnaise-cheese topping evenly over the top of the tomato slices in the pie.

- Spread the topping right up to the crimped edges of the pie crust.

CRABS & CRABMEAT

BEAUFORT DEVILED CRAB FINGERS

These enticing crab appetizers are tender and delicious, with just a hint of heat

This recipe is dedicated to Beaufort, South Carolina's most illustrious resident, the author Pat Conroy, whose richly detailed novels capture perfectly the sights, voices, and flavors of the beautiful Carolina Lowcountry. Blue crabs are a significant part of the culinary fabric of the Beaufort area, from communal backyard "crab cracks" to Daufuskie Island's legendary deviled crab to the famous Frogmore Stew.

This recipe takes the deviled crab concept, kicks up the flavor by a few degrees, and makes it "portable" as an appetizer or as a fun dinner entree. Claw crabmeat is perfect for this, as it has good color and a nice strong crab flavor that stands right up to the bold seasonings. *Yield: 36 appetizers*

Ingredients:

1 medium white or sweet onion, finely chopped

2 stalks celery, finely chopped

1 clove garlic, minced

1 small hot red pepper or 1 medium jalapeño, minced

2 tablespoons canola or light olive oil

$^1/_2$ cup finely crushed saltines

$^1/_2$ cup fresh white bread crumbs

2 scallions, finely chopped

1 tablespoon Worcestershire sauce

1 tablespoon Dijon mustard

$^1/_2$ teaspoon black pepper

1 tablespoon lemon juice

1 pound crab claw meat, shell bits and cartilage removed

1 egg white, lightly beaten

1 cup panko crumbs

$^1/_3$ cup melted butter

Paprika for dusting

Fresh lemon juice (optional)

Beaufort Deviled Crab Fingers

- Sauté onion, celery, garlic, and hot peppers in oil over medium heat until softened. Let cool.

- Combine the cooked vegetables with next 7 ingredients. Fold in crab-meat and egg white until just blended.

- Spread the panko crumbs on a plate. Form mixture into cylinders. Drizzle with melted butter and dust with paprika.

- Bake 15 to 20 minutes at 375°F until golden brown. Sprinkle with lemon juice, if desired.

The basic recipe for a classic deviled crab starts with sautéing 1/4 cup finely chopped celery and 1/4 cup finely chopped pepper in 1/2 cup butter with salt and pepper to taste. Add in 2 pounds white crabmeat, 1 pound claw crabmeat, 6 large beaten eggs, 1 tablespoon dry mustard, 1 tablespoon Worcestershire sauce, and 1/3 cup crushed crackers. Bake in buttered casserole 30 minutes at 425°F.

Classic Tartar Sauce: In a glass bowl, combine 1/2 cup mayonnaise with 1 tablespoon minced pickles, 1 tablespoon minced olives, 1 tablespoon minced onion, and 1 tablespoon minced parsley. Mix well. Chill before serving with any kind of fried seafood. Also get creative and make tartar sauce with capers, hard-boiled eggs, fresh chervil, lemon juice, pimientos, Dijon mustard, or minced chives.

Form Mixture into Cylinders

- Form the crabmeat mixture into 36 finger-sized cylinders.

- The easiest way to do this is to divide the mixture in half, then divide those two amounts of mixture in half again.

- Divide each of these 4 amounts of mixture into 9 equal amounts.

- Roll each of the 36 finger-sized cylinders into firm fingers, then roll the fingers in the panko crumbs. Place them on a baking pan spaced apart.

Bake until Golden Brown

- The melted butter that is drizzled on the crab fingers adds flavor and aids in the cooking process.

- Dust the crab fingers with a little paprika, which is more for color and presentation than taste.

- Once baked, the fingers will have a nice, warm golden brown look to them.

CRABS & CRABMEAT

SWEET & SPICY CRAB LEGS

A 5-pepper spice rub and a garlicky citrus butter flavor these crab legs

If you love steamed crab legs but feel that they can sometimes be a little dull, then here's a recipe that will make your crab legs (or at least your taste buds) get up and dance!

It starts with a peppery spice rub added to softened butter flavored with garlic and orange juice. Then, all that flavor is brushed onto lightly cracked snow crab legs and broiled until the butter and spices soak in and flavor the sweet crabmeat inside.

Look for crab legs with a sweet sea smell and minimal shell discoloration. Check that exposed meat looks moist and white. Let frozen crab legs defrost slowly and completely. This recipe works well with king crab legs also. *Yield: 2–4 servings*

KNACK FISH & SEAFOOD COOKBOOK

Ingredients:

1 1/2 teaspoons black peppercorns

1 1/2 teaspoons white peppercorns

1 teaspoon green peppercorns

1 teaspoon red pepper flakes

2 teaspoons sweet paprika

2 teaspoons coriander seed

3/4 cup butter, softened

1 tablespoon orange juice concentrate

4 large cloves garlic, minced

1 teaspoon salt

3–4 pounds snow crab legs

Sweet and Spicy Crab Legs

- Combine the first 6 ingredients in a spice mill and grind to a slightly coarse powder (or place the spices in a doubled plastic bag and crush them with a meat mallet or rolling pin).

- Mix the spices with the butter, orange juice concentrate, garlic, and salt.

- Crack the crab legs in a few spots to let the flavorings penetrate, then brush the spiced butter generously onto crab legs.

- Broil for 3 to 4 minutes per side to heat through.

MAKE IT EASY

Spice rubs can be purchased in gourmet shops, or they can be made with ingredients from your spice rack. If you like sweet and spicy flavors, combine 2 tablespoons of ground cumin, 1 tablespoon of paprika, 1 tablespoon of brown sugar, 1 tablespoon of chili powder, and 1 teaspoon of oregano. Store in a jar with a tight-fitting lid.

Basting sauces can be used to flavor all kinds of seafood. They are easy to make. Simply allow 1 stick of unsalted butter to soften at room temperature. With a fork, blend in various ingredients, such as 2 tablespoons of fresh basil, 2 tablespoons of minced fresh chives, 3 to 4 minced garlic cloves, or 2 tablespoons of chopped fresh dill with the juice of $1/2$ lemon. Store in the refrigerator until needed.

Make 5-pepper Spice

- Many serious cooks have a spice mill, or a coffee grinder that is dedicated to the use of grinding spices.

- Spice mills and coffee grinders can be purchased in most gourmet stores.

- Spices can also be crushed with a rolling pin or meat mallet.

- If you use a meat mallet, make sure you use the smooth side of the mallet for pounding the spices.

Brush on Spiced Butter

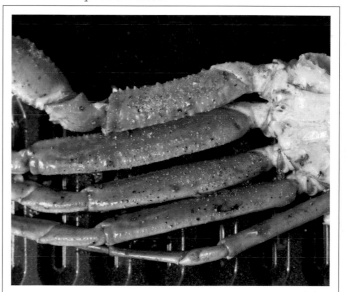

- The more a person cooks, the more confident he or she will become.

- Don't be afraid to make slight changes in a recipe. For instance, try making this dish with orange peel instead of orange juice concentrate.

- Or, if you don't have any fresh garlic, use the garlic powder from your spice rack.

- Remember to buy new bottles of spices now and then because so much flavor escapes during storage.

CRISPY STUFFED SOFT SHELLS

These soft-shell crabs, flavored with mushrooms, shallots, and garlic, are a real delight

In classic stuffed mushrooms, it's the crabmeat that goes inside the mushrooms; this time, though, the tables are turned, and it's the crab that gets stuffed!

Soft-shell crabs are a unique treat full of sweet crab flavor. Before you experience them, it's a bit hard to imagine eating a whole crab, shell and all, but with soft shells that's what you do. The shell is very soft, but fries up crisp. Soft-shell crabs are only available fresh for a few weeks in spring, but can be had frozen year-round. When buying fresh, be certain that they are alive before you have them cleaned and dressed. If frozen, defrost them slowly in the refrigerator to retain their sweet flavor. *Yield: 4 servings*

KNACK FISH & SEAFOOD COOKBOOK

Ingredients:

2 eggs, beaten

¼ cup milk

½ teaspoon salt

1 clove garlic, crushed

2 tablespoons butter

2 tablespoons minced shallots

12 ounces "Baby Bella" or white mushrooms, diced

1 tablespoon minced parsley

¼ teaspoon dried thyme

¼ teaspoon black pepper

¼ teaspoon salt

1 teaspoon flour

¼ cup milk

½ cup flour

½ cup fine bread crumbs

2 tablespoons finely grated Parmesan cheese

8 cleaned and dressed soft-shell crabs

Crispy Stuffed Soft Shells

- Combine first four ingredients in a bowl; chill.

- Melt butter over medium heat; add next six ingredients. Sauté until mushrooms release juices.

- Add 1 teaspoon flour, cook 2 minutes. Slowly add ¼ cup milk, stirring until thickened. Let cool. Divide stuffing between crabs, placing some under each half of shell.

- Combine flour, crumbs, and cheese on a plate. Dip crabs in egg mixture, then breading; fry in ¼ inch of oil (365°F) 4 to 6 minutes per side.

178

Less is more for some cooks when it comes to soft-shell crabs. They contend that all you need is salt, pepper, flour, and butter. Dry 12 cleaned soft-shell crabs with a paper towel. Season with salt and pepper. Dust with flour. In a large skillet, cook the crabs in batches in just enough butter to prevent sticking until they are golden brown, about 5 minutes per side.

Even easier is this dipping sauce, which also can be served with stone crabs. In a glass bowl, combine 2 tablespoons of dry mustard with 1/4 cup of sour cream and 1/4 cup of mayonnaise. Season to taste with salt, pepper, and Worcestershire sauce. Mix well. Serve this mustard dipping sauce with lemon wedges on the side.

Stuffing the Soft Shells

- In a sauté pan over medium heat, melt the butter. Add the minced shallots, diced mushrooms, minced parsley, thyme, pepper, and salt. Sauté until the mushrooms release their juices.

- Add flour. Cook for 2 minutes. Add milk. Stir until thickened. Allow to cool.

- Divide this stuffing equally among the 8 soft-shell crabs.

- Hold a crab in 1 hand with your thumb holding open the top shell flap. With a spoon, stuff each crab shell.

Avoiding Oil Spatters

- Splatter shields in different sizes will come in handy when you are pan-frying.

- These fine mesh screens will help contain oil splatters, and that will keep your stovetop clean.

- A splatter shield can be placed over the top of a skillet or frying pan while food is cooking.

- Because it is made of a fine metal mesh screen, the splatter shield does not act as a lid, and you can see through it.

CRABS & CRABMEAT

POACHED WHOLE LOBSTER

The king of crustaceans, lobster poached in wine and seasonings makes a regal presentation

When it comes to celebrating special occasions, nothing says luxury quite like lobster. Fresh lobster meat from the Atlantic lobster *(Homarus americanus),* when properly prepared, is wonderfully sweet, briny, and uniquely fragrant. A whole lobster may seem like a challenge, but they are actually simple to cook and are not all that difficult to dismantle.

Very large lobsters may look impressive, but are actually less tender and flavorful. It's better to serve 2 smaller lobsters than 1 large one. Make sure the poaching stock barely simmers during the cooking time; high temperature can toughen the lobster meat. Serve with your choice of warm clarified butter or garlic aioli. *Yield: 2 servings*

KNACK FISH & SEAFOOD COOKBOOK

Ingredients:

4 quarts water

2 cups white wine

1 large carrot, cut into chunks

2 stalks celery with leaves, coarsely chopped

1 medium onion, coarsely chopped

1 tablespoon black peppercorns

1 tablespoon coriander seed

2 tablespoons sea salt (or other non-iodized salt)

3 bay leaves

1 small hot pepper, split (or 1 teaspoon red pepper flakes)

2 whole live lobsters (1 1/4–1 1/2 pounds each)

Poached Whole Lobster

- In a large covered stockpot, bring the first 10 ingredients to a boil. Cover and simmer 10 minutes.

- While the poaching liquid is simmering, place the live lobsters in the freezer to desensitize them.

- When the poaching liquid is ready, return it to a boil, ease the lobsters into the water, and cover.

- Cook the lobsters 10 to 12 minutes (10 minutes for 1¼ pound; 12 minutes for 1½ pound). Serve with warm clarified butter or garlic aioli.

• • • • RECIPE VARIATIONS • • • •

Clarified Butter: Place 2 sticks of butter, cut into chunks, in a small glass bowl. Place the bowl in a pan containing an inch of simmering water. Remove the bowl from the pan when the butter has melted. Allow the butter to cool. Skim and discard the milky white solids that have risen to the top. Carefully pour off the clarified butter. Leave the watery residue at the bottom of the bowl.

Garlic Aioli: Blend 2 to 3 minced garlic cloves into a cup of mayonnaise. This is even better if you make your own mayonnaise from scratch. Take it to an even higher level by using roasted garlic instead of raw garlic. Garlic aioli is wonderful with poached or boiled lobster. It also makes a terrific spread to use when you make sandwiches.

Easing the Lobsters In

- Some cooks believe that the most humane way to cook a fresh lobster is to first place the lobster in the freezer for 10 minutes. This desensitizes the lobster.

- Always ease the lobster head first into the simmering water, and cover the pot with a lid.

- Boiling is better than steaming a lobster.

- Lobsters flavor the cooking water, which in turn flavors the lobsters. When steamed, all that flavor is left in the bottom of the pot.

Making Clarified (Drawn) Butter

- To clarify butter, place the butter in a large glass bowl in a warm oven (225°F).

- Let the butter stand until it melts and you can see three distinct layers.

- Skim off and discard the top layer of foamy curd with a fork, then pour or spoon off the clarified butter in the middle.

- Discard the bottom layer of watery sediment.

PORTUGUESE LOBSTER ROLLS

This savory lobster sandwich is a tasty and unusual version of the New England classic

There has long been a sizeable Portuguese population in New England, drawn by the fishing industry, and they have added the flavors of their sunny homeland to the culinary palette of the area.

This recipe is a variation on New England's famed lobster roll sandwich which in its most basic form is just chunks of lobster blended with mayonnaise and served in a toasted split-top hot dog roll. In this version, lobster meat is paired with cubes of Yukon Gold potatoes and seasoned with shallots, tarragon, and sherry vinegar for a taste of Portugal. Serve these in halved, toasted Portuguese rolls with mixed baby greens and a dusting of colorful paprika. *Yield: 4 servings*

Ingredients:

4 medium Yukon Gold potatoes (about ³/₄ pound)

¹/₄ cup mayonnaise

1 tablespoon minced shallots (or white part of scallions)

2 tablespoons minced parsley

¹/₂ teaspoon dried tarragon, crushed (or 1 teaspoon minced fresh tarragon)

2 teaspoons sherry vinegar (or white wine vinegar with ¹/₄ teaspoon brown sugar)

¹/₄ teaspoon salt

¹/₄ teaspoon white pepper

8 ounces cooked lobster meat

4 Portuguese rolls (or small hoagie rolls)

Mixed baby greens or baby spinach

Paprika for dusting

Portuguese Lobster Rolls

- Peel and cut the potatoes into ½ inch cubes. Boil in salted water until just tender (about 8 minutes); place in ice water until cool. Drain well.

- Combine mayonnaise, shallots, parsley, tarragon, sherry vinegar, salt, and pepper. Fold in the lobster and the potatoes. Refrigerate until cool.

- Cut rolls in half lengthwise, cut a pocket in each half, and lightly toast under broiler or in oven.

- Fill toasted rolls with greens and top with lobster salad. Dust with paprika.

Making the Lobster Salad

- It's important that the potatoes be cut into uniform ½-inch cubes.

- Likewise, the cooked lobster meat should also be cut into bite-size chunks.

- You should be able to see clearly the chunks of lobster in the salad.

- When combining the salad ingredients, gently fold them together. You don't want to mash the potatoes.

Filling the Lobster Rolls

- With a bread knife, cut the Portuguese rolls in half lengthwise. Small hoagie rolls can also be used to make these lobster rolls.

- Cut a pocket into each half, scooping out some of the bread.

- Other times, hot dog rolls are used, which come with their own ready-made pockets.

LOBSTER ENDIVE SALAD

A pleasing balance of flavors and textures make this lobster salad a special treat

This salad is perfect for special occasions when you want to impress. It's easy to prepare and features buttery lobster meat, tangy blue cheese, crisp bacon, and crunchy toasted walnuts on a bed of delicate white Belgian endive.

Choose the smallest, whitest endives you can find (larger ones can be bitter), with moist, tightly compacted leaves with no brown discoloration at the tips. Arrange the nicest leaves on the plates artfully; thinly slice the remainder.

You can use raw lobster meat or canned lobster (the refrigerated kind) for this recipe. If using frozen lobster, thaw it slowly in the fridge for best flavor. Real, fresh butter is an absolute must. *Yield: 4 servings*

Ingredients:

¹/₂ cup chopped walnuts or pecans

1 pound small white Belgian endive

4–5 ounces crumbled blue or gorgonzola cheese

8 slices cooked bacon, crumbled

1 tablespoon butter

2 cups lobster meat (about 12 ounces)

Chives for garnish (optional)

Lobster Endive Salad

- Toast nuts in dry skillet over medium-low heat, stirring frequently, until fragrant, 3 to 5 minutes. Set aside.

- Separate endives into leaves; discard cores. Arrange the nicest leaves on 4 plates; thinly slice remaining leaves crosswise and mound loosely on plates. Sprinkle with blue cheese and bacon.

- Melt the butter in the skillet and sauté lobster (briefly if already cooked; 2 to 3 minutes if raw).

- Arrange lobster on plates and top with nuts. Serve with a light vinaigrette.

•••• RECIPE VARIATIONS ••••

Maine Lobster Salad: Boil or poach 1 lobster for every 2 guests. Remove meat from tail and claws. Use tail meat for salad. Reserve claws for garnishing. Allow 1 tablespoon of mayonnaise for every cup of cooked lobster meat (cut into small chunks). Mix well and refrigerate. Place lobster salad on crisp lettuce leaves. Sprinkle lightly with paprika. Top each salad plate with a whole lobster claw.

Lobster Quiche: Sauté ½ cup chopped green onions in 2 tablespoons butter. Add 1 to 2 cups fresh lobster cut into chunks. Combine 3 beaten eggs with 1 tablespoon tomato paste, 2 cups scalded cream, ¼ teaspoon nutmeg, 2 tablespoons sherry, and 4 tablespoons shredded Gruyère cheese. Add lobster to pre-baked pie shell. Pour egg mixture over lobster. Bake 350°F 30 to 40 minutes.

Arrange the Salad Elements

- Arrange the nicest endive leaves on each salad plate in a starburst pattern.

- Thinly slice the remaining endive leaves crosswise. Mound some of these sliced leaves in the center of each plate. Sprinkle with the blue cheese and bacon.

- Arrange the sautéed lobster in the middle of each plate.

- Top the lobster with the toasted nuts.

Sauté Lobster in Butter

- In the same skillet that you toasted nuts, melt the butter over medium-high heat.

- Cut the lobster meat into bite-size pieces.

- Add the lobster to the sauté pan. Toss the lobster to coat well with the melted butter.

- If raw, cook the lobster meat for 2 to 3 minutes. If already cooked, heat the lobster just briefly.

PAN-SEARED CURRIED LOBSTER
Pan-seared lobster tail is richly flavored with Indian spices in this delightfully aromatic dish

The luxurious sweetness of lobster meat and the bold flavors of Indian cuisine infuse the lobster tails and gives them a rich, golden color, while the caramelizing effect of the searing sweetens the spices with lobster essence.

A mild curry powder is used here; choose one that suits your taste. You can also use garam masala, a dry spice mixture available in Indian groceries that is used as a base for curry powder blends. Add some additional turmeric for a richer golden color.

Frozen lobster tails should be defrosted slowly and completely before cooking. Fresh or defrosted tails should be cooked same or next day for optimum flavor. *Yield: 2 servings*

Ingredients:

2 (5- to 7-ounce) lobster tails

1/4 teaspoon sea salt

Freshly grated black pepper

2 teaspoons mild curry powder

2-3 tablespoons canola or peanut oil

1 large clove garlic, peeled and crushed

1 serrano or other small chile pepper, split, seeds removed

1/2 teaspoon coriander seeds

1/2 teaspoon yellow mustard seeds

Seeds from 1 cardamom pod (optional)

1/4 cup heavy cream

Optional garnish: Chopped cilantro leaves

 Pan-seared Curried Lobster

- Split lobster tails, leaving bottom shell partially connected. Fold open. Discard digestive tract, rinse, pat dry. Sprinkle with salt, pepper, and curry powder.

- Heat the oil. Sauté garlic clove and chile until garlic colors lightly. Remove both from pan.

- Sear lobster, adding seeds to pan. Remove lobster from pan.

- Stir in cream and heat through. Adjust salt; drizzle sauce over lobster.

Garam masala in its many versions is the primary spice blend used in the kitchens of northern India. It can be a blend of 2 or 3 spices and herbs, and it can contain a dozen or more. Some are fiery, while others are aromatic. Garam masala should be used judiciously, added to dishes at different times during the cooking process.

• • • • RECIPE VARIATION • • • •

Basic Garam Masala: In a skillet, dry roast the following until darkened: 2 cinnamon sticks broken into pieces, 3 bay leaves, 2 tablespoons cumin seeds, 1 tablespoon coriander seeds, 2 teaspoons cardamom seeds, 2 teaspoons black peppercorns, and 1 teaspoon cloves. Stir frequently. Allow to cool. Grind and blend with 1 teaspoon ground mace. Store in an airtight container for up to 4 months.

Splitting the Top Shell

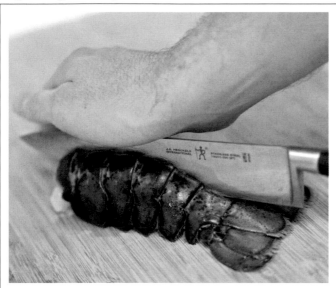

- Place the lobster tail on a cutting board. Hold the tail firmly in place.

- With a very sharp chef's knife, cut the tail in half lengthwise.

- Push the knife through the top shell and the body, but do not cut through the under shell.

- The tail can now be spread open to expose the lobster meat inside the shell.

Searing the Lobster Tails

- To sear, place the lobster tails meat side down in the skillet.

- Allow the lobster tails to cook for 1 to 3 minutes, or until their edges turn red.

- Add the seeds to the skillet. Turn the lobster tails over. Cook for another 1 to 3 minutes.

- When done, remove from the pan.

LOBSTER & MUSHROOM RISOTTO

A timesaving adaptation that produces creamy rice with superb lobster and mushroom flavor

Though not a true risotto (which requires a lot of time and stirring), this version delivers all the rich flavors and creamy goodness of the real thing.

Starting with a base of sautéed cremini mushrooms, garlic, onions, and olive oil, flavors are layered and combined until the final moment when lobster is gently folded throughout.

You don't have to use Arborio (the traditional risotto rice), but do buy the best short-grain or medium-grain rice you can find; long-grain or "converted" rice won't work here.

Low-sodium stock is a must, as you want to control the salt level. Parmesan or Asiago work equally well, but use quality cheese and grate it just before using. *Yield: 4 servings*

Ingredients:

2 tablespoons extra virgin olive oil

1 1/2 cups chopped cremini (Baby Bella) mushrooms

2 cloves garlic, minced

1/2 cup chopped onion

1 1/2 cups short- or medium-grain rice

1/2 cup dry white wine

1 cup water

1 cup low-sodium chicken or vegetable stock

1/4 cup milk

1/4 teaspoon white pepper

Salt (optional)

1/2 cup finely grated Parmesan or Asiago cheese

1/4 cup chopped parsley leaves

1 cup cooked lobster meat, in chunks

Optional garnishes: Parmesan or Asiago shavings, toasted pine nuts, lemon zest

Lobster and Mushroom Risotto

- Sauté mushrooms, garlic, and onions in olive oil until softened. Add rice and stir for 1 minute. Pour in wine and stir until absorbed.

- Add the water, stock, milk, and white pepper. Bring just to a boil; reduce heat, cover, and simmer 15 minutes.

- Stir in the cheese; adjust salt if needed (remember that the lobster will add some saltiness).

- Gently fold in the parsley and lobster chunks. Serve immediately.

What makes risotto so special? The right ingredients and proper cooking, slow and gentle. In a true risotto, each grain should be slightly al dente, but as a whole the dish is creamy and smooth. Rice known as "superfini" in Italy is the correct rice to use when making risotto. Arborio and carnaroli are the two types to look for when shopping for the right rice.

The other necessities for making a proper risotto include a heavy pot, preferably with a copper bottom and a firm handle to hold onto while you're stirring the rice; a wooden spoon because a metal spoon will damage the tender grains of rice; unsalted butter, dry white wine, a good chicken or vegetable stock, and finely grated Italian cheese (Parmesan or Asiago).

Stir in the Rice

- In a heavy pot, heat the olive oil. Add the chopped mushrooms, minced garlic, and chopped onions. Cook until softened.

- Add the rice. Stir for 1 minute, coating the grains of rice well.

- Arborio, the Italian rice used traditionally in risotto, is recommended, but a high-quality or medium-grain rice can also be used.

- Do not use long-grain or converted rice.

Fold in Lobster and Parsley

- After the water, chicken stock, milk, and white pepper have been added to the rice, bring the mixture to a boil. Cover the pot and simmer for 15 minutes.

- Stir in the grated cheese. Check the taste, and add salt if needed.

- Using a wooden spoon or flexible spatula, fold in the chopped parsley.

- Just before serving, gently fold in the chunks of cooked lobster meat.

MAPLE-GLAZED LOBSTER

An elegant lobster dish, with a mysteriously familiar peppery sweetness that you'll really enjoy

Though very quick and easy to make, this recipe will give you a meal that any top restaurant would be proud to serve. It's perfect for special occasions, especially intimate dinners for 2, or any time you want to spoil yourself with a bit of culinary opulence.

The glaze is made from a simple mixture of soy sauce, maple syrup, and black pepper; the soy is tempered by the maple, which mellows as it cooks. Coarse pepper adds a gentle bite.

Arugula greens have an appealing touch of bitterness, which contrasts nicely with the lobster. You can substitute fresh baby spinach or mixed baby greens. Toast the hazelnuts in a dry pan for a few minutes until fragrant. *Yield: 2 servings*

Ingredients:

1/4 cup light soy sauce

1/4 cup maple syrup

1/2 teaspoon coarse ground black pepper

1 1/2 tablespoons butter

1 small yellow onion, diced

8 ounces arugula leaves, rinsed and dried

1/4 teaspoon salt

1/4 cup chopped hazelnuts, lightly toasted

2 lobster tails (5–8 ounces each)

8 thin bamboo skewers

Maple-glazed Lobster

- In a saucepan, simmer first 3 ingredients until reduced by half. Remove from heat.

- Melt butter in skillet; add onion, arugula, and salt. Cook, stirring, 3 to 5 minutes. Remove from heat, stir in hazelnuts; keep warm.

- Split lobster tails in half; discard tract. Remove meat, lay straight, and thread each piece on 2 parallel skewers. Trim any rough edges.

- Pat dry. Brush with glaze; broil under high heat, 1 to 2 minutes per side. Remove skewers. Serve lobster over hazelnut greens.

Zesty Coleslaw: With this lobster dish, no ordinary coleslaw will do. In a large glass bowl, whisk ¼ cup oil into 1 tablespoon Dijon mustard and 1 tablespoon balsamic vinegar. Add 1 heaping teaspoon sugar. In a serving bowl, combine 3 cups shredded cabbage, 1 cup finely diced red bell pepper, and ½ cup diced scallions. Pour the dressing over the vegetables. Toss thoroughly. Chill before serving.

Grilled Potatoes: As long as you're grilling the lobster, grill some potatoes too. Thread chunks of raw potato onto skewers. Drop the skewers gently into a deep pot of boiling salted water. Cook for 10 minutes. Pull the skewers out of the water. Pat dry with paper towels. Brush the potatoes with olive oil. Season with salt and pepper. Put the skewers on the hot grill for 2 minutes per side, or until all sides are golden brown.

Splitting the Tails

- Place the lobster tail on a cutting board. Hold the tail firmly in place.

- With a very sharp chef's knife, cut the tail in half lengthwise.

- Push the knife all the way through the top shell, the body, and the under shell, splitting the tail in 2 pieces.

- Remove and discard the gray intestinal tract that runs down to the tail.

Threading the Tenderloins

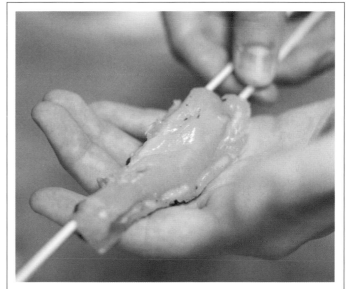

- Soak bamboo skewers in water for at least 30 minutes.

- Remove the lobster meat from the shells that have been split in half.

- Trim any rough edges on the lobster tenderloins for a neat presentation.

- Thread each tenderloin onto 2 parallel bamboo skewers. This will prevent the lobster meat from spinning around the skewers and ensures even cooking.

MARYLAND-STYLE BAKED SCALLOPS

Serve this scallop dish as a delicious entree, or in individual ramekins as an appetizer

Redolent with garlic, parsley, and Old Bay seasoning, this dish comes together very quickly and is on the table, bubbly and delicious, in no time.

Dry-pack scallops have no water added and shrink less than regular or frozen scallops. If you can't find dry-pack scallops, you can add another ¼ to ½ pound to make up for shrinkage.

Drain regular scallops well before cooking. This recipe can be made ahead; combine ingredients as directed in recipe, cover, and refrigerate. Remove from refrigerator 15 to 20 minutes before you bake it. Baked scallops also make an excellent appetizer; distribute the same ingredients in individual buttered ramekins. Bake 10 to 15 minutes. *Yield: 4 servings*

Ingredients:

2 pounds bay scallops, (dry-pack preferred; if using thawed, drain well)

2 tablespoons minced garlic

¼ cup chopped parsley leaves

4 ounces (1 stick) melted butter, divided

1½ cups panko or lightly toasted fresh bread crumbs

1 tablespoon Old Bay or other seafood seasoning

¾ cup grated Parmesan cheese

Maryland-style Baked Scallops

- Preheat oven to 375°F. Spread the scallops evenly in a buttered medium-sized baking dish or in individual buttered ramekins.

- Sprinkle the scallops with the garlic and parsley; drizzle with half of melted butter. Stir gently to mix.

- Combine the bread crumbs with the seafood seasoning and spread evenly over the top. Drizzle with remaining melted butter.

- Sprinkle with Parmesan cheese and bake 15 to 20 minutes until top is browned and bubbly.

YELLOW ● LIGHT

This recipe calls for bay scallops, the sweetest in flavor. If really fresh, bay scallops require very little cooking and can even be eaten raw. Warning: Inferior scallops are sometimes passed off as bay scallops. Taste is a reliable test for the real thing. Bay scallops tend to be uniform in size. Counts range from 50 or 60 per pound up to 100 per pound.

Season the Scallops

- These scallops have layers of flavor, beginning with a sprinkling of minced garlic and chopped parsley.

- Next, drizzle the scallops with melted butter.

- Spread the bread crumbs and seafood seasoning over the top of the scallops. Drizzle with the remaining melted butter.

- Sprinkle grated Parmesan cheese over the entire baking dish for a final layer of flavor.

Bake until Golden Brown

- This dish can be served in individual buttered ramekins as an appetizing first course.

- Or the scallops can be brought to the table in a large baking dish for family-style service.

- Either way, the scallops are baked in a preheated 375°F oven for 15 to 20 minutes.

- The top of the scallops should be golden brown and bubbly.

SEARED BALSAMIC SCALLOPS

A dramatic dish that highlights sweet, briny scallops with prosciutto and a balsamic glaze

Searing scallops caramelizes the surface and creates delightfully complex flavors. Here, jumbo scallops are brushed with a sweetened glaze of balsamic vinegar and wrapped in salty Italian prosciutto ham before searing. A bed of white beans and basil in a quick pan sauce adds a creamy contrast.

Buy very fresh scallops for this recipe. Natural, dry-pack scallops are rarely white; their color can range from coral pink to beige. Water-added scallops are often white, but shrink significantly when cooked. It's worth seeking out dry-pack scallops, as regular scallops are too moist to sear properly.

Buy top quality, super-thin imported prosciutto for its superior flavor. *Yield: 2 servings*

Ingredients:

¹/₂ cup balsamic vinegar

2 tablespoons light brown sugar

8 jumbo (under 10 per pound size, also known as U10), dry-pack sea scallops

8 paper-thin slices prosciutto

2 tablespoons olive oil

¹/₄ cup white wine

2 cloves garlic, minced

¹/₄ cup finely diced celery

2 teaspoons minced fresh basil

1 (15-ounce) can white beans (such as cannellini), rinsed and well drained

Seared Balsamic Scallops

- In a saucepan, simmer vinegar over medium-low heat until thickened (5 to 7 minutes). Stir in sugar; cook 2 minutes. Let cool.

- Brush scallops top and bottom with vinegar. Wrap scallops, folding prosciutto slices lengthwise to fit; secure with toothpicks.

- Sear scallops in oil over medium-high heat, 1½ to 2 minutes per side; remove from pan. Keep warm.

- Lower heat to medium. Sauté remaining ingredients 2 to 3 minutes until heated. Remove toothpicks from scallops; serve on top of white beans.

Wrap Scallops with Prosciutto

- Make the balsamic glaze, and allow it to cool. Brush the tops and bottoms of the 8 sea scallops with the balsamic vinegar glaze.

- Wrap 1 paper-thin slice of prosciutto around each scallop.

- If necessary, fold each slice of prosciutto in half lengthwise for it to fit better around each scallop.

- Secure the prosciutto in place with a toothpick.

Sear the Balsamic Scallops

- In a large skillet over medium-high heat, add the olive oil.

- To sear, place prosciutto-wrapped sea scallops in the hot oil.

- Cook the scallops for 1½ to 2 minutes per side.

- Remove the scallops from the skillet. Keep the scallops warm while you complete the dish. Be sure to remove toothpicks before serving.

195

SCALLOP-STUFFED TOMATOES

Ripe plum tomatoes combine with scallops and an Italian cheese topping in this appealing dish

You can bring the flavors of outdoor summer dining to your table in any season with these filled red ripe tomatoes.

The tomatoes are stuffed with a lemon-scented scallop, garlic, and parsley sauté, then topped with basil, cream, and Grana Padano cheese. They come from the oven bubbly and fragrant, carrying memories of sea air and summer sun.

Frozen scallops are fine here; defrost and drain them well before using. Roma (aka plum) tomatoes are available year-round and have consistently good flavor. Grana Padano cheese is an excellent grating cheese that melts well and has a flavor similar to good Parmesan, but a bit more mellow. Use freshly grated Parmesan as a substitute. *Yield: 4 servings*

Ingredients:

12 large Roma tomatoes

1 teaspoon olive oil

1 pound bay scallops

2 large cloves garlic, finely minced

1/4 cup parsley leaves, chopped

1 tablespoon finely shredded lemon zest

4 ounces grated Grana Padano or Parmesan

2 tablespoons finely minced fresh basil leaves

1 cup whipping cream

Scallop-stuffed Tomatoes

- Cut tops off tomatoes, scoop out pulp and seeds. Place tomatoes in a small, lightly oiled baking dish. If necessary, cut a tiny slice from bottom so tomatoes will stand upright.

- Briefly sauté the scallops with the garlic, parsley, and lemon zest until just opaque. Divide scallops among the tomatoes.

- Combine the cheese, basil, and cream; spoon mixture into and over each tomato.

- Bake at 375°F for 20 to 25 minutes until bubbly. Pass under broiler to color, if desired.

You might want to try this recipe using beefsteak tomatoes, which have a greater complexity of flavor than Roma tomatoes. In addition, the beefsteaks are larger and easier to stuff. It's also a good idea to rub salt on the interior of the hollowed-out tomato, which should be placed upside down on paper towels to drain before being stuffed. The salt sweats the tomato and enhances its flavor.

••••• RECIPE VARIATION •••••

Bay Scallop Avocado Appetizers: In a food processor, pulse the pitted flesh of a ripe avocado. Add to that $1/2$ cup sour cream, $1/2$ cup mayonnaise, and 1 teaspoon Dijon mustard. Pulse to mix well. Pour into a serving bowl. Chill at least 1 hour before serving with 3 pounds of bay scallops that have been poached in water and white wine. Serve with toothpicks for dipping.

SCALLOPS

Scoop Out the Tomatoes

- With a very sharp knife, slice off the top of each tomato (about ¼ of an inch).

- Holding the tomato in 1 hand, insert the tip of a paring knife at an angle just outside the tomato's core.

- With a sawing motion, move the knife around the core until it is cut free.

- Using a small spoon, scoop out the seeds and pulp.

Fill Tomatoes with Cheese

- Place the hollowed-out tomatoes in a baking dish. To help them stand upright, cut a thin slice off the bottom to make a flat surface.

- Stuff each tomato with some of the sautéed scallop mixture.

- In a glass bowl, combine the grated cheese, minced basil, and cream. Mix well.

- Spoon this mixture into and over each tomato.

SPICY SCALLOP LINGUINE

A zesty scallop pasta sauce, rich with Italian flavors and hints of exotic spice

Though the word *arrabbiata* means "angry" in Italian, this pasta dish will make your mouth very happy!

Pasta All'Arrabbiata is a Roman classic, and is almost always served as a meatless dish; here we bring in sweet bay scallops to add a taste of the sea. A hint of cumin and cinnamon lend a mysterious, exotic depth without making their presence known, and a squeeze of lemon at the end adds a vibrant note to this delightfully piquant dish.

This is a very quick and easy sauce to make and goes well with other pasta shapes. And like many Italian dishes this one is just as good the next day—if there are any leftovers, that is! *Yield: 4–6 servings*

Ingredients:

1 cup chopped onion

1 tablespoon finely minced garlic

2 tablespoons minced parsley

1 tablespoon olive oil

1/4 cup white wine

2 (15-ounce) cans petite diced tomatoes

2 tablespoons tomato paste

1/2 teaspoon crushed red pepper flakes

1/4 teaspoon ground cumin

1/4 teaspoon cinnamon

1/2 teaspoon black pepper

1 pound linguine

1/2 cup green peas (fresh or frozen)

1 1/2 pounds bay scallops

1/4 cup whole fresh basil leaves

Lemon wedges

Parmesan cheese (optional)

Spicy Scallop Linguine

- Sauté the onions, garlic, and parsley in the olive oil over medium heat until softened. Add wine, cook for 2 minutes.

- Stir in tomatoes, tomato paste, pepper flakes, cumin, cinnamon, and pepper. Simmer gently 20 minutes, stirring occasionally.

- While the sauce is cooking, prepare the pasta according to package directions. Drain well; keep warm.

- Return sauce to medium-high heat; add peas, scallops, and basil. Cook until scallops are lightly firm. Toss pasta with sauce and top with a little lemon juice.

Scallops Amatriciana: Sauté ¼ pound diced bacon in olive oil until lightly browned. Add 3 cloves minced garlic, 1 cup chopped onion; cook 10 minutes. Add 1 teaspoon red pepper flakes, ½ teaspoon black pepper, 2 tablespoons tomato paste, 2 cans petite diced tomatoes. Simmer 20 minutes. Add 1 pound bay scallops, ¼ cup chopped basil leaves. Cook 5 to 7 minutes; serve over cooked spaghetti.

• • • • • • GREEN ● LIGHT • • • • • • •

Italian chefs rely on the water in which their pasta has cooked for all sorts of uses. It is a salted and slightly starchy broth that can be added to a pasta dish that's a bit too dry. Since the pasta cooking water is neutral, it won't change the existing flavors in a dish. The next time you drain your pasta, scoop out a cup of the water and set it aside in case you need it to finish off the pasta dish you're creating.

Cook Off the Alcohol

Toss Pasta with Scallop Sauce

- Cooking the wine briefly removes the alcohol and concentrates the flavor.

- Avoid using cooking wine; it's inferior quality and full of salt. Only cook with wine you would enjoy drinking.

- Defrosting frozen peas in a bowl of cool water 10 to 15 minutes before cooking restores their moisture and plumps them up again.

- Always use quality canned tomato products. They make a noticeable difference in the results.

- Toss thoroughly so that all the pasta is coated in the sauce.

- If you don't have wooden pasta forks to toss with, salad tongs work well also.

- If you want to add more zing to the sauce, add ½ teaspoon of cayenne pepper along with the pepper flakes.

- If you find it's too spicy, you can temper the heat by adding ¼ cup of cream and some additional grated cheese to make a gentler Creamy Arrabbiata.

SCALLOP "SLIDERS" WITH BACON

A zesty bacon remoulade and peppery seared scallops take "sliders" to a new level

Here is a deliciously different take on the popular mini-sandwich that's terrific for game day gatherings, outdoor parties, or spicy midnight snacks. These cook quickly and their bold flavors are sure to please even die-hard meat eaters.

You can use pre-cooked bacon pieces (the real kind, not bits) to save time when making the remoulade. Add more cayenne or a few dashes of your favorite hot sauce to kick up the heat, if you wish. Use only dry-pack scallops for this recipe, as a regular "wet pack" of defrosted frozen scallops will have too much moisture to sear properly. Don't try to move the scallops around while they're cooking: they will release easily when they've formed a crust. *Yield: 8 appetizers*

Ingredients:

½ cup mayonnaise

2 tablespoons crumbled cooked bacon

2 teaspoons minced sweet pickle

1 teaspoon tomato paste

1 teaspoon spicy brown mustard

½ teaspoon dried chives

½ teaspoon paprika

Pinch of cayenne pepper (optional)

8 small slider rolls (or potato dinner rolls)

Softened butter

8 jumbo (under 10 per pound size, also known as U10) dry-pack sea scallops

1½ tablespoons Worcestershire sauce

1 teaspoon coarse-ground black pepper

2 Roma tomatoes, sliced

Green leaf lettuce

Scallop "Sliders" with Bacon

- Combine first 7 ingredients (plus cayenne, if using); refrigerate. Split rolls and butter lightly. Pass rolls under broiler until golden. Keep warm.

- Brush scallops top and bottom with Worcestershire; sprinkle with black pepper.

- Rub a cold skillet with a thin coat of butter. Turn heat to medium-high; when butter smokes, add scallops and press down gently to sear.

- Cook 1½ to 2 minutes until scallops loosen; flip scallops and repeat. Serve on rolls with tomato slice, lettuce, and bacon remoulade.

• • • • RECIPE VARIATION • • • •

Classic Remoulade: In a glass bowl, combine 1 cup mayonnaise, 1 finely minced garlic clove, 1 finely chopped hard-boiled egg, 2 tablespoons finely chopped parsley, 1 teaspoon tarragon, 1 teaspoon capers, 1 teaspoon Dijon mustard, and 1 teaspoon anchovy paste (or 2 mashed anchovy fillets). Mix well. (Some cooks omit the hard-boiled egg and capers, and add black pepper to taste.)

ZOOM

Sliders are a hot trend that many of us hope will never go the way of so many other trendy foods. The term "slider" began years ago as U.S. Navy slang. Sailors called hamburgers "sliders" because they were so greasy, they would slide down your throat. These days sliders are on the menu at many upscale restaurants. And they aren't the least bit greasy.

Brush Scallops with Worcestershire

- This dish has a great deal of zing, beginning with the Worcestershire sauce that is brushed on the tops and bottoms of the scallops.

- Add to that a sprinkle of coarse-ground black pepper.

- After you cook the scallops, serve them on slider rolls with sliced tomatoes and lettuce.

- The finishing touch is the bacon remoulade, another bit of zing.

Press to Sear Scallops

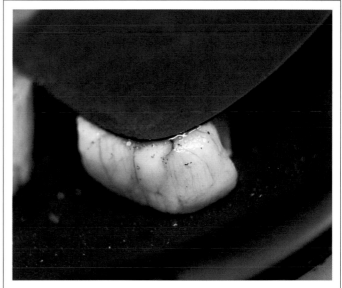

- Rub a cold skillet with a thin coat of butter.

- Place the skillet over medium-high heat. When the butter starts to smoke, add the scallops, pressing down gently to sear them on 1 side.

- The scallops should loosen after 2 minutes.

- With a spatula, flip the scallops over. Gently press down to sear their other side.

SCALLOP & SHRIMP MINI PIZZAS

Mini seafood "pizzas" on a flaky crust are a fun lunch or crowd pleasing appetizer

Everyone will love these easy to make (and eat) goodies. The scallops and shrimp are marinated in a revved-up Italian dressing, then used to top a flaky biscuit crust spread with a cream cheese "sauce." You can add other toppings, like olives or pepperoni, or let each family member or guest decorate their own pizzas before baking.

Frozen shrimp and scallops are fine for this recipe, just let them defrost slowly in the fridge and drain them well. Any style of biscuit will work, but the flaky layer varieties have good flavor and texture for these. You can use a different cheese, if you prefer; choose something that melts well and has a nice bite (mozzarella is too mild). *Yield: 10 appetizers*

Ingredients:

30 large raw shrimp, peeled and deveined

30 bay scallops

$1/2$ cup bottled Italian dressing

$1/2$ teaspoon red pepper flakes

$1/2$ teaspoon dried rosemary, lightly crushed

2 cloves garlic, minced

1 roll (10-count) refrigerated "flaky layer"–type biscuits

6 ounces flavored cream cheese (chive or vegetable)

$1/3$ cup grated Asiago cheese

Optional toppings: sliced olives, pepperoni strips, capers, pimientos, diced sun-dried tomatoes

Scallop and Shrimp Mini Pizzas

- Combine the first 6 ingredients in a bowl; chill 10 to 15 minutes. Preheat the oven to 375°F.

- Separate the biscuits on a nonstick baking sheet and gently stretch them out into 4- to 5-inch circles. Spread about a tablespoon of cream cheese on each.

- Bake biscuits until just beginning to color. Top each with 3 shrimp, 3 scallops, and your choice of toppings; sprinkle with grated cheese.

- Return pizzas to oven and bake another 3 to 5 minutes.

History of Pizza: Pizza originated in Naples, Italy. It was not until after World War II that pizza became known in the U.S. when American soldiers returned home hungry for the flat yeast breads they had sampled while stationed in Italy. Pizzerias started to open in New York, Boston, New Haven, and Baltimore, cities that had large Italian-American populations.

Scampi or Pesto Pizza: Make pizza as directed, but flavor shrimp and scallops instead with plenty of roasted garlic, shredded mozzarella cheese, thinly sliced white onions, a sprinkle of oregano, and chopped parsley. Or use freshly made pesto, shredded mozzarella cheese, sliced plum tomatoes, sun-dried tomatoes, and kalamata olives. Either way these pizzas will be a hit with family and friends!

Stretch Out the Biscuits

- Pop open a roll of flaky-layer biscuit dough, available in the refrigerator section of the supermarket.

- Separate the 10 biscuits on a nonstick baking sheet.

- Gently stretch out the biscuit dough to form circles that are 4 to 5 inches in size.

- Depending on the size of your baking sheet, you may have to do this in batches.

Add Toppings to Pizzas

- Once the pizza begins to brown, you should remove it from the oven to add your toppings.

- In addition to the seafood, you can add your choice of toppings to make this dish your own.

- Some suggestions include mushrooms, olives, and green peppers. Don't forget the grated cheese.

- Then, bake the pizzas for another 3 to 5 minutes.

OYSTER & BABY CORN STEW

No one who tastes this oyster stew will ever believe how simple it is

So simple, yet so very delicious, freshly made oyster stew is a real eye-opener for those who have only ever had the canned variety.

There are many elaborate recipes for oyster stew, but this is the way that many oystermen prepare it: simply, without flour or other thickeners, so that the rich succulence of the oysters themselves can shine through. This version adds baby corn for its subtle flavor and appealing texture.

Use plump, refrigerated (not canned) oysters. If using freshly shucked oysters, you'll need approximately 10 to 12 medium oysters to equal 1 half-pint. Be sure to shuck them over a bowl to save all their flavorful "liquor" and strain it well before adding it to the pan. *Yield: 2 servings*

Ingredients:

2¹/₂ cups half-and-half

1 can or jar (approx. 12 ounces) baby corn, rinsed, well drained (cut into small pieces, if desired)

¹/₂ teaspoon sea salt (or other non-iodized salt)

¹/₄ teaspoon white pepper

Pinch of cayenne pepper

¹/₄ cup unsalted butter

¹/₂ pint oysters, undrained

Oyster and Baby Corn Stew

- Heat half-and-half, baby corn, salt, white pepper, and cayenne in a saucepan over medium heat until hot, but still below a simmer. Keep warm.

- In a sauté pan, melt the butter, then heat the oysters and their liquor over low heat just until the edges

  ruffle. Add the oysters and their liquor to the saucepan and mix gently.

- Check the seasonings; add additional salt, pepper, or cayenne if desired.

- Serve immediately with oyster crackers or lightly buttered toast.

Oyster stews are holiday traditions for some families. The rich, creamy creation is suitably festive, for oysters have long been associated with champagne and special occasions. But this has been the case only in the past century. Prior to that oysters were everyday food for English peasants, much like lobsters were eaten regularly by servants in New England.

RECIPE VARIATION

Oyster Cream Soup: In a pot over medium heat, melt 3 tablespoons butter. Add 3 tablespoons minced shallots, 2 finely diced carrots, and a finely diced leek. Sauté 2 minutes. Add 2 cups white wine, 4 cups water, 2 cups clam juice, salt, and pepper. Bring to a boil; reduce and simmer 20 minutes. Add 3 cups cream and 36 fresh oysters. Poach 2 to 3 minutes. Stir in fresh herbs just before serving.

Use Fresh or Shucked

Heat Oysters and Liquor

- You will need ½ pint of plump oysters for this recipe. Do not use canned oysters.

- If you plan to shuck your own, you will need 10 to 12 medium-size oysters. Oysters should be stored cup side down in the refrigerator for no more than 2 days.

- Shuck the oysters over a bowl to catch all the oyster liquor. Stain it before use.

- You can also buy freshly shucked oysters under refrigeration at seafood markets.

- Check the shucked oysters for tiny shell shards.

- In a sauté pan over low heat, gently cook the oysters and their liquor just until the edges around the oysters begin to "ruffle" or curl. This will take approximately 1 minute.

- Add the heated oysters and their liquor to the saucepan containing the half-and-half.

- Stir gently. Check the seasonings.

CRUNCHY FRIED OYSTERS

Fried oysters are a crunchy, briny, savory delight for lunches, sandwiches, or snacks

The perfect fried oysters are crunchy on the outside with tender, lightly cooked oysters nestled inside. Fried oysters are not only terrific for meals or snacks, but they're the star of that famous New Orleans sandwich, the oyster roll.

If you're using refrigerated jar oysters, drain them well (freeze the oyster liquor for later use). Pat them dry before using.

You can substitute "unsalted top" saltines for the oyster crackers. White cornmeal is perfectly fine instead of yellow. (If you don't have cornmeal, but you do have polenta or grits, you can pulse either in a spice grinder until finely ground.)

Be sure to scoop any browned bits from the oil between batches. *Yield: 4 servings*

Ingredients:

1/2 cup all-purpose flour

1 cup finely crushed oyster crackers

1/2 cup yellow cornmeal

1/2 teaspoon black pepper

2 large eggs

1/2 teaspoon Old Bay or other seafood seasoning

2 pints oysters, well drained

Canola or peanut oil for frying

Crunchy Fried Oysters

- Put the flour in a small bowl. Mix the cracker crumbs, cornmeal, and pepper in another bowl.

- Beat the eggs with the seasoning until foamy.

- Dredge the oysters first in flour (shake off excess), then dip in the egg mixture, then coat thickly in the cracker and cornmeal mixture.

- Heat half an inch of oil in a heavy skillet to 360°F. Fry the oysters in batches until golden brown. Drain on paper towels.

Oyster Rolls: K-Paul's Louisiana Kitchen in New Orleans makes a wonderful oyster roll, what they call an Oyster Po'boy. They stuff perfectly fried oysters into a hollowed-out loaf of fresh bread, smeared with mayonnaise. They also serve their famous oysters (seasoned, battered, and deep-fried) with a fresh spinach and Pernod liqueur cream sauce on jalapeño toast points.

Coleslaw with a Lemon Twist: The perfect side dish to fried oysters: In a large glass bowl, combine 1 head of cabbage that you've shredded with 2 finely chopped celery stalks, 2 shredded carrots, 2 chopped scallions, 1 finely chopped cucumber, the juice from 2 lemons, 1/4 cup of salad oil, 2 tablespoons of mayonnaise, salt, and pepper to taste. Mix well. Chill before serving.

Finely Crush Oyster Crackers

Coat in Cracker Mixture

- You can crush oyster crackers or saltines in several different ways.

- The easiest method is to pulse the crackers in a food processor until they are finely crushed.

- You can also crush crackers in a plastic bag by pounding them with the flat side of a meat mallet.

- A heavy can or empty wine bottle can also be used to pound the crackers in the plastic bag.

- Place all-purpose flour in 1 bowl. In a second bowl, combine crushed oyster crackers with cornmeal and black pepper. In a third bowl, beat eggs with seafood seasoning until foamy.

- Dredge each oyster in the flour, and shake off excess.

- Dip each oyster in the beaten eggs.

- Coat each oyster generously in the crushed oyster cracker mixture.

OVEN-ROASTED HICKORY OYSTERS

A flavor-enhancing compound butter gives these oven-roasted oysters their outdoor taste

Like clambakes in the Northeast, oyster roasts in the South are a highly anticipated seasonal tradition. When the weather turns cooler, the oysters are plump and ready, and the first community oyster roasts of the season become social affairs.

This recipe is based on the salty pleasure of roasted oysters, with their gentle sweetness and hint of smoke. Here,

a compound butter puts savory Worcestershire and hickory flavoring inside the oysters as soon as they open.

Choose moist, tightly closed oysters from a reputable purveyor. Oysters should be kept cool, but not buried in ice (they'll freeze to death). *Yield: 2 servings*

Ingredients:

½ stick (4 tablespoons) of butter, slightly softened

1 teaspoon Worcestershire sauce

½ teaspoon liquid hickory smoke seasoning

Pinch of brown sugar

2 pounds coarse salt crystals, such as ice cream salt (or substitute kosher salt)

1 dozen large oysters in the shell

Saltines

Hot pepper sauce

Cocktail sauce

Oven-roasted Hickory Oysters

- Combine first 4 ingredients. Form into a cylinder in plastic wrap. Refrigerate.

- Preheat oven to 450°F. Spread the salt evenly in a baking pan. Nestle oysters, cupped shell down, in the salt. Tap any open shells; discard any that don't close.

- Roast until shells open (about 10 minutes); cut butter into 12 pieces and insert a piece into each oyster. Roast 3 minutes more.

- Serve in the shell with saltines, hot pepper sauce, and a dish of cocktail sauce.

ZOOM

Oysters have a rough layered shell, usually white to gray in color. They grow in nutrient-rich estuaries. Oysters are sold under a variety of names, which indicate their place of origin. They range from small to large with varying briny flavors. If you are ever invited to an oyster tasting, you will be amazed at the many different oysters and how their grayish-white meat varies in taste and texture.

Make the Compound Butter

Nestle Oysters in Salt

- Compound butters are flavored butters. They should be tightly wrapped. Leftover butter should be kept in the freezer.

- For this recipe, combine the softened butter in a glass bowl with the Worcestershire sauce, liquid hickory smoke seasoning, and the brown sugar. Mix well.

- Scrape all the flavored butter onto a piece of plastic wrap.

- Form the butter into a cylinder shape. Wrap tightly and refrigerate.

- In a large baking pan with sides, spread the coarse salt crystals or kosher salt in an even layer.

- Nestle the 12 oysters (still in their shells), cup side down, into the bed of salt.

- The oyster shells should be tightly closed.

- Tap any oysters that are slightly open. Discard any oyster shells that don't close.

209

BUTTERY CREOLE OYSTER PILAF

A new take on an old favorite, with butter-poached oysters and smoked sausage

Pilaf (sometimes spelled "pilau" or "perlau" and in the South pronounced "perloo") is a rice dish often containing spices, nuts, and/or fruit such as raisins or chopped dates. Pilafs by any name are a traditional side dish with roasted meats.

Here, a pilaf is raised to entree status with the addition of smoked sausage and buttery oysters. Almonds, golden raisins (also called sultanas), and scallions add flavor, as does the hint of aromatic nutmeg.

Any type of smoked sausage would be fine in this recipe; andouille is an excellent choice for its complex flavor. Use a good-quality rice that has its own flavor. We've used both jasmine rice and basmati with good results. *Yield: 4 servings*

Ingredients:

8 ounces smoked sausage, cut in ¹/₂-inch pieces

3 scallions, green and white parts separated, thinly sliced

¹/₂ cup slivered blanched almonds

¹/₄ cup golden raisins

1 tablespoon canola or light olive oil

1¹/₂ cups long-grain rice

¹/₂ teaspoon nutmeg

¹/₄ teaspoon white pepper

2 cups chicken stock

1 pint oysters, well drained (¹/₂ cup of oyster liquor reserved)

3 tablespoons butter

Buttery Creole Oyster Pilaf

- In a covered skillet, cook sausage, white parts of scallions, almonds, and raisins in oil 5 minutes. Stir in rice, nutmeg, pepper, stock, and reserved oyster liquor.

- Bring to simmer, cover, and cook 15 minutes. Remove from heat.

- In a small saucepan over low heat, melt butter with green parts of scallions. Turn heat to medium-low and add oysters.

- Cook oysters slowly until edges ruffle. Spread rice on a heated platter; spoon oysters and butter over top.

GREEN ● LIGHT

Oysters are especially popular during the holiday season, making an appearance in turkey stuffings, scalloped dishes, and on the half-shell. It used to be that oysters could be purchased only in months with an "R" in their name, as in September through April. But modern technology has enabled the farming of oysters so consumers can buy oysters year-round.

• • • • RECIPE VARIATION • • • •

Oyster Stuffing: Sauté $1/2$ cup chopped onions and $1/2$ cup chopped celery in $1/4$ cup butter 5 minutes. Add $1/4$ teaspoon seafood seasoning, $1/2$ teaspoon garlic powder, and $1/2$ cup chicken broth. Bring to boil. Pour into bowl containing 5 cups bread cubes, 1 pint shucked and chopped oysters with liquor, and 4 hard-boiled chopped eggs. Mix well. Bake in greased dish 350°F 30 minutes.

Prepare the Flavor Base

- In a large deep skillet with a cover, combine the sausage pieces with the thinly sliced white part of the scallions, slivered almonds, and golden raisins.

- Cook for 5 minutes over medium-high heat.

- Stir in the rice, nutmeg, white pepper, chicken stock, and reserved oyster liquor.

- Bring to a simmer. Cover and cook for 15 minutes. Remove skillet from the heat.

Poach Oysters in Butter

- In a small non-reactive saucepan over low heat, melt the butter.

- Add the thinly sliced green part of the scallions.

- Raise the heat slightly to medium-low. Add the oysters, making sure they are free of any tiny shell shards.

- Gently cook the oysters just until their edges start to "ruffle" or curl. This will take approximately 1 minute.

OYSTERS

OYSTERS PROVENÇAL

Garlicky and satisfying, this oyster dish is a taste of France's beautiful, sunny south

In Provence, that storied region in the south of France, life takes a slower pace. There always seems to be time to linger no matter what your agenda might have been. The relaxed attitude carries over into the kitchen. Food is taken seriously, especially the freshness of ingredients, but "fussiness" is essentially unknown. Good ingredients are allowed to speak with their own voices, with minimal added flavoring.

This oyster dish brings together some of the classic Provençal elements—wine, shallots, tomatoes, zucchini, garlic, rosemary—and adds to them a taste of the sea. The resulting broth is fragrant and ambrosial, and is absorbed by the grilled peasant bread. *Yield: 4 servings*

Ingredients:

¹/₄ cup extra virgin olive oil, divided

4 large, thick (¹/₂-inch) slices peasant bread

4 cloves garlic, peeled and crushed

2 large shallots, minced (or 1 small onion, minced)

1 large green bell pepper, chopped

4 Roma tomatoes, seeded and chopped

2 medium zucchini, chopped

2 teaspoons fresh rosemary, chopped (or 1 teaspoon dry)

¹/₄ teaspoon salt

¹/₂ teaspoon coarse ground black pepper

¹/₄ cup rosé or blush wine (such as white zinfandel)

1 pint oysters in their liquor

Oysters Provençal

- Brush 2 tablespoons of the olive oil over the bread. Broil or pan-sear the bread until nicely toasted. Rub each slice all over with a crushed garlic clove.

- Mince crushed garlic and sauté in olive oil until softened. Add the next 7 ingredients. Cook 5 minutes.

- Add wine; simmer 3 minutes. Stir in oysters and liquor; cook until edges ruffle. Adjust salt.

- Place a piece of grilled bread in a shallow bowl. Spoon oysters and sauce over the bread.

The landlocked parts of Provençe that are hours from the Mediterranean Sea are fortunate to have a wealth of fresh fish at the weekly market in Vaison. This enables the fine French cooks to create sea bass cooked in parchment with warm pistou, a sauce of olive oil, basil, and garlic; steamed salmon with a warm lemon vinaigrette; and cod that is wrapped in pancetta and seared.

Eastern, Pacific, and Olympia oysters are the major species harvested in the coastal waters of the United States. Eastern oysters are traditional half-shell oysters, harvested from New England waters to the Gulf Coast. Pacific or Japanese oysters are found from northern California to British Columbia. Olympia oysters are indigenous to the Pacific Ocean. Belon oysters are farmed on both coasts.

Toast the Rustic Bread

Spoon Oysters over Bread

- Brush some of the olive oil over the 4 thick slices of peasant bread.

- Broil or pan-sear the bread until nicely toasted on both sides.

- The peasant bread can also be grilled. Be careful not to burn the bread.

- Rub each slice of toasted bread with a garlic clove.

- Depending on which oysters you use, this finished dish can have a variety of flavors.

- Some oysters taste briny or metallic, while others are mild and even buttery.

- Oysters pick up flavors from their surroundings, wherever they are harvested.

- In general, oysters from the colder northern waters have a brinier flavor, and oysters from the warmer southern waters are milder.

BAKED OYSTERS CORDON BLEU
Oysters topped with ham, Swiss cheese, and chives are a surefire winner

Oysters and ham go together remarkably well, and this recipe takes finely minced ham, grated Swiss cheese, and minced chives and creates a topping for baked oysters that has the added zing of hot pepper sauce.

Seek out moist-looking, tightly closed oysters; discard any that don't close when tapped. If they aren't stable on the

baking sheet, you can set them in a layer of coarse or kosher salt to steady them. Any oysters that don't open after 5 minutes should be returned to the oven for a few minutes more. Discard any that don't open after 10 minutes. Use a potholder or heavy glove when opening oysters to help protect your hands from the shells and the knife. *Yield: 3–4 servings*

Ingredients:

8 ounces finely minced ham

4 ounces grated Swiss cheese

2 tablespoons minced chives (or green parts of scallions)

$1/2$ cup panko or lightly toasted fresh bread crumbs

1 teaspoon hot pepper sauce

$1/4$ teaspoon black pepper

2 tablespoons mayonnaise

16 medium oysters, scrubbed and rinsed

Paprika for dusting (optional)

Baked Oysters Cordon Bleu

- Preheat the oven to 425°F. Thoroughly combine the first 7 ingredients.

- Place the oysters on a baking sheet; tap any open shells and discard any that don't close.

- Bake the oysters 5 minutes until the shells open

slightly. Let cool. Pour off oyster liquor and save for another use. Pry oysters open and discard top shell.

- Top the oysters with the ham mixture and bake 10 to 12 minutes until lightly browned and bubbly. Dust with paprika, if desired.

Cordon Bleu is French for "blue ribbon". It is also the world's largest hospitality education institution with 20 schools on 5 continents. One of its most famous graduates is Julia Child. The origin of the school dates back to 1578, when French knights wore crosses on blue ribbons around their necks. The knights became known for their extravagant banquets, known as "cordon bleu."

Oysters Casino: Allow 6 oysters per guest. Carefully pry open the oysters. Over each oyster on the half shell, sprinkle a few drops of lemon juice, a little bit of minced green pepper, and a 1-inch square of bacon. Bake in a 400°F oven for 10 to 12 minutes, or place under the broiler for 5 minutes. Season with salt and pepper.

Remove the Top Shell

- Place the oysters on a baking sheet cup side down. Discard any shells that don't close when tapped.

- In a 425°F oven, bake the oysters for 5 minutes, or until shells open slightly. Allow shells to cool.

- Wear an oyster glove, or hold the oyster in a thick kitchen towel.

- Pry the oyster open with an oyster knife. Slide the knife under the top shell to sever the muscle. Pop the top shell off.

Top Oysters with Ham

- Save the top shell that you pry off from each oyster.

- Place a spoonful of the ham and cheese mixture on the top of each oyster on the half shell.

- Place the topped oysters on a baking sheet.

- If needed, invert the saved top oyster shells on the baking pan and use them to keep the topped oysters level.

GREEK CLAM & CHICKPEA STEW

This savory stew is a festival of Greek flavors in one enticing bowl

The uniquely blue waters of the Mediterranean have provided a wealth of seafood for centuries. Greek fishermen harvest the sea's bounty, and resourceful cooks transform it into a plethora of wonderful seafood dishes.

This recipe is inspired by those dishes and ingredients: garlic, tomatoes, wine, and herbs form the flavor basis for the baby clams and scallops. Chickpeas (aka garbanzos or ceci beans) add an earthy note to the savory broth.

Look for tiny clams with thin shells that are tightly closed (or close tightly when tapped); discard any that don't close. If using frozen cooked clams in the shell, defrost them in the fridge and add them at the very end just to heat through.
Yield: 2 servings

Ingredients:

3 cloves garlic, minced

1 tablespoon full-flavored olive oil

1 teaspoon dried oregano

$1/2$ teaspoon dried thyme

$1/2$ cup vermouth

1 can chickpeas, rinsed and drained

1 can (28-ounce) whole tomatoes, crushed and drained

1 tablespoon tomato paste

2 cups chicken stock or 1 can chicken broth

2 large slices French or Italian bread

2 ounces Greek feta cheese

Additional olive oil

1 pound baby ("butter") clams (in shell)

$1/2$ pound small bay scallops

4 slices of lemon

1 tablespoon chopped parsley

Greek Clam and Chickpea Stew

- In a large saucepan over medium heat, sauté garlic until softened. Add oregano, thyme, and vermouth; cook down 1 minute.

- Add chickpeas, tomatoes, tomato paste, and stock. Simmer 20 to 25 minutes, uncovered, skimming any foam.

- Lightly toast bread under broiler. Top with crumbled feta, drizzle with olive oil; broil until cheese softens.

- Add clams, scallops, and lemon to saucepan. Cover and cook until clams open. Divide between 2 bowls, sprinkle with parsley. Serve with feta toast.

Mediterranean Sauce: In a bowl, combine the juice of 1 lemon, 1 cup olive oil, 2 diced tomatoes, 3 parsley sprigs (chopped), 1 basil sprig (minced), 1 tarragon sprig (minced), 2 teaspoons chopped capers, and 2 teaspoons chopped green olives. Finely dice a baby carrot, baby zucchini, and baby summer squash, and add. Season with salt and pepper. Spoon sauce over broiled fish. Garnish with fava beans.

Clams Diablo: In a large saucepan, sauté $\frac{1}{2}$ cup chopped onions, $\frac{1}{4}$ cup chopped celery, and 1 crushed garlic clove in 2 tablespoons olive oil. Add 1 can of cut-up peeled tomatoes with the juice, $\frac{1}{4}$ cup red wine, $\frac{1}{2}$ teaspoon thyme, and $\frac{1}{4}$ teaspoon red pepper flakes. Bring to a boil. Reduce heat. Simmer 10 minutes. Add 24 littleneck clams. Cover; cook 10 minutes. Serve with crusty Italian bread.

Make the Feta Toast

- Place the slices of French or Italian bread on a baking sheet. Place the baking sheet under the oven broiler to toast the bread. Be careful not to burn the bread.

- Top the toasted bread with the crumbled feta cheese.

- Drizzle the toasted bread with olive oil.

- Place the toasted bread back under the broiler just until the cheese melts.

Cook the Baby Clams

- In a large saucepan over medium heat, sauté the minced garlic until softened.

- Add the oregano, thyme, and vermouth. Cook for 1 minute.

- Add the chickpeas, canned tomatoes, tomato paste, and chicken stock. Simmer for 20 to 25 minutes, uncovered.

- Add the baby clams still in their shells, bay scallops, and lemon slices. Cover and cook until the clams open.

CLAM FRITTERS WITH SALSA VERDE

Canned clams are a real timesaver when making these colorful and appetizing fritters

A homemade salsa verde is the perfect dipping sauce for these tasty treats. Make it first and refrigerate it so that it's cool and refreshing when the hot fritters are ready.

Canned clams are great for adding to soups, stews, dips, and other dishes where you want a briny seafood taste and an interesting texture. Always buy good-quality canned clams.

These fritters, with the addition of sweet corn, scallions, bell peppers, and canned green chiles, stretch a small amount of clams a long way with flavor to spare. You can substitute some of the clam juice in place of an equal amount of the milk for a more assertive clam flavor. *Yield: approx. 24 fritters*

Ingredients:

2 cans (4 ounces each) green chiles
$1/2$ cup parsley leaves, loosely packed
$1/4$ cup cilantro leaves, loosely packed
1 large jalapeño pepper, chopped
3 large cloves garlic, chopped
Juice of $1/2$ of a small lime
Salt (optional)
$1/2$ cup drained, chopped canned clams
1 cup thawed frozen corn kernels
3 scallions, chopped
2 tablespoons chopped red bell pepper
$1/2$ teaspoon paprika
$1/4$ teaspoon black pepper
1 cup all-purpose flour
1 teaspoon baking powder
1 teaspoon salt
1 egg, beaten
Milk
Canola or peanut oil for frying

Clam Fritters with Salsa Verde

- Pulse first 6 ingredients in a blender or food processor until almost smooth; adjust salt, if needed. Cover and chill.

- Combine clams and next 9 ingredients in a bowl. Mix in enough milk to make a thick batter.

- Heat $1/2$ inch of oil in a heavy skillet to 360°F. Gently drop batter by the tablespoon into oil and fry $1 1/2$ to 2 minutes per side until golden.

- Drain on paper towels. Serve with the chilled salsa verde.

Easy Clam Fritters: Combine 1¾ cups sifted flour, 1 tablespoon baking powder, ½ teaspoon nutmeg, and ½ teaspoon salt. In another bowl, combine ½ pint chopped clams, 2 beaten eggs, 1 cup milk, 2 teaspoons grated onion, and 1 tablespoon butter. Combine the 2 bowls to make the batter. Drop the batter by the teaspoonful into oil that is 350°F. Fry 3 minutes or until golden brown.

Clams Oreganate: Pry open 12 littleneck clams, leaving the meat on the half shell. Arrange the clams in a shallow pan. Combine 6 minced garlic cloves, 1 tablespoon oregano, 2 tablespoons minced parsley, and ½ cup fine dry bread crumbs. Divide this stuffing equally over the clams. Drizzle each one with a little olive oil. Bake in a 400°F oven for 10 minutes, or broil until browned.

Prepare the Salsa Verde

Fry the Clam Fritters

- Drain the 2 cans of green chiles. In a blender or food processor, combine the green chiles, parsley, cilantro, jalapeño pepper, garlic cloves, and lime juice.

- Blend or pulse the salsa verde ingredients until almost smooth.

- Taste the mixture to see if any salt is needed.

- Pour the salsa verde into a serving bowl. Cover and refrigerate.

- In a bowl, combine the chopped clams with the corn, scallions, red bell pepper, paprika, black pepper, flour, baking powder, salt, and beaten egg.

- Add just enough milk to make a thick batter.

- In a heavy skillet, heat ½ inch of oil to 360°F. Gently drop the batter by the tablespoon into the hot oil.

- Fry the fritters until they are golden, up to 2 minutes per side. Drain the fritters on paper towels.

CLAMS & MUSSELS

CLAM & ARTICHOKE LINGUINE

Marinated artichokes and fast-cooking clams are the secret of this quickie pasta dish

Everybody needs a handful of easy and satisfying dishes in their repertoire for when they need to get dinner on the table really quickly. This recipe requires very little preparation and derives its amazing flavor from just a few ingredients.

Marinated artichokes are a real timesaver when you're in a rush; they've got a sophisticated texture and come packed in a marinade that serves as the basis for a sauce. Make sure you buy the ones packed in seasoned oil and vinegar (not seasoned water). You can buy small cans of sliced black olives to save time also. Buy fresh clams from a reputable purveyor; cheap clams are no bargain. Discard any that won't close when tapped. *Yield: 4 servings*

Ingredients:

1 pound linguine

2 tablespoons extra virgin olive oil

2 large cloves garlic, minced

1 cup white wine

$1/4$ cup minced parsley leaves, divided

1 small bay leaf

1 (7- to 10-ounce) jar Italian-style marinated artichokes, undrained

2 tablespoons sliced black olives

$1/2$ teaspoon red pepper flakes

24 littleneck clams (plus a few extra)

Salt (optional)

Clam and Artichoke Linguine

- Cook linguine in salted water according to package directions. Meanwhile, heat the olive oil in a large covered pan and sauté garlic until softened.

- Add the wine, half of the parsley, and next 4 ingredients. Bring to a boil, add the clams; cover and cook, shaking pan frequently, 3 to 5 minutes until clams open.

- Discard any closed shells. Remove bay leaf and adjust salt, if needed.

- Divide linguine between 4 large bowls; spoon clams and sauce over pasta. Sprinkle with parsley.

Manila Clams with Linguine: This dish can also be made with Manila clams, the sweetest and smallest hard-shell clams you'll find at a fish market. The shells are pretty with wide bars of color over a finely ridged shell. Farmed in the Pacific Northwest, Manila clams need only 3 to 5 minutes to steam open. They are generally used in pasta dishes and soups.

Baked Shrimp and Artichokes: In an ovenproof skillet, sauté 4 cloves of minced garlic in $1/3$ cup of butter over medium heat. Add 2 pounds of medium-large shrimp that have been peeled and deveined. Stir to coat well. Add 2 small jars of marinated artichokes, their marinade, and $1/4$ cup of dry white wine. Move the skillet to a 400°F oven. Bake for 10 minutes. Serve with lemon wedges.

Cook Off the Alcohol

- In a large pan with a cover, heat the olive oil.

- Sauté the minced garlic in the hot oil until softened.

- Add the wine, half of the minced parsley, the bay leaf, marinated artichokes, sliced black olives, and red pepper flakes.

- Bring to a boil, which will cook off some of the alcohol in the wine.

Add Clams to Sauce

- The flavor base of this sauce comes from the littleneck clams and the liquid they release when their shells open up.

- You might want to add another dozen littleneck clams to this sauce to save for another meal.

- The extra clams can be removed from the sauce and refrigerated.

- The meat in those clams can be used as an appetizer or in a salad.

CLAMS & MUSSELS

CLASSIC MUSSELS "MARINER STYLE"
This classic French bistro preparation is surprisingly easy to make and so delicious to eat

Moules Mariniere, the French name for this dish, actually translates more accurately to "mariner's wife mussels." Generations of unsung fishermen's wives were responsible for preparing hearty meals from the catch of the day.

This deceptively simple dish takes a few ingredients and uses them to raise the humble bivalve to the gastronomic heavens. In the process, it also produces a really heavenly sauce that tastes like the reason for crusty bread's existence.

Fresh, farmed-at-sea mussels are most often sold in net bags already debearded. They often require little more than a quick scrub and rinse to be ready. Wild mussels will require more effort to clean. *Yield: 2 servings*

Ingredients:

2 tablespoons butter

1 cup chopped yellow or white onions

1 tablespoon minced shallots (or white part of scallions)

1 small bay leaf

1/2 cup chopped parsley leaves

1/2 teaspoon coarse ground black pepper

1 cup white wine

2 pounds mussels, debearded and scrubbed

Classic Mussels "Mariner Style"

- Melt the butter over medium heat in a stockpot or large covered pan. Sauté the onions, shallots, and bay leaf for 5 minutes.

- Add the parsley, pepper, and wine; bring to a simmer and cook 1 minute more. Raise heat to high; gently add the mussels, and cover.

- Cook, shaking the pan frequently, 5 to 7 minutes until shells have opened. Divide mussels between 2 large bowls, discarding any unopened ones.

- Spoon sauce over mussels and serve with crusty bread.

Steamed Mussels: In a large skillet, heat 3 tablespoons olive oil. Add 1 thinly sliced onion, 4 minced garlic cloves, and 1 cup finely diced celery. Sauté until onion is soft. Add 2 pounds mussels, 1 cup dry white wine, and a pinch of thyme. Cover and cook over medium-high heat for 3 to 4 minutes. Turn off heat. Let stand for 2 minutes. Sprinkle with freshly chopped parsley.

Mussels au Gratin: Steam open 4 pounds of mussels. Break off and discard the top half of each shell. Arrange mussels on the half shell in a baking dish. Sauté minced garlic, chopped onion, and chopped parsley in lemon juice and olive oil. Add 1 cup of cracker crumbs and $1/2$ cup grated Parmesan cheese. Evenly top each mussel with stuffing mixture. Bake in 400°F oven for 5 to 10 minutes.

Sauté the Shallots

Spoon Sauce over Mussels

- To mince a shallot, peel the shallot and place it flat-side down on a cutting board.

- Slice crosswise almost all the way to the root end.

- Make as many parallel cuts as possible through the top of the shallot down to the cutting board.

- Lastly, make very thin slices perpendicular to the cuts already made in the shallot.

- For many seafood lovers, the best part of this dish is sopping up the sauce with crusty bread.

- Serve the large bowls of mussels with plenty of French bread, or any kind of loaf that has a firm crust.

- Italian bread, sourdough and artisan loaves are all good choices.

- This hearty dish is best served at informal dinners where everyone will enjoy dunking their bread into the broth.

CLAMS & MUSSELS

SWEET & TANGY BAKED MUSSELS

An unusual, sweetly zesty way to prepare mussels for mealtime or as fun appetizers

You put the lime in the coconut, as the song says, but you also put in pineapple, and pickled jalapeños, too. Then you use it to top briny mussels and sprinkle them with sesame seeds. The result? A fun ride for your taste buds that gives any meal or occasion a touch of South Seas flair.

Pickled jalapeños come in jars and cans, either whole or sliced, and are a very easy way to add a little something special to almost any savory dish. You can substitute fresh jalapeños, but remember to always wear gloves when handling hot peppers. Fresh pineapple is excellent in this recipe if it's available, but canned is fine. Pass these under the broiler for additional color. *Yield: 3–4 servings*

Ingredients:

1 cup crushed pineapple, well drained

1/2 cup shredded coconut

2 tablespoons chopped pickled jalapeño peppers

1 tablespoon lime zest

24 mussels (plus a few extra), debearded and scrubbed

1/4 cup sesame seeds

Sea salt (or other non-iodized salt)

Sweet and Tangy Baked Mussels

- Combine first 4 ingredients in a bowl. Preheat oven to 400°F. Tap any open mussel shells; discard any that don't close.

- Place mussels on a baking sheet and bake briefly until shells open slightly. Remove and let cool.

- Pry shells apart and loosen mussels; discard shell half with tendon and place mussels back in remaining shell.

- Top with pineapple mixture and sprinkle each with sesame seeds and a pinch of salt. Bake 10 to 12 minutes or until lightly browned.

Pineapple Salsa: In a large glass bowl, combine ½ cup diced fresh pineapple with ½ cup diced tart apples and ½ cup diced mango. Add 2 tablespoons minced red onion, 1 tablespoon minced ginger, and ¼ cup chopped cilantro. Add 1 diced tomato, 1 minced jalapeño pepper, the juice of 2 limes, and 2 tablespoons fresh passion fruit juice. Mix well. Chill before serving. This is great on grilled fish.

Mussels with Dijon Mustard Dipping Sauce: Steam open 4 pounds of mussels. In a saucepan, bring 1 tablespoon each white wine vinegar and finely chopped shallots to a boil. Allow to cool. Add 1 tablespoon water. Whisk in ½ cup unsalted butter, a little bit at a time. Whisk in 1 tablespoon Dijon mustard. Season to taste with salt and pepper. Serve in individual dipping bowls with bowls of cooked mussels.

Discard Shell with Tendon

Top with Pineapple Mixture

- Preheat oven to 400°F. Place mussels on a baking sheet or in a baking pan. Bake mussels briefly until their shells open slightly.

- Remove the mussels from the oven, and let them cool.

- Pry the mussel shells apart. Discard the shell containing the tendon.

- Place the shell containing the mussel on a baking sheet.

- In a glass bowl, combine the crushed pineapple with the shredded coconut, chopped pickled jalapeño peppers, and lime zest. Mix well.

- Using a spoon, top each mussel with the pineapple mixture.

- Sprinkle the pineapple-topped mussels with sesame seeds and a pinch of salt.

- Bake in a 400°F oven for 10 to 12 minutes, or until lightly browned.

CLAMS & MUSSELS

SAVORY "BEER MUSSELS"

A different reading of a popular phrase is the basis of this boldly flavored dish

We've all heard of "beer muscles," a delusional condition brought on by excessive beer consumption that convinces the sufferer he possess the strength of Popeye after a six-pack of genetically-enhanced spinach. Of course, he's wrong! Thankfully, the condition is temporary, and his vitality can be easily restored with a bowl of these delicious mussels.

This is a no-holds-barred flavor fest: caramelized onions, whole grain mustard, amber beer, a handful of jalapeños, and a healthy dose of black pepper are absolutely guaranteed to wake up the senses and instill vigor.

A hearty bread like rye or pumpernickel served alongside is vital for absorbing all the savory sauce. *Yield: 2 servings*

Ingredients:

3 tablespoons butter

1 large sweet onion, chopped

1 teaspoon sugar

1 teaspoon black pepper

2 (12-ounce) bottles amber beer

1¹/₂ tablespoons whole grain or coarse ground mustard

¹/₄ cup pickled jalapeño slices

2 pounds mussels, debearded & scrubbed

1 tablespoon minced chives (or 1 small scallion thinly sliced)

Salt to taste

Savory "Beer Mussels"

- Cook the onions in butter over medium heat in a large covered pan until softened. Add sugar and black pepper; sauté until caramelized.

- Add beer and mustard. Simmer, covered, 10 minutes.

- Return sauce to a boil, add the jalapeño slices and the mussels; cover and cook, shaking pan frequently, until the mussels open (about 7 minutes).

- Divide between 2 large bowls, discarding any unopened mussels; sprinkle with chives or scallions. Serve with rye or pumpernickel bread.

Caramelize the Onions

Add Jalapeños and Mussels

- In a large pan, melt the butter over medium heat. Add the chopped sweet onions and cook until softened.

- Add the sugar and black pepper. Sauté until caramelized.

- For the best results in caramelizing onions, use a pan with a nonstick surface. Cook onions over medium heat for about 45 minutes.

- The best onions to use are the sweet varieties: Vidalia, Maui, and Walla Walla.

- To the pan containing the caramelized onions, add the amber beer and mustard. Mix well. Cover and simmer for 10 minutes.

- Increase the heat, and bring the sauce to a boil.

- Add the slices of pickled jalapeño and the mussels.

- Cover and cook, shaking the pan frequently, until mussels open, about 7 minutes.

WEB SITES & ONLINE VIDEOS
Information for cooking seafood

With a wide variety of books, magazines, Web sites, and videos available, it's easier than ever to find all the information and materials you need to cook delicious fish and seafood meals for your family and friends. Many offer step-by-step instructions that will help you learn to select and prepare fish with confidence. A wealth of online videos can bring such lessons to life for visual learners, who can replay them as needed.

On the Internet, culinary inspiration is only a click away: You can visit food blogs and Web sites written by passionate, innovative cooks, search a variety of general recipe Web sites, or ask for tips and advice from experts and home cooks alike on the many food-related forums.

Seafood Cooking Web Sites

About.com Fish & Seafood Cooking
http://fishcooking.about.com/
A great place to start to learn about cooking your favorite fish.

AboutSeafood.com
www.aboutseafood.com/
Recipes and helpful information about cooking seafood from the National Fisheries Institute.

Chef2Chef Seafood Recipes
www.chef2chef.net/recipes/section/seafood/page1.php
Seafood recipes from Chef2Chef, a site where home cooks can get advice from professional chefs.

Food Blog Search
http://foodblogsearch.com
Search thousands of food blogs for seafood recipes and more.

How to Cook Fish
www.howtocookfish.info
A well-named site with recipes, techniques, and a seafood glossary.

Hugging the Coast Daily Food Blog
www.huggingthecoast.com
Daily food and cooking blog from one of the authors of *Knack Fish Seafood Cookbook*. Home of the Fish for Friday Recipe of the Week

Seafood Watch: A Consumer's Guide to Sustainable Seafood
www.montereybayaquarium.org/cr/seafoodwatch.aspx
The definitive site for sustainable seafood news around the world.

The Sushi FAQ
www.sushifaq.com/
Everything you need to know about enjoying sushi and sashimi.

***U.S. News & World Report:* 11 Best Fish—High in Omega-3s and Environment-Friendly**
www.usnews.com/health/diet-fitness/slideshows/best-fish
Simple guide to help you choose heart-healthy and sustainable fish in a hurry.

Online Seafood Cooking Videos

5min.com Seafood Videos

www.5min.com/Tag/seafood

Hundreds of videos about cooking seafood . . . all under 5 minutes long!

eHow's Tips for Preparing Seafood Video Series

www.ehow.com/videos-on_997_tips-preparing-seafood.html

A growing collection of seafood cooking videos from eHow and Expert Village.

Epicurious Seafood Videos

www.epicurious.com/video/technique-videos/technique-videos -seafood/1915458785

Nice selection of fish preparation videos from the popular food site Epicurious.

Howcast Fish Cooking Videos

www.howcast.com/categories/410-Fish

Short how-to videos that will help you prepare fresh seafood.

Howstuffworks Seafood Guide Videos

http://videos.howstuffworks.com/recipes/seafood-guide-videos .htm

Add new skills when cooking fish or brush up on the basics here.

How2Heroes: Seafood

http://how2heroes.com/videos/seafood/

Find exciting gourmet seafood video recipes guaranteed to stir your appetite.

iFood.tv Seafood Videos

www.ifood.tv/network/seafood/videos

iFood.tv member videos sharing culinary delights from the sea.

Look and Taste Fish Videos

www.lookandtaste.com/our-videos/fish/5/

For video recipes for Crab Cracker to Salmon Scallopini, this is the place to go.

Rouxbe Online Cooking School Seafood Videos

http://rouxbe.com/how-to-cook/fish-cooking-recipes

Learn new cooking skills in the comfort of your home from this subscription-based online cooking video site.

Seafood Secrets Video Recipes

www.seafoodsecrets.com.au/pages/recipes/how_to_cook_ seafood_videos.htm

Nice collection of seafood how-to videos from the Australian site, Seafood Secrets.

Vimeo Seafood Videos

www.vimeo.com/tag:seafood

Find inspiration from these seafood-related videos on Vimeo.

YouTube

www.youtube.com

To find hundreds of delicious seafood videos, just type in "seafood" in their massive search engine.

ADDITIONAL READING
Find tips and culinary advice in these helpful books

Fish and Seafood Cookbooks

Adler, Karen and Fertig, Judith M. *Fish & Shellfish, Grilled & Smoked.* Harvard Common Press, 2002
Fans of outdoor cooking will enjoy this book about the joys of grilled and smoked fish filled with hundreds of recipes by two members of an all-women barbecue team called the 'Que Queens.

Berkowitz, Roger and Doerfer, Jane. *The New Legal Sea Foods Cookbook.* Broadway, 2003
Co-authored by the owner of the acclaimed New England restaurant chain Legal Sea Foods, this book features easy fish recipes that almost anyone will love.

Bittman, Mark. *Fish: The Complete Guide to Buying and Cooking.* Wiley, 1999
With more than 500 recipes from *New York Times* food columnist Mark Bittman, this book also shares the ins and outs of selecting fresh fish.

Brennan, Ralph and Bourg, Gene. *Ralph Brennan's New Orleans Seafood Cookbook.* Vissi D'Arte Books, 2008
Comprehensive and definitive guide to New Orleans seafood cooking by restaurateur Ralph Brennan.

Brody, Jane E. and Flaste, Rick. *Jane Brody's Good Seafood Book: A Guide to Healthy Eating with More Than 200 Low-Fat Recipes.* W.W. Norton & Co., 1994
For those looking to reduce their consumption of unhealthy fats, this book is a treasure trove of lowfat recipes.

Carpenter, Hugh and Sandison, Teri. *Fast Fish.* Ten Speed Press, 2005
Looking to make something delicious and healthy in a hurry? Think fish and let the tasty recipes in this book inspire you.

DeBorde, Rob. *Fish on a First-name Basis: How Fish Is Caught, Bought, Cleaned, Cooked, and Eaten.* St. Martin's Press, 2006
A folksy cookbook full of hand-drawn illustrations and entertaining asides about cooking fish by a writer for Food Network's *Good Eats*.

Dekura, Hideo, Treloar, Brigid, and Yoshii, Ryuichi. *The Complete Book of Sushi.* Periplus Editions, 2004
Everything you need to know to make sushi in your own home, sharing a nice range of sushi recipes from traditional to contemporary, as well as step by step tips.

Green, Aliza. *Field Guide to Seafood: How to Identify, Select and Prepare Virtually Every Fish and Shellfish at the Market.* Quirk Books, 2007
When you first start to shop at fish markets, choosing from a wide variety of fish can be overwhelming. This book will help you buy and prepare some of the less common fish as well as such tried and true favorites as shrimp and salmon.

Loomis, Susan Herrmann. *The Great American Seafood Cookbook.* Workman Publishing Company, 1988
An extensively researched cookbook featuring more than 250 recipes from all over the United States.

Moonen, Rick and Finamore, Roy. *Fish Without a Doubt: The Cook's Essential Companion.* Houghton Mifflin Harcourt, 2008
Encyclopedic guide that will help you make the most of sustainably caught seafood.

Peterson, James. *Fish & Shellfish: The Cook's Indispensable Companion.* William Morrow Cookbooks, 1996
Take seafood cooking to the next level with this comprehensive cookbook.

Stein, Rick. *Rick Stein's Complete Seafood: A Step by Step Reference.* Ten Speed Press, 2008
A large, very informative, and well-organized book about all aspects of preparing fish. Perhaps the ultimate reference for serious seafood cooks.

Thompson, Fred. *The Big Book of Fish & Shellfish: More Than 250 Terrific Recipes.* Chronicle Books, 2006
If most of the fish you eat is from restaurants, this book will have you cooking your favorite fish at home in no time.

231

Magazines

Cooking Light
www.cookinglight.com

Cook's Illustrated
www.cooksillustrated.com

Food & Wine
www.foodandwine.com

Saveur
www.saveur.com

Author Favorites

Cajun & Creole Cooking by Crescent Books (1992)

The California Pizza Kitchen Cookbook by Larry Flax and Rick Rosenfield (Macmillan, 1996)

The Complete Book of Spices by Jill Norman (Viking Studio Books, 1991)

The Complete Fish Cook by Barbara Grunes and Phillis Magida (Contemporary Books, 1990)

The Dean & DeLuca Cookbook by David Rosengarten (Alfred A. Knopf, 1996)

Complete Guide to Seafood Cookery by the Rhode Island Seafood Council (1984)

The Complete Seafood Cookbook by Bettina Jenkins (Charles E. Tuttle, 1995)

The Dictionary of Italian Food and Drink by John Mariani (Broadway Books, 1998)

Doin' the Charleston by Molly Heady Sillers (Chrisreed Publishers, 1984)

The Fannie Farmer Cookbook by Marion Cunningham (Alfred A. Knopf, 1990)

Fish—The Complete Guide to Buying and Cooking by Mark Bittman (Macmillan Publishing, 1994)

Fish & Shellfish by James Peterson (William Morrow & Company 1996)

The Fish Book by Kelly McCune (Harper & Row, 1988)

Ginger East to West by Bruce Cost (Aris Books, 1984)

Go with the Grain by the Rice Council of America (Wimmer Brothers Books, 1982)

A Gringo's Guide to Authentic Mexican Cooking by Mad Coyote Joe (Northland Publishing, 2001)

McCormick & Schmick's Seafood Restaurant Cookbook (Arnica Publishing, 2005)

A New England Fish Tale by Martha Watson Murphy (Henry Holt, 1997)

New Orleans by the Bowl by John Demers (Ten Speed Press, 2003)

Patricia Wells at Home in Provence by Patricia Wells (Scribner, 1996)

Perfect Vegetables by the Editors of Cook's Illustrated Magazine (America's Test Kitchen, 2003)

The Providence and Rhode Island Cookbook by Linda Beaulieu (Globe Pequot Press, 2006)

Risotto—A Taste of Milan by Constance Arkin Del Nero and Rosario Del Nero (Harper & Row, 1988)

Roy's Feasts from Hawaii by Roy Yamaguchi (Ten Speed Press, 1995)

The Sea-Fare's Culinary Treasures by George Karousos (Gramma S.A., 1989)

Seafood—A Collection of Heart Healthy Recipes by Janis Harsila and Evie Hansen (National Seafood Educators, 1990)

Seafood As We Like It by Anthony Spinazzola and Jean-Jacques Paimblanc (Globe Pequot Press, 1985)

250 True Italian Pasta Dishes by John Coletta (Robert Rose, 2009)

EQUIPMENT RESOURCES

Find what you need to make your time in the kitchen a little easier

RESOURCES

Places to Buy Kitchen Equipment

Amazon.com Kitchen & Dining

www.amazon.com

From small appliances to tableware, Amazon's Kitchen & Dining Department has a large selection from which to choose.

Barbecues.com

www.barbecues.com/

Everything you need for outdoor cooking and entertaining.

Chefscatalog.com

www.chefscatalog.com

Featuring an extensive selection of quality cookware and kitchen equipment.

Cooking.com

www.cooking.com

With more than 60,000 items, it's no wonder that it's such a popular online shopping destination for home cooks.

Cutlery and More

www.cutleryandmore.com/

Quality kitchenware from All-Clad to Zojirushi.

Lodge Cast Iron Cookware

www.lodgemfg.com/

Founded in 1896. Lodge is the oldest family-owned cookware foundry in America.

OXO

www.oxo.com

Makers of innovative and ergonomically designed kitchen gadgets, kitchen tools, utensils, and more.

Pampered Chef

www.pamperedchef.com/

Lots of interesting products for those who love to cook.

Williams-Sonoma

www.williams-sonoma.com/

The holy grail of quality kitchenware sites.

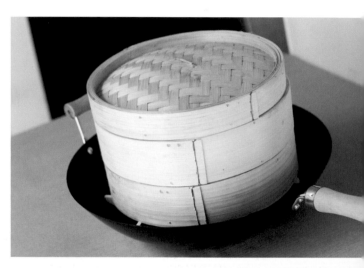

METRIC CONVERSION TABLES
Approximate U.S. Metric Equivalents

Liquid Ingredients

U.S. MEASURES	METRIC	U.S. MEASURES	METRIC
$\frac{1}{4}$ TSP.	1.23 ML	2 TBSP.	29.57 ML
$\frac{1}{2}$ TSP.	2.36 ML	3 TBSP.	44.36 ML
$\frac{3}{4}$ TSP.	3.70 ML	$\frac{1}{4}$ CUP	59.15 ML
1 TSP.	4.93 ML	$\frac{1}{2}$ CUP	118.30 ML
$1\frac{1}{4}$ TSP.	6.16 ML	1 CUP	236.59 ML
$1\frac{1}{2}$ TSP.	7.39 ML	2 CUPS OR 1 PT.	473.18 ML
$1\frac{3}{4}$ TSP.	8.63 ML	3 CUPS	709.77 ML
2 TSP.	9.86 ML	4 CUPS OR 1 QT.	946.36 ML
1 TBSP.	14.79 ML	4 QTS. OR 1 GAL.	3.79 L

Dry Ingredients

U.S. MEASURES	METRIC	U.S. MEASURES		METRIC
$\frac{1}{16}$ OZ.	2 (1.8) G	$2\frac{4}{5}$ OZ.		80 G
$\frac{1}{8}$ OZ.	$3\frac{1}{2}$ (3.5) G	3 OZ.		85 (84.9) G
$\frac{1}{4}$ OZ.	7 (7.1) G	$3\frac{1}{2}$ OZ.		100 G
$\frac{1}{2}$ OZ.	15 (14.2) G	4 OZ.		115 (113.2) G
$\frac{3}{4}$ OZ.	21 (21.3) G	$4\frac{1}{2}$ OZ.		125 G
$\frac{7}{8}$ OZ.	25 G	$5\frac{1}{4}$ OZ.		150 G
1 OZ.	30 (28.3) G	$8\frac{7}{8}$ OZ.		250 G
$1\frac{3}{4}$ OZ.	50 G	16 OZ.	1 LB.	454 G
2 OZ.	60 (56.6) G	$17\frac{3}{5}$ OZ.	1 LIVRE	500 G

FIND INGREDIENTS

If you're looking for something special here are some places to try

Catalogs and Online Resources

Charleston Seafood

www.charlestonseafood.com/

A wide variety of fresh fish shipped overnight anywhere in the United States.

CleanFish Sustainable Seafood

http://cleanfish.com/find.htm

Find environmentally friendly fish and seafood from local markets in your area.

The Cook's Garden

http://www.cooksgarden.com/

Everything you need to grow your own herbs, fruits, and vegetables.

Faraway Foods

http://farawayfoods.com/index.html

Mustard, sauces, marinades, seasonings, and more from around the world.

FoodReference.com

www.foodreference.com/

Stumped about a particular ingredient or spice? Just type it in the search bar of this comprehensive food reference site to learn more about it.

La Tienda

www.tienda.com/

Artisanal seafood, specialty olive oil, vinegar, spices, and ingredients that celebrate the cuisine of Spain.

Legal Sea Foods

www.legalseafoods.com/

Shrimp, lobster, and other seafood delivered to your door from the acclaimed New England seafood purveyor.

Marx Foods

www.marxfoods.com/

Gourmet seafood, bulk foods, and exotic spices.

HOTLINES & ASSOCIATIONS

Get useful information, advice, support, and tips

Phone Number and Web Sites

American Dietetic Association's Home Food Safety
(800) 877-1600, Extension 4793
A hotline that will help you with your food safety questions.

Foodsafety.gov
www.foodsafety.gov/
Information about the latest food recalls can be found here.

Kosherquest.com's List of Kosher Fish
www.kosherquest.org/bookhtml/FISH.htm
For those following a kosher diet or serving guests that do, this information is essential.

Partnership for Food Safety Education (Fight Back)
(202) 220-0651
Learn more about safe handling of food.

USDA Cooperative Extension System Office Finder
www.csrees.usda.gov/Extension/index.html
Find your local cooperative extension office that shares information about cooking, vegetable gardening, and food preservation.

U.S. Food and Drug Administration's Center for Food Safety and Nutrition Hotline
(888) SAFEFOOD
Get up-to-date info about food and product recalls, food handling, and more.

U.S. Food and Drug Administration Seafood Hotline
(800) FDA-4010
Food safety, preparation, and storage tips from the FDA.

GLOSSARY

Beat: To manipulate food with a spoon, mixer, or whisk to combine.

Bread: To coat fish with crumbs or crushed crackers before baking or frying.

Brine: A mixture of salt, sugar, and water used to season fish before cooking.

Broil: To cook food close to the heat source, quickly. Used in slow cooking to add color and flavor.

Broth: Liquid extracted from fish, used as the basis for most soups.

Brown: Cooking step that caramelizes food and adds color and flavor before cooking.

Coat: To cover food in another ingredient, as to coat fish fillets with bread crumbs.

Chill: To refrigerate a food or place it in an ice-water bath to rapidly cool it.

Chop: To cut food into small pieces, using a chef's knife or a food processor.

Chowder: A soup thick with vegetables and meats, usually seafood, thickened with cream and cheese.

Deglaze: To add a liquid to a pan used to sauté meats; this removes drippings and brown bits to create a sauce.

Dice: To cut food into small, even portions, usually about ¼ inch square.

Grate: To use a grater or microplane to remove small pieces or shreds of skin or food.

Grill: To cook over coals or charcoal, or over high heat.

Herbs: The edible leaves of certain plants that add flavor to food, including basil, marjoram, thyme, oregano, and mint.

Marinate: To allow fish or vegetables to stand in a mixture of an acid and oil, to add flavor and tenderize.

Melt: To turn a solid into a liquid by the addition of heat.

Pan-fry: To cook quickly in a shallow pan, in a small amount of fat over relatively high heat.

Sauté: To cook a food briefly in oil over medium-high heat, while stirring it so it cooks evenly.

Seasoning: To add herbs, spices, citrus juices and zest, and pepper to food to increase flavor.

Shred: To use a grater, mandoline, or food processor to create small strips of food.

Simmer: A state of liquid cooking, in which the liquid is just below a boil.

Spices: The edible dried fruits, bark, and seeds of plants, used to add flavor to food.

Steam: To cook food by immersing it in steam. Food is set over boiling liquid.

Toss: To combine food using two spoons or a spoon and a fork until mixed.

Whisk: Both a tool, which is made of loops of steel, and a method which combines food until smooth.

INDEX

Page references at main entries indicate general information on topic.